HALLELUJAH

Gill & Macmillan
Hume Avenue
Park West
Dublin 12
www.gillmacmillanbooks.ie

© Jonathan Bardon 2015

978 07171 6354 0

Design by Tanya Ross www.elementinc.ie
Edited by Síne Quinn
Indexed by Eileen O'Neill
Printed and bound by ScandBook AB, Sweden

This book is typeset in Adobe Calson 10pt on 12pt.

The paper used in this book comes from the wood pulp of
managed forests. For every tree felled, at least one tree is
planted, thereby renewing natural resources.

A CIP catalogue record for this book is available from the
British Library.

5 4 3 2 1

Hallelujah

THE STORY

A MUSICAL GENIUS

THE CITY THAT BROUGHT HIS
MASTERPIECE TO LIFE

JONATHAN BARDON

Gill & Macmillan

For Carol

Acknowledgements

In the early 1950s shortly after long-playing records had been invented, my father, Eric Bardon, arrived at our home in Booterstown in south Dublin with a turntable which, with some difficulty, was duly attached to the radio. Since he restricted his purchases to just two or three LPs a year and, like the rest of his family, had a very limited knowledge of classical music, he took care to consult an expert before buying. That expert was a customer of the Munster & Leinster Bank in Donnybrook, where my father was a teller for many years. One day, returning from work, my father dismounted his bicycle with delight. We gathered round to watch him take out from a paper bag not one, but three, records he had been advised to purchase: the complete Handel's *Messiah*, with Sir Adrian Boult conducting the London Philharmonic Orchestra and Choir, and the soloists Jennifer Vyvyan (soprano), Norma Proctor (alto), George Maran (tenor) and Owen Brannigan (bass).

Not being able to tell a crotchet from a quaver, I nevertheless got to know the oratorio extremely well by playing the vinyl discs endlessly. Indeed, much later on when I first heard two more authentic interpretations, one conducted by Sir Neville Marriner and the other by Christopher Hogwood, my initial reaction was to be offended by the sprightlier tempi of both recordings. As a student I would often wander along the Liffey quays to browse in second-hand bookshops and to return by ascending Fishamble Street. My first surprise was that the Musick Hall was no longer there and the second that there was no plaque to mark where it once had been. (A plaque is there today.) When in 1984 I came to write a book on Wood Quay, which is adjacent to Fishamble Street, there was no question but that it had to feature a brief account of the first performance of *Messiah*.

My interest in finding out more about the event revived when I decided to make it one in a series of five-minute radio programmes, the text of which was subsequently included in *A History of Ireland in 250 Episodes* published in 2008. The journey of exploration to find out why Handel was invited to Dublin, why he accepted, why he decided to give *Messiah* its première in the Irish capital, and why it was so enthusiastically received there, proved to be more tortuous but also more engrossing than I had expected. I was extremely fortunate to find that I could draw on a wide range of scholarly works and other well-researched publications. In telling the story I am especially reliant on the published findings of specialists. I hope that these writers will consider acknowledgement of their work in the references and bibliography in part an expression of my gratitude. Though he was in the throes of completing his biography of Sir Lewis Namier, David Hayton, a distinguished authority on early eighteenth-century Ireland and on parliamentary history, and a former joint editor of *Irish Historical Studies*, set aside a very considerable amount of time to go through the draft chapters and to make very helpful suggestions. Trevor Moore allowed me to draw on his expertise as a composer and musician. My sincere thanks to them both. However, any errors which may have crept into the text are entirely my own. Victor Blease, Eddie McCamley, Roy Maxwell and, above all, my wife Carol Tweedale, valiantly undertook the task of reading draft chapters to comment on how the text might be received by the non-specialist, and their advice urging adjustment and further clarification was much appreciated. A group of men of my own vintage who meet once a month in Belfast to discuss Ireland's past, the island's present condition and the country's cultural heritage were amongst those who provided many valuable insights. They are: Maurice Blease, Victor Blease, Douglas Carson, David Coffey, Brian Garrett, Liam Kearney, John Knox, Eddie McCamley, Alister McReynolds, Peter Spratt, Thompson Steele and Barry White. My thanks to the staffs of the National Library of Ireland in Dublin, the Handel House Museum and the Foundling Museum in London, and the Linen Hall Library and the McClay Library of Queen's University in Belfast. Sincere thanks also to Richard Hawkins, John K. Hunter, Fiona Aryan, the Very Reverend Dr Hugh P. Kennedy, Adrian Bannan, Kieran Fagan and Stephen Bleade. Rosemary Hunter, Róisín Sweeney, Ruth Tweedale and Dan Bardon who gave me introductions, made helpful comments and answered queries.

Sinéad O'Kelly spoke to me after she had toured Ireland with the Irish Baroque Orchestra to perform as the soprano soloist in *Messiah*. What struck her most forcibly – in addition to being profoundly moved by the music – was the way that Handel 'paints the words of the text with the music he writes'. No other composer, in her experience, paid such close attention to the meaning of the text in a libretto and took such care to write music to match it. Sinéad spoke as a professional opera singer. Others who at different times have helped me to understand how uplifting, fulfilling and joyful it has been to take part as amateur choristers in *Messiah* include: Joanna Mules, Michael Burns, Marcus Patton, Noel Thompson, John Hunter and Brian Garrett. The cellist, uillean piper and composer, Neil Martin, described the moment he took part as a nine-year-old in singing the Hallelujah chorus at the Belfast school of Music Christmas concert as 'life changing'.

Margaret and Norbert Bannon, in a succession of generous invitations to performances in Dublin, have converted me into an enthusiast for grand opera. Máire Casement and her late husband, Dermot Neary, reinforced that enthusiasm by organising regular attendance at Castleward Opera in Co. Down. My wife Carol has succeeded in broadening my musical tastes to the extent that twice in recent years I have stood with her (without moving for more than three hours) very contentedly in the grounds of the Royal Dublin Society in Ballsbridge to hear the matchless Bruce Springsteen play. I am profoundly grateful to Carol: the value of her support throughout the writing of this book has been incalculable.

Roger Boyle, the Earl of Orrery, once observed that Jonathan Swift was attended by 'a constant seraglio of very virtuous women'. Reading this quotation again I am prompted to adjust it, applying it to the staff of Gill & Macmillan who have worked with me on this project in the most supportive way – 'Conor Nagle, the commissioning editor, is attended by a constant seraglio of very talented, lively and imaginative women'. They are: Catherine Gough, Jen Patton, Jennifer Brady and Teresa Daly. I am also exceedingly grateful to Síne Quinn who edited the text for this book with painstaking care and sensitivity, as well as impressing me frequently with her knowledge and insights.

A Note on Dating

In 1582 Pope Gregory XIII introduced the New Style or Gregorian calendar which began the year on 1 January. Scotland and nearly all states on the European mainland adopted this calendar. Until 1752 England and Ireland stuck with the Old Style or Julian calendar, in which the beginning of the year was Lady Day, 25 March. By 1700 the Old Style calendar was 11 days behind the New Style.

In this book, as is the usual practice, dating is according to the Old Style for the day and the month, but according to the New Style for the year. For example, Handel performed his masque *Acis & Galatea* in the Fishamble Street Musick Hall on 20 January 1741 Old Style or 31 January 1742 New Style, but is dated here as 20 January 1742.

Contents

Chapter 1
'Year of the Slaughter': A Grim Prologue

BLIADHAIN AN ÁIR

Every year energetic Dubliners rise early to climb Killiney Hill,
south of the city, to greet the dawn on midsummer's day. As
they look down to watch the first rays touch some of the most
sumptuous private residences in the country and brighten a part
of the Irish Sea, often compared with the Bay of Naples, only a
few of them will know why there is an obelisk at the summit, or
why there are remains of a huge wall surrounding the hill. These
constructions are evidence of a great relief scheme to provide work
for the starving in 1741, funded by John Mapas of Rochestown, one
of the few wealthy Catholic landowners remaining in south County
Dublin at the time. And close to a grand Palladian mansion in Co.
Kildare, Castletown House, stands another obelisk – huge, elaborate
and 70 feet high – erected by the orders of Lady Katherine, widow
of a former Speaker of the Irish House of Commons, William
Conolly. This too had been put up at the same time and for the
same purpose – to provide work for the starving. Two years later in
1743 a Major Hall of Churchtown, south of the city, erected a very
large conical stone building, broad at the base and narrow at the top,
with a spiral stairway on the outside. This was no gentleman's folly:
known for a time as the 'Inkbottle' and later as the 'Bottle Tower', it
had been built as a barn to hold such a large store of grain so that no
one in the area would ever starve to death again.[1] These are modest
reminders of what today is a little-known event, an episode which
was nevertheless one of the greatest tragedies in the history of
modern Ireland, a famine so terrible that it was recalled as *bliadhain
an áir*, 'Year of the Slaughter'.

It was also a crisis that persuaded members of the 'Charitable
Musical Society for the Release of Imprisoned Debtors' in Dublin
that an unprecedented step should be taken to raise the relief funds

so desperately needed. As tens of thousands were perishing from hunger and fever, members of this charity joined forces with the governors of Mercer's Hospital and the Charitable Infirmary in the city, to invite over from London the greatest composer they knew of, George Frideric Handel. They would ask him to conduct a benefit concert of compositions of his own choosing in the Society's new Music Hall in Fishamble Street. It was in this way that the sacred oratorio, *Messiah*, came to be given its first performance in Dublin on 13 April 1742.

The 'Great Frost'

On 29 and 30 December 1739 'the most violent storm ... for several years past' brought with it bitter cold from the east. As the New Year began three ships foundered in Dublin Bay – a French vessel bringing in casks of brandy, a Riga fly-boat laden with flaxseed, and a Liverpool sloop with a cargo of salt and earthen ware. All the passengers on the sloop were drowned and the body of its captain was found on Merrion Strand 'covered over with ice'.

Throughout January 1740 Arctic weather gripped Ireland, so intense that vast numbers of fish were found dead around the shores of Strangford Lough and Lough Neagh. In north Tipperary a whole sheep was roasted on top of 19 inches of ice on the River Shannon at Portumna, 'at the eating of which they had great mirth, and drank many loyal toasts'.[2] Afterwards a hurling match was played on the ice between two teams of gentlemen. So sharp was the frost that people from Tyrone walked directly across the frozen waters of Lough Neagh as they travelled to the market in Antrim town.

Lasting seven weeks, this 'Great Frost' froze the sea around both English and Irish ports, halting the shipping of coal from Cumbria, Ayrshire and south Wales across the Irish Sea to Dublin. Desperate citizens tore up hedges and ornamental shrubs around the city, and 14 men were arrested for felling trees in Phoenix Park. At night Dublin's streets were plunged into darkness: most street lamps had no fuel left since waterwheels could not turn to press enough rapeseed to replenish them with oil; and lamplighters found that the few still with oil were quickly extinguished by the extreme cold.[3]

Ireland was not alone: all of western Europe north of the Alps and the Pyrenees was gripped by this intensely cold weather. Air masses spread from northern regions of the Russian Empire as blocking anticyclones – an extension of the semi-permanent high-pressure region near the North Pole – reversed the direction of the usual south-westerly flow. The winter of 1739-1740 proved the longest and coldest in modern western European history. As early as the end of October 1739 ice had put an end to voyages in the Baltic. All the rivers in Germany were already frozen by the first of November. At Kew outside London measured rainfall for the last six months of 1739 had accumulated to an extraordinary 16.17 inches. Then bitter easterly winds, blowing at gale force without ceasing for a week at the end of 1739, caused temperatures to drop close to or below 0°F (-17.7°C) over most of England. The Denmark Sound froze solid in February 1740 enabling people to travel by sledge between Elsinore and Sweden. The Zuyder Zee in the Dutch Republic froze over completely. A million head of sheep perished in Bohemia; in Burgundy's wine-growing region a third of the vines were killed; minimum temperatures of −18°F (-27.7°C) in Uppsala and −26°F (-54°C) in Warsaw were recorded; and even in Pavia in northern Italy temperature readings fell below freezing point every single day in February, on one occasion to 3°F (-16 °C). Scotland was more fortunate: there heavy falls of snow covered winter corn with a protective blanket, unlike in many other countries where frost killed the seed in the ground.[4]

'THE MOST DREADFUL CALAMITY THAT EVER BEFELL THIS POOR KINGDOM'

Over nearly all of Europe the winters for the previous ten years had been exceptionally mild and generally harvests had been bountiful. This had not been the case for Ireland: here the Great Frost hit the ordinary people of the island particularly hard as it followed a succession of half a dozen years of abnormal weather severely reducing farm yields. The most vulnerable, found mostly in the southern half of the country, were those who depended on the potato both for food and as a cash crop. Now the temperature plummeted so greatly that potato stores in straw-covered clamps in the ground were turned to inedible pulp. As Michael Rivers, a Co. Waterford merchant, observed, the frost:

has already destroyed a great part of the potatoes that lie in the cabins that lodge them and most of the potatoes of our country that are in the ground, by which the poor are likely to suffer greatly.[5]

Three weeks later Richard Purcell wrote from north Cork:

The eating potatoes are all destroyed, which many will think will be followed by famine among the poor, and if the small ones, which are not bigger than large peas and which be deepest in the ground, are so destroyed as not to serve for seed, there must be sore famine in 1741 … If no potatoes remain sound for seed, I think this frost the most dreadful calamity that ever befell this poor kingdom.[6]

Around Upper and Lower Lough Erne the usual cost of a barrel of potatoes was between 8s and 10s; in 1740 the price had risen to 32s a barrel. The price asked in Dublin for a barrel of oats went up from 7s to 12s, and by May 1741 it had reached 15s.

In Dublin a fund was launched to deal with the crisis. Donations were collected in the more prosperous Church of Ireland parishes in the east of the city to provide relief to artisans and weavers in the Liberties. During the last week of January nearly 80 tons of coal and 10 tons of meal were freely distributed. The viceroy, the Duke of Devonshire, ordered that £100 be taken from the state coffers to be added to Dublin's appeal fund.

So many wild birds had been killed by the cold that there was an eerie silence across the land. This poem appeared in *Faulkner's Dublin Journal*:

> No lark is left to wake the morn,
> Or rouse the youth with early horn;
> The blackbird's melody is o'er
> And pretty robin sings no more.
>
> No thrush to serenade the grove
> And soothe the passions into love,
> Thou sweetest songster of the throng,
> Now only live in poet's song.

Huge numbers of cattle and sheep had been killed by the extreme cold. On 3 February Jonathan Swift, Dean of St Patrick's Cathedral, hoped that 'we have almost done with this cursed weather'[7] and, indeed, soon after the temperature began to rise. It was no longer safe to walk over the frozen River Liffey. But when the thaw set in the usual rains did not follow. In consequence, there was little or no grazing for those animals that had survived the frost. 'The cattle are all dying,'[8] it was reported from Lismore in Waterford at the end of March. In April a correspondent from north Wexford wrote to the Dublin newspaper, *Pue's Occurrences*:

> Without rain what is to become of us? The corn that is sowed is perishing, the corn we have in our haggards is so prodigious dear the poor cannot purchase it … As for flesh meat they cannot smell to it, they have lost all their sheep long ago, and now their last stake, their little cows are daily and hourly dropping for want of grass.[9]

This abnormal drought was not confined to Ireland. On 24 May the *London Advertiser* reported: 'Grass and Corn were all burnt up, and the Fields looked as red as Foxes'.[10] By the second week of June 1740 corn prices in Ireland were twice what they had been in January; at Drogheda a mob boarded and smashed up a vessel laden with corn; and in the capital at the end of May the *Dublin News-Letter* reported:

> The bakers having made but little household bread, the populace were so greatly enraged that they broke open their shops that night and on Sunday; some sold their bread and gave them money, others took it away, and in this manner they went through the city.

On the following Monday the mob roamed out of the city to seize meal from mills in Harolds Cross and its neighbourhood. As they attempted to restore order, soldiers called out from the Royal Barracks killed several rioters. Troops had to patrol the markets and streets for the ensuing five days and nights. Fourteen men and one woman were charged with rioting and theft of food. Five were acquitted; three were publicly whipped; and three more were gaoled for three months each.

The remaining four received seven-year sentences to be transported to the New World; however, all escaped from their prison ship off the coast of Waterford and one got back home to Dirty Lane in Dublin only to be re-arrested after assaulting a gardener – he was executed two months later.[11] The drought was so severe that the streams that usually turned the water wheels to power corn mills and woollen tuck mills dried up. In the tinder-dry conditions fires raged in many towns: 150 houses burned down in Carrick-on-Suir, Co. Tipperary, 53 in Wexford town, and 20 in the village of Moate, Co. Westmeath.

The harvest in the autumn of 1740, depleted though it was, brought some relief. Then bad weather returned. Violent gales blew in September, followed by blizzards along the east coast in October, covering Belfast in what were described as 'prodigious' quantities of snow. Indeed, the autumn of 1740 was probably the coldest in two centuries in all of Great Britain and Ireland. Two terrible storms hit the country in November, accompanied by more snow and frost. On 9 December the heavens opened with such force that floods were reported across the island, washing houses and 'whole trees' into the River Liffey, and one correspondent from Navan, Co. Meath, described 'the greatest flood in the River Boyne that was ever known in the memory of man'.[12] On the following day temperatures dropped and the Arctic weather returned. A foot of snow fell in the Midlands on 13 December. Once again rivers froze over with 'the people sliding and skating everywhere' on the Liffey.[13]

PRIMATE BOULTER ORGANISES RELIEF

The Irish Parliament then met only every second year. When the session ended in May 1740 William Cavendish, 3rd Duke of Devonshire, returned to England with his viceregal entourage, not to come back to Ireland for another 18 months. His place at the head of government in Ireland was taken, as was the usual practice, by the three Lords Justices. On this occasion they were: the Church of Ireland primate, Hugh Boulter, Archbishop of Armagh; the Speaker of the Irish House of Commons, Henry Boyle; and Robert Jocelyn, Baron Newport, the Lord Chancellor. On 15 December 1740 Samuel Cooke, Lord Mayor of Dublin, made a formal visit to Dublin Castle to consult with the Lords Justices 'on proper measures to reduce the price of corn'.[14]

The Lords Justices responded swiftly. A meeting of the Irish Privy Council was called and each high sheriff was instructed to record all the stocks of grain held by merchants and farmers in their particular county. A detailed return survives only for Co. Louth: it revealed that in all the county there were 85,000 barrels of grain, indicating that only one household in five in the county had enough food to see them through the following months. There is no reason to believe that the rest of Ireland was in any better condition.

Archbishop Boulter, though advanced in years, acted with great energy. He started a scheme of relief in Dublin on New Year's Day 1741. Rations were to be given free to genuine residents of the city who were now destitute 'by the deadness of trade and dearness of bread' so that they would not be forced to beg on the streets.[15] The city's workhouse in James Street, which had been transformed into a foundling hospital, was turned into a food depot; the institution's governors being on hand to sign meal-tickets for those entitled to be assisted. By mid-January 3,000 were being fed every day. By April the numbers had reached 4,400. At first the archbishop was paying for this out of his own pocket; it cost him £18 a day. Then George Berkeley (the noted philosopher and Bishop of Cloyne), Dean Swift, and a number of noblemen rallied round to contribute and raise funds. Some prominent citizens, including the Lord Mayor, were so grateful to Archbishop Boulter that in March they commissioned the painting of his portrait. In Waterford nearly 2,000 were being served boiled oatmeal two days a week, and the authorities were especially active in Cork city.[16] Over most of the rest of the country, however, there was an almost complete absence of an organised system of relief. A devastating famine was now sweeping across the island, together with its handmaiden: fever.

'A BLOODY FLUX AND A VIOLENT FEVER RAGES'
Extreme fluctuations in the weather not only ruined crops and killed domestic stock but also led to widespread epidemics of fatal diseases. The severe and protracted cold winter of 1739-1740 lengthened the time people stayed indoors, huddled together, and this close personal contact – especially in cramped and poorly ventilated dwellings – intensified the risks of contracting deadly louse-born and respiratory afflictions. Then the long drought that

followed helped the diffusion of bacteria that led to enteric diseases, particularly dysentery and typhoid fever. In any case, when their bodies were weakened by hunger and hypothermia, people more easily fell prey to infections such as dysentery, then known as 'the bloody flux'. John Usher, a land agent at Lismore, Co. Waterford, wrote to his employer in London in February: 'a bloody flux and a violent fever rages so all over the country that scarce a day passes that we do not bury fifteen or sixteen even in this small place … For my own part, were it not for the business of this place I would fly for my life'.[17]

Now the killing diseases were typhus and relapsing fever, infections spread mainly by the human body louse. Typhus produced delirium, vertigo, a high fever, bloodshot eyes and small, round, pinpoint purple-red spots caused by haemorrhages just under the skin. In the second week of the disease victims suffered delirium and became helpless, unable to move, eat or drink without assistance. Most victims died from heart failure or complications such as bacterial pneumonia. From west Cork Sir Richard Cox wrote: 'By all I can learn, the dreadfullest civil war, or most raging plague never destroyed so many as this season'.[18] The Rev. Philip Skelton, curate of Monaghan parish, reported that there were 'whole parishes in some places … almost desolate; the dead have been eaten in the fields by dogs for want of people to bury them'.[19]

The wealthy and powerful also succumbed to fever. They included Sir Alexander Staples, a leading Dublin merchant, and three judges: Lord Chief Justice Sir John Rogerson, 'lamented by the poor to whom he was a constant benefactor'; Prime Serjeant Richard Bettesworth, MP for Midleton, Co. Cork; and Chief Baron Wainwright who died in his home at Mount Merrion, a few miles south of Dublin.[20]

A FEARFUL HARVEST

Out of a population of around 2,400,000, between 310,000 and 480,000 died that year of 1741 as a direct result of famine and fever. A greater proportion of the population died in this *one* year than during the *five* years of the Great Famine in the 1840s when the population was more than three times larger. All Europe experienced famine conditions in 1741, but no country,

except for Norway, suffered as much as Ireland. How can this
extraordinarily high death toll for Ireland be explained? After all, the
extreme weather affected all of western and northern Europe and,
indeed, adverse conditions for farming continued longer elsewhere,
particularly in Scandinavia, than in it did in Ireland.

The answer seems to be that those in authority failed to put into
effect the most elementary measures needed to safeguard the destitute
from hunger and starvation. Though the dearth in Prussia was acute,
and the state was at war, timely and efficient action by its government
prevented a catastrophe. In France, the King's controller general,
Philibert Orry, engaged the Parisian banker, Isaac Thellusson, to buy
up cereals wherever he could. Thellusson even obtained corn from
Ireland and set about his work so enthusiastically that Orry, to his
embarrassment, was left with a huge stock of unsold grain by the
autumn of 1741 to the value of around 13 million livres. In England
the Elizabethan Poor Law obliged each parish to provide relief to
the old, the sick, the destitute and the 'casual poor'. This included
'outdoor relief' in the form of food, fuel and clothing, and in this
way a mortality crisis was averted during 1739-41.[21] In Scotland the
system of poor relief was not compulsory but it seemed to work as
well as the obligatory system in England.

Acute famine conditions and the deaths of tens of thousands were
to be found primarily in outlying possessions of dynastic powers.
Norway was then merely a province, part of the territory held by
the Danish monarchy; Sweden still ruled Finland; and what is
now Belgium was one of the scattered dominions of the Austrian
Habsburgs. All three governments failed to do enough and mortality
levels were very high in consequence and, in the case of Norway, equal
to that in Ireland.[22]

Ireland was in theory a separate kingdom, but in fact a British
possession ruled by George II. Though an Irish Parliament met in
Dublin, ultimate authority rested in London. The 1720 Declaratory
Act had confirmed that Westminster could legislate for Ireland,
should it wish to. More important, the British Privy Council had a
supervisory role over Irish legislation through Poynings' Law, enacted
in its original form in 1494; it was able to amend or suppress Irish
bills which could not then be revived or re-amended. Here there
was no system of obligatory poor relief. Parishes were expected – but

not compelled – to provide relief. In spite of its title, the Church of Ireland was not the church of most of the island's inhabitants. Only a few of those who were in distress during the Great Frost and the Year of the Slaughter were members of that church's congregation. Those in authority were of a different religious persuasion to most of those being struck down by famine and fever. Some prominent landlords with estates in the most distressed areas were absentees, living most of the time on the other side of the Irish Sea. In short those responsible for governing Ireland, at both a national and a local level, lacked the funding, the staff, the machinery to provide relief, and in some cases the will, to prevent a catastrophe in time of crisis, especially in the countryside.

REMANDED IN CUSTODY

The death toll seems to have been at its highest in the province of Munster. Though hordes of starving families poured into Dublin seeking relief, often in vain, vigorous action by Archbishop Boulter and others, and timely importation of corn from the American Colonies, kept down the loss of life from hunger and fever in Ireland's capital city. Nevertheless, no part of the country escaped the consequences of this terrible famine. The desperation of so many kept the courts inordinately busy. Speaker Boyle was informed that magistrates in the Munster circuit were 'grievously offended daily with miserable spectacles, expiring wretches and noisome smells'.[23] Most had been remanded in custody for the theft of cattle or of food, because:

> provisions are so scarce that 'tis impossible to supply all, and there is now scarce a night passes without accounts from different parts of the country of cows, sheep or some kinds of provisions being stole, and the jails are already so full that the consequence is greatly to be dreaded.[24]

Lord Chancellor Jocelyn, writing to Philip Yorke, Earl of Hardwicke, on 29 March 1741, expressed the view that the health of judges would be 'worn down' by the great number brought before them in the courts. Many judges handed out sentences of death for those convicted of the theft of food. At county assizes in 1741 there were 67 capital convictions, around three times the average for the previous two years. In 1742 the figure was double that figure again as magistrates dealt with the backlog of those on remand from the year before. Of all death sentences in the years 1739-1748, 82 per cent were handed down in 1741 and 1742. In some places leniency was shown: there were so many crammed into prison on remand for the theft of food in Co. Kildare that most were given their freedom in batches after simply being branded on the hand.[25] There was no question, however, of releasing those incarcerated who could not pay their debts – the objects of concern of the Charitable Musical Society.

GAOL INMATES: 'THEIR EYES ARE FALLING OUT AND THEIR BONES PIERCING THEIR SKINS'

The maintenance of business confidence depended heavily on knowing that the law as it applied to debtors and insolvents was fully enforced. The government in turn was anxious to ensure that the courts did their duty. Parliament frequently concerned itself with the issue with the result that the law became extremely complicated.[26] The outcome for those who could not meet the demands of their creditors did not change, however: incarceration in prison. Irish legislation provided for the recovery of small debts by a variety of means, but there was no law which made it possible to recover larger sums through process against a debtor's property. Neither land nor liquid assets such as bills of exchange could be seized for payment of debt, except in cases of bankruptcy. Only a few could be classed as bankrupts – for the most part they were wholesalers whose businesses had failed. Everyone else with no hope of paying their debts – including shopkeepers, tavern proprietors, farmers, drovers and artisans – could not be classed as 'bankrupts' and were designated 'insolvents'. In short, the fate of the great majority of those who could not answer their creditors was imprisonment. Indeed, it is more than likely that many members of the Charitable Musical Society had relatives or friends who had at one time or another endured the life-threatening experience of being cast into one of the city's gaols for debt.[27]

Debtors and insolvents could be held in any of Dublin's six prisons, in particular: the national debtors' prison, the Four Courts Marshalsea in Molesworth's Court, off Fishamble Street; Kilmainham Gaol on the banks of the River Camac which specialised in imprisoning debtors of Dublin county; and Newgate in Cornmarket, a prison principally for criminals but debtors were also sent there. Without a doubt, conditions in Newgate were worse than in any other gaol in Ireland. All those sentenced by the judges of the King's Bench, the Lord Mayor, or Justices of the Peace for the City of Dublin were directed to be sent there. However, only the poorest were held in Newgate because constables could be bribed to take them instead to gaols less vile and life-threatening. The committee charged by the Irish Parliament to enquire into Irish gaols, reported in 1729 that 'none are sent to' Newgate 'but those of the poorer sort who are not worth fleecing'.[28] This was most vividly illustrated by the revelation that John Audovin, during his six weeks incarceration in the Black Dog gaol (a former tavern in Newhall Street) while he was *waiting to be executed*, had to spend the extremely large sum of £300, most of it to prevent a transfer to Newgate.[29]

The post of head gaoler of Newgate was given to the man who made the highest bid and could offer substantial financial securities. Since the salary was trifling, he recouped his outlay and made his money by charging his prisoners for their accommodation and many extras. Prisoners from outside the city boundary got neither bread nor bedding and so, to survive, they had to beg money from their families and friends to meet the gaoler's extortionate demands. Those from the city itself got a six-penny loaf of bread every eight days (which in 1741 weighed only four pounds), described as 'a poor substance (God knows) in this dreadful season'.[30] Not until 1764 were those applying to become gaolers forbidden to pay 'a fee, emolument or gratuity' and only from then did they have to display prominently a table of fees in the prison.[31] Right up to this date, in a practice known as 'brocking', money was extorted from new arrivals at Newgate and in the City Marshalsea. According to a letter in the *Freeman's Journal*, if money was:

> not immediately paid by the newcomer, he or she, will be stripped, naked (and in the case of resistance be pinned fast with cords) to be carried to the necessary house and there ducked until almost suffocated and their cloaths pledged until the sum is paid.[32]

Faulkner's Dublin Journal, published very close to Newgate, did what it could to arouse the compassion of readers. In March 1741 it reported that four prisoners in that gaol

> have within these few days died through real hunger, as it most shockingly appeared from their having eaten their tongues almost out of their heads, and many other such spectacles of poverty, their eyes are falling out, and their bones piercing their skins.

Donations received by the newspaper were converted into bread, cheese and beer to be given to the prisoners.[33]

By the spring of 1741 more than 140 prisoners were crammed into Newgate. Most were on remand for the theft of food but many, too, were debtors. As the preamble to an Irish relief act had acknowledged back in 1737, 'such unhappy debtors have always been deemed the proper objects of public compassion'.[34] The voluntary body whose main object was to free as many as possible of these 'unhappy debtors' was the Charitable Musical Society.

A MUSICAL JOURNEY THROUGH 'HELL': TO THE SIGN OF THE CROSS-KEYS AND ON TO THE BULL'S HEAD TAVERN IN FISHAMBLE STREET
The origins of the Charitable Musical Society which was to be primarily responsible for inviting Handel to Dublin, and which was to erect the music hall in which *Messiah* was first performed, are to be found in the shadow of Christ Church. Here, dominating steeply rising ground on the Liffey's south bank, this venerable cathedral overlooked the city's busiest district. Faced by the Tholsel, the headquarters of Dublin's civic government, on Skinners' Row and flanked by no fewer than four parish churches, Christ Church was hemmed in on all sides. The cathedral's chapter house and medieval cloister had long since been swallowed up by the Four Courts of Chancery, King's Bench, Common Pleas and Exchequer and, what had once been residences for ecclesiastical dignitaries, had now been converted into inns, shops and printing houses. Those being brought for trial from Christ Church Lane had to enter 'Hell', a dark narrow passage – covered with an arch adorned with an image of the Devil carved in oak – nearly ten feet below the cathedral floor leading directly to the courts. It was here in Christ Church Yard –

not quite 100 feet long and no more than 50 wide, bustling with attorneys, legal clerks, witnesses, plaintiffs, aldermen, vergers and vendors – that John Neal (or O'Neil) had begun making recorders, flutes and violins early in the eighteenth century. From 1721 he was selling sheet music imported from England and two years later he began printing his own, his first publication being a *Choice Collection of the Newest Airs, Minuets and Play House Tunes*. Then in 1724, Neal, now in partnership with his son William, published the earliest printed collection of Irish music, including pieces by Ireland's great harpist, Turlough Carolan. In time at least 28 musical publications – ranging from works by Corelli and Handel to John Gay's *The Beggar's Opera* – issued from the Neal printing press. The Neals were also accomplished performers on a variety of instruments and much in demand after a day's work to play in the neighbouring taverns.

At an early stage these men with a shared passion for music, meeting for convivial impromptu concerts in inns and each other's homes, saw the opportunity to raise money for worthy causes. In 1710 a club formed to put on plays to raise money for charity had been set up by a respected shopkeeper, Gregory Byrne. A few years later, in a tavern called the Sign of the Cross-Keys, just a few yards away from the Neals' workshop in Christ Church Yard, Byrne's club was absorbed to become the nucleus of a new charitable society, now concerned with musical performances rather than dramatic productions. When the charitable society's first president, Patrick Beaghan, died in 1723, John Neal presided as his successor for many years thereafter. Since the Cross-Keys inn was too cramped for their planned vocal and instrumental performances, they arranged to hold their meetings in the Bull's Head Tavern in Fishamble Street.[35] This inn was accessed through another stygian passage matching 'Hell' on the other side of Christ Church Yard.

'Hell' seems to have been aptly named: the condemned were taken from one of the four courts down across Christ Church Yard through this dark lane out into Fishamble Street and downhill to the narrow entry leading to the Four Courts Marshalsea in Molesworth's Court. John Harding had published the *Dublin News-Letter* next to this prison in this cul-de-sac. He had put himself in peril by printing one of the notorious *Drapier's Letters*

in 1724. Harding refused to reveal that 'the Drapier', the author
of these satirical tracts, lampooning the government and declared
treasonable by the Irish Privy Council, was none other than
Jonathan Swift. For this Harding was cast into the Marshalsea. The
Dublin News-Letter survived, its production transferred to Skinners'
Row, but Harding did not: the privations suffered in a dark, disease-
ridden prison cell were too much for him and he died shortly after
being released. A poem entitled 'A Poem to the whole People of
Ireland', relating to M.B. Drapier, by A.R. Hosier, printed in the
Blind Key by Elizabeth Sadlier, 1726 explained in the second verse:

> He left, with his widow, two children behind,
> And little, God help her! to keep them from starving;
> But hop'd, for the Drapier's sake, friends she would find,
> Or that for his own merit they'd think her deserving.

The sufferings of Sarah, Harding's widow, were not over. In October
1725 it was ordered by the House of Lords that she be taken into
custody for printing a poem entitled 'Wisdom's Defeat', commenting
on the passing of an address to the King by the Lords, which was by
them declared to be 'base, scandalous, and malicious, highly reflecting
upon the honour of their House, and the Peerage of this Kingdom'.
The sheriffs of the city of Dublin were ordered to direct 'the said
scandalous pamphlet to be burnt by the hands of the common
hangman; and that they see the same done between the hours of
twelve and one, before the gate of the Parliament House, and also
before the Tholsel of the city'. Sarah Harding was duly imprisoned
but, unlike her husband, she survived the experience.[36]

   The grim Four Courts Marshalsea was largely hidden by other
buildings from the eyes of what were by now the fashionable residents
of Fishamble Street. During the reign of Charles II, fishmongers
and butchers who for centuries had held their markets here had been
ordered to transfer their trades north of the river to Ormond Market.
The stench of the fishambles, fleshambles and tanning pits no longer
tainted the air and thus the character of Fishamble Street, which ran
steeply down the east side of Christ Church, had been transformed.
This thoroughfare was fast becoming one of Dublin's best-known
venues for music. Half way down Fishamble Street, opposite St John's

church, the Philharmonick Room had been built for the Musical
Academy (which renamed itself the Philharmonick Society in 1741)
as a replacement for its hall in Crow Street. Several large cage-work
houses still stood in this street, though several had been destroyed,
including the London Tavern, by a fire which had broken out in the
London Entry between Castle Street and Fishamble Street in 1729.
(Cage-work houses were substantial half-timbered structures erected in
the sixteenth century: external and internal walls had been constructed
of squared oak beams joined by mortises, tenons and wooden pegs, with
the spaces between filled with plaster and brick, and roofed with tiles,
shingles or slates.) The Bull's Head Tavern was the largest cage-work
house still standing on the western side of Fishamble Street. Belonging
to the Dean and Chapter of Christ Church, it had once been leased
as a town house by the Plunketts, the earls of Fingall, and still bore on
its front that family's coat of arms. The Bull's Head Tavern was much
prized as a venue for convivial meetings and celebrations and it became
the regular home of the Charitable Musical Society.

THE CHARITABLE MUSICAL SOCIETY RAISES FUNDS TO LIBERATE IMPRISONED DEBTORS

The charitable musical club formed in the Cross-Keys inn, named
at first the 'Bull's Head Society' after the tavern where performances
were held, met every Friday evening. When a concert was over,
members finished the night with 'catch singing, mutual friendship,
and harmony'.[37] It cost five shillings – 'an English crown' – to
become a member and a committee arranged a programme of
musical events for each year. The society's annual dinner was held
in December; the season for their entertainments ended in May;
and the proceeds were allocated to various laudable purposes. At
first funds were given to the Dublin Society (a society founded in
1731 to promote scientific and practical improvement, now the
Royal Dublin Society), but then the Bull's Head Society formed
a committee to visit gaols in the city and to pay for the liberation
of incarcerated debtors. The release of insolvents from prison
thereafter became the principal charitable object of the society.
Laurence Whyte, teacher of mathematics and an active member,
was concerned to draw attention to the exceptional inclusiveness
of this charitable organisation. Its members ranged from titled

gentlemen to humble artisans and – a particularly striking feature
– it appears to have had no difficulty including Catholics. Whyte
had close connections with many Catholic families and may even
have been a Catholic himself. He wrote a long poem to describe the
society during the time that John Neal was president. It begins:

> While honest Neal the mallet bore,
> Who filled the chair in days of yore,
> There lawyers met, and eke physicians,
> Attorneys, proctors, politicians;
> Divines and students from the College,
> Men full of speculative knowledge;
> Captains and coll'nel's all in red,
> Who in the school of Mars were bred.
> Some beaux and prigs, with nice toupees,
> With wast-coasts lac'd down to their knees;
> Some poets, painters, and musicians,
> Mechanicks, and mathematicians,
> For tradesmen there gave no offence,
> When blessed with manners or good sense;
> Some gentlemen, some lords and squires,
> Some Whigs, and Tories, and Highflyers;
> There Papists, Protestants, Dissenters,
> Sit cheek by jole, at all adventures,
> And thus united did agree
> To make up one Society.
> That some drink jill, and others beer,
> Was all the schism they had to fear.[38]

For a time the society moved to the George in Fishamble Street and
after that to The Bear in Winetavern Street; by then it had changed
its name to 'The Charitable and Musical Society'. As the society
attracted more members it moved back again to the Bull's Head
Tavern. Here it adopted titles which during the 1730s ranged from
'The Bull's Head Club in Fishamble-street for Releasing Prisoners'
to 'The Charitable Musical Society for the Relief of Insolvent
Debtors' and 'The Charitable Musical Society for the Release of
Imprisoned Debtors'.[39]

'THE CHARITABLE MUSICK HALL IN FISHAMBLE-STREET, WHICH IS FINISHED IN THE GENTEELEST MANNER'

John Neal's son, William, acted as treasurer of this body through all its changes of name and venue. It was he who masterminded the construction of the 'Great Musick Hall', often referred to as 'Mr Neal's Great Room'. This auditorium was built specifically to put on concerts for the benefit of their charity, while the society continued to hold convivial evenings in the more intimate surroundings of the Bull's Head Tavern. The society engaged Richard Cassels (or Castle) to build the Great Musick Hall in Fishamble Street on a site facing the Bull's Head Tavern. Cassels, the most distinguished architect then working in Dublin, had first been brought over from Germany in 1727 by Sir Gustavus Hume to build his country mansion, Castle Hume, by the shores of Lough Erne. Thereafter he moved to Dublin where he built great houses for the nobility in cut stone. Cassels's commission for the Fishamble Street Musick Hall came more or less at the same time as his contract to design the city's most splendid mansion so far, Tyrone House in Marlborough Street, for Marcus Beresford, Viscount Tyrone.

The Musick Hall in Fishamble Street, when it was completed in 1741, was Ireland's largest concert venue. It could seat 700. At the eastern end it had a 'throne' for the president of the society. The following year Laurence Whyte described it in verse:

> As Amphion built of old the Theban wall,
> So Neal has built a sumptuous Musick Hall;
> The one by pow'rful touches of his lute;
> The other by the fiddle and the flute.
> Join'd with some others of harmonic sound,
> He rais'd this lofty fabric from the ground;
> Where heaps of rubbish in confusion stood,
> Old walls, old timber, and some rotten wood;
> From their old chaos they new forms assume, –
> Here stands the Hall, and there the drawing room,
> Adorn'd with all that workmanship can do
> By ornaments and architecture too.
> The oblong area runs from east to west.
> Fair to behold, but hard to be exprest;
> At th' eastern end the awful throne is plac'd,

With fluted columns and pilasters grac'd,
Fit for the noblest President to rest,
Who likes the arms of Ireland for his crest.
In different classes, at the western end,
Musicians with their instruments attend;
While they diffuse their harmony around,
The concave arch reverberates the sound.
The architect has here display'd his art,
By decorations proper for each part:
The cornice, dentills, and the curious mould,
The fret-work, and the vaulted roof behold;
The hollow arches, and the bold design,
In ev'ry part with symmetry divine.[40]

The hall was formally opened on 2 October 1741 with a Charitable Musical Society concert. To help defray expenses, the new building was hired out to suitable organisations and individuals. For example, two ladies, Mrs Hamilton and Mrs Walker, organised an 'Assembly' there every Saturday evening – advertisements they inserted in the press described the venue as 'The Charitable Musick Hall in Fishamble-street, which is finished in the genteelest manner'.[41]

The extreme weather of 1740 and the famine that followed it in 1741 placed a heavy burden on the city's charitable organisations. In Dublin's grim, insanitary gaols, debtors and insolvents, men and women who were the objects of concern for the Charitable Musical Society, languished together with other criminals and great numbers on remand charged with the theft of food. The funds raised by the society to help these imprisoned men and women must have been impressive. *Faulkner's Dublin Journal* had this report in its 14-17 March 1741 issue:

The Committee of the Charitable Musical Society appointed
for this year to visit the Marshalseas in this City, and release
the Prisoners confined therein for debt, have already released
188 miserable persons of both sexes. They offered a reasonable
Composition to the Creditors. And many of the Creditors being
in circumstances almost equally miserable with their Debtors, due
regard was paid by the Committee to this Circumstance.

As well as paying off the creditors, the Society had also to pay the fees
demanded by the gaolers before the debtors could be freed.[42]

'THUS DEVONSHIRE, OUR SORROWS TO ALLAY, INVITES THE NATION TO HEAR HANDEL PLAY'

Just when the Charitable Musical Society for the Release of
Imprisoned Debtors decided to take the step of inviting Handel to
come to Dublin is not known. The society's committee thought it
made good sense to join forces with two other charities in the city
with impeccable credentials.

One was the Charitable Infirmary in Cook Street, founded by
six Catholic physicians who had pooled their resources in 1718
to provide – initially – just four hospital beds. It is thought to be
the oldest voluntary hospital in either Ireland or Great Britain.
Thanks to charitable persons who 'came cheerfully into an annual
subscription' there were nine beds by 1724. In 1728 the Charitable
Infirmary moved north of the Liffey to larger premises on Inn's
Quay, on a site now occupied by the present Four Courts. John
Watson Stewart's 1740 *Gentleman's and Citizen's Almanac* outlined
the services provided:

In this House, great numbers of maimed, wounded, and
diseased poor, are constantly relieved. There are above 36 beds,
with provision and all necessaries for interns, who are received
into the house, and constantly attended; as well as medicines
and advice gratis for all externs, who flock in numbers thither
daily. The charity is altogether supported by the voluntary
contributions of the well-disposed.

The surgeons attending provided their services 'without fee or reward'.[43]

The second voluntary body to join with the Charitable Musical
Society was Mercer's Hospital, founded in 1734 by Mrs Mary
Mercer who had given a large house at the end of Stephen Street to
be turned into a hospital for the reception of 'lunatics and persons
afflicted with the King's evil [scrofula], cancer, leprosy, falling
sickness, etc.'[44] Dublin Corporation had given £50 towards fitting out
the house, and a very substantial legacy from a Captain Hayes had
made it possible to build a large extension enabling the institution
to increase the number of its beds to 62. Mercer's Hospital was
unquestionably the city's most prominent charity which was able to
draw Dublin's élite, including the Lord Lieutenant when he was in
town, once or twice a year to its benefit performances in the 'Round
Church', St Andrew's, in Suffolk Street. Indeed, these concerts
had given the citizens of Dublin their first opportunity to listen to
Handel's sacred music. Peers of the realm readily accepted nomination
as governors but, apart from acting as stewards at the benefit
performances, only Lord Tullamore and Lord Mountjoy appear to
have made an appearance at board meetings.[45]

Most biographies of Handel inform readers that the Duke of
Devonshire delivered the invitation to Handel to come to Dublin.
That is possible but by no means certain. The assumption that
the viceroy issued the invitation arises from a long poem written
by Laurence Whyte. His collection, *Original Poems on Various
Subjects*, published in 1742, was 'most humbly dedicated' to 'the
Right Honourable, Honourable, and Worthy Members of the most
Ancient, Charitable, and Musical Society at Mr. Neal's new Music-
Hall in Fishamble-street, Dublin: Consisting of Lords, Knights,
Gentlemen and Citizens'. The collection included this poem
with an almost impossibly long title, *A poem On The general Effect
and Excellency of Musick, but now more particularly on the famous
Mr. Handel's Performance, and Compositions, who has lately been
invited into this Kingdom, by his Grace the Duke of Devonshire, Lord
Lieutenant of* Ireland. The second verse begins:

> Our *Isle*'s from Famine and Contagion free,
> What now remains but *Song* and *Harmony*,
> But *Devonshire*, to make it more compleat,
> Has brought us *Handel* in his Science great,

Grand in his Aspect, Faculties, and Skill,
With Compositions flowing from his Quill

If only because he was in receipt of regular payments from the King, Handel would have needed royal permission to come to Ireland. This required a senior official to request leave from London and, since the three charities could not do this, the Duke or Sir Robert Wilmot, the London representative of the Irish government, may well have obliged them by doing so. As the music historian David Hunter has observed: 'From Devonshire's viewpoint the issuance of an invitation was an easy way to claim credit for providing the élite with a stellar diversion after the despair of the previous twenty-one months'.[46] Handel and the Duke were probably not acquainted, for Devonshire, unlike his viceregal predecessors, did not subscribe to opera in London.

Whyte's long poem is a panegyric, concerned as much to heap praise on the viceroy as on the visiting composer. Written during Handel's visit to Ireland, and more than two months before the première of *Messiah*, a notice in *Pue's Ocurrences* specifically referred to the invitation:

> Shortly to be published A Poem by Laurence Whyte on the General Effect and Excellency of Music, particularly, on the famous Mr. Handel's performance, who has been lately invited into this Kingdom by his Grace the duke of Devonshire, lord lieutenant of Ireland, for the Entertainment of the Nobility and Gentry.

And, indeed, the poem did not hesitate to give the Duke credit for bringing over a composer who had been taking Dublin society – 'the Nation' – by storm:

> Thus *Devonshire*, our Sorrows to allay,
> Invites the Nation to hear *Handel* play,
> Soon as his Grace appear'd on *Irish* Ground,
> Our two Year's Famine were in *Lethe* drown'd ...
> This Blessing, cou'd *Hybernia* once obtain,
> No more shou'd any murmur or complain.

When Handel received an invitation at the behest of the three charities he could begin to see the advantages of travelling over to Ireland. After all, the charities requested only one benefit performance and all the rest of his time in Dublin could be spent organising and directing his own concert series. The success of the composer's visit to Oxford in 1733 may well have encouraged him to expect a handsome financial return in the Irish capital. The role of Matthew Dubourg would have been pivotal. Handel had known him ever since he had heard the child prodigy play the violin standing on a stool in London. Dubourg had been engaged to lead the orchestra in several of Handel's operas in the capital before being appointed Master of the State Music in Dublin Castle. He regularly travelled back to London and would have explained to Handel what Dublin could offer in the way of instrumentalists, choristers, venues and the like. Dubourg must have given Handel assurances that interest in the city would be such that he could profit from the whole venture.

There may well have been an understanding made with representatives of the charities that Handel would try out a new composition for them in Dublin. Never at any stage was *Messiah* referred to, not even during the first couple of months of the composer's stay in Ireland.[47] Clearly Handel was giving himself time to assess the mood of his Dublin audiences, metaphorically keeping the score of his sacred oratorio in his back pocket until he felt that they were ready to hear its first performance.

Chapter 2
Handel: The German Creator of the English Oratorio

A LONDON AUDIENCE ENTRANCED

On 24 February 1711 the cream of London society crowded into the
city's splendid Queen's Theatre in the Haymarket for the first night
of the opera *Rinaldo*. The complicated plot was frankly ludicrous: the
young crusader Rinaldo, during the siege of Jerusalem, finds that his
beloved Almirena has been abducted by the sorceress Armida. With
the help of the Furies and his commander Goffredo, Rinaldo drives
off monsters guarding a magic mountain, turns a hanging garden into
a desert with the wave of a magic wand, and rescues the heroine from
certain death at the hand of the sorceress who avoids being hacked
down in an instant for her wickedness by promptly converting to
Christianity.[1]

This première was rapturously received. The audience was awestruck
by the sumptuous costumes, the seductive sirens, the fire-breathing
dragons and the elaborate scenery, which included a mountain reaching
up to the roof of the stage, flocks of live chaffinches flying between
the onstage trees, realistic impressions of thunder and lightning, and
fireworks – patrons being assured by the *Spectator* that in case of an
accident 'there are several Engines filled with Water, and ready to
play at a Minute's Warning'.[2] Those who were present forgave the
fact that stagehands forgot to move some wing flats causing the sea to
appear wrongly among the trees, that a chariot failed to materialise for
the pagan champion Argante, and that some ladies had their finery
spoiled by songbirds defecating from above. Above all, the audience
was entranced by the rich, dramatic music, especially the rendering of
magnificent arias by Niccolò Grimaldi, Elisabetta Pilotti and other
star singers imported from Italy. And Handel, the composer, trusted –
correctly as it turned out – that few would notice that most of the music
for the opera was recycled material, cherry-picked from a wide range of
his earlier compositions.[3]

'THE TOWN IS RUN MAD AFTER A NEW OPERA'

Born Georg Friederich Händel in Halle in the state of Saxony
in 1685, he began his career as an organist, and then moved to
Hamburg in 1703 where he became a harpsichordist-conductor.
Possibly invited by Prince Ferdinando de Medici, son of the Grand
Duke Cosimo of Tuscany, Handel then travelled to Italy. There,
though he quickly became known as 'The Saxon', he was happy
to sign himself Giorgio Federico Hendel. It was in Italy that the
composer spent some of the most formative years of his musical
career. This German Lutheran, whose grandfather had been a pastor,
whose first employer had been a Calvinist minister, now accepted the
patronage of Cardinal Pietro Ottoboni in Rome, and in 1707 wrote
a setting of Psalm 110, *Dixit Dominus domino meo*, forming part of
the Vesper Offices. His first Italian opera, *Rodrigo*, had its première
in Florence. Handel struck up a friendship with the composer
Alessandro Scarlatti, and followed him to Venice. By the spring of
1708 he was back in Rome where his new patron, Marchese Francesco
Maria Ruspoli, commissioned him to write for that Easter a large-scale
oratorio on Christ rising from the dead. *Oratorio per la resurrezione
di Nostro Signor Gesu Cristo* was given a magnificent staging in the
Marchese's palace – 1,500 printed word-books had been made available
for the huge audience and members of it were able to follow the text by
the light of no fewer than 16 candelabras.

By the autumn of 1708 Handel was in Naples, possibly to keep
out of the way of armies rampaging through much of Italy that year.
Indeed, Ruspoli himself was on campaign leading a regiment out of
Rome in September. In Naples Handel was commissioned by Cardinal
Vincenzo Grimani to compose the serenata *Aci, Galatea e Polifemo*,
a dramatic cantata for the wedding of the Duke of Alvito to Donna
Beatrice di Sanseverino. The following year he was working on his
opera *Agrippina* ready for the 1709-10 winter season in Venice. This
proved to be his greatest triumph, so far. Later, his biographer John
Mainwaring declared that the 'theatre, at almost every pause, resounded
with shouts and acclamations of *viva il caro Sassone* and other
expressions of approbation too extravagant to be mentioned'.[4]

In 1710 Handel was on his way north. He had been offered the
prestigious post of Kapellmeister (a position which placed him in
charge of the orchestra and choir) to the court of Georg Ludwig,

Elector of Hanover, with a salary of 1,000 thaler. The Elector's mother, Sophia, wrote to the Queen of Prussia that Handel 'plays the harpsichord marvellously to the enjoyment of the Electoral Prince and Princess'.[5] Later the Electoral Prince, as King George II, would be Handel's most stalwart patron. During this time Handel got an invitation from Charles Montagu, the Duke of Manchester, to come to London. The Duke had met Handel when he was Britain's ambassador to Venice; since then he had been searching for singers and musicians on behalf of his friend John Vanbrugh, the dramatist and promoter who had designed the Queen's Theatre in the Haymarket. The Elector of Hanover had his own good reason for giving his Kapellmeister leave to go to London: Queen Anne had had 13 pregnancies but not one child had survived and her husband Prince George had died in 1708. To avoid a Catholic succession, the queen was by now fully reconciled to the accession after her death of her distant relative, the Elector of Hanover. Besides, Anne was already developing a strong liking for Handel's compositions.

The first Italian opera performed in London had been Giovanni Bononcini's *Camilla* staged at Drury Lane in March 1706. From then on London society seemingly could not get enough of Italian opera. Jonathan Swift – still in London and yet to be appointed Dean of St Patrick's cathedral in Dublin – was appalled, as he wrote to a friend:

> The Town is run mad after a new Opera. Poetry and good Sense are dwindling like Echo into Repetition and Voice … these Opera's will be the ruin of the Nation … A good old Lady five miles out of Town askt me tother day, what these Uproars were that her Daughter was always going to.[6]

In short the Elector's Kapellmeister had arrived in a city with an élite hungering for Italian music, divas, castrati and spectacle. Handel was quick to do his best to meet that need. London had recently bypassed Paris to become the largest city in Europe and, at the centre of a thriving and expanding colonial empire, the nobility coming 'to town' as each winter approached had the deep pockets required to fund the lavish entertainment for which so many of the gentry craved. England had internationally famous poets and writers but, since the untimely death of Henry Purcell in 1695, it had produced no composer that could be placed in the first rank. Handel was in a very advantageous position to fill that vacancy.

Rinaldo's run of 15 performances was considered a brilliant success, and established Handel's name in England. His company was eagerly sought after. The composer accepted invitations to several of the private concert clubs then flourishing in London, including one which met in the house of the merchant Thomas Britton in Aylesbury Street off Clerkenwell Green. Britton sold coal from the ground floor of his home, and then converted the upper storey into a concert room. Handel played here along with several who in time would become his good friends. One of these was a young boy, Matthew Dubourg. He made his solo debut in Britton's concert room, standing on a stool: he would become a great violin virtuoso, an accomplished musical director and an occasional composer, and – 30 years later – he would lead the orchestra at the first performance of *Messiah* in Dublin.[7]

Handel returned briefly to Hanover and got permission to go abroad again. Failing to keep a promise to return in good time, Handel was dismissed from service to the court in 1713. This was not an acrimonious parting: the Elector knew that Handel now needed a larger stage than Hanover could offer. In any case, the two men would very soon be collaborating closely.

Back in London Handel was introduced to Richard Boyle, 3rd Earl of Burlington, a young man who had acquired a passion for Italian opera on a tour of Italy. It was at one of Burlington's lavish soirées that, in the company of the poet Alexander Pope and Queen Anne's doctor, John Arbuthnot, Handel was introduced to Jonathan Swift. Swift by that stage seems to have reconciled himself somewhat to the craze for Italian opera. Burlington became Handel's patron for a time. Queen Anne granted Handel a pension of £200. She was too corpulent and immobile to come to the Haymarket opera house but, since she loved music and could sing and play the harpsichord, she invited musicians to perform at St James's Palace. On 6 February 1711, for example, guests were sumptuously entertained and during the afternoon 'was perform'd a fine Consort, being a Dialogue in Italian, in Her Majesty's Praise, set to excellent Musick by the famous Mr *Hendel* … with which Her Majesty was extreamly well pleas'd'.[8]

HANDEL BECOMES A NATURALISED ENGLISHMAN

Queen Anne died on 1 August 1714: Arbuthnot wrote to Swift soon afterwards, 'I believe sleep was never more welcome to a weary traveller than death was to her'.[9] Georg Ludwig, Elector of Hanover, was now also George I of England. There was much understandable anxiety in government circles as to whether or not this Elector, who had such a tenuous claim by blood to the throne, would win general acceptance. The Jacobite rebellion in Scotland in 1715 demonstrated the insecurity of this Hanoverian succession at the outset.

When King George arrived in London politicians there were relieved to find that the rumour that he could speak no English was incorrect and, in fact, that he and his family were also fluent in French.[10] Handel played his part in the propaganda drive to win backing for his former employer. He composed the orchestral suite, *Water Music*, to escort the monarch and his retinue in a spectacular voyage up the Thames (which, incidentally, ensured that he got the six months back pay owed to him). The grateful George I provided the composer with regular commissions thereafter. Handel's financial security was enhanced further when James Brydges, Earl of Carnarvon and later the Duke of Chandos, agreed to become a patron and commissioned him to compose a series of anthems. The composer did not become a naturalised Englishman until 1727, but England had become his home and he had anglicised his name, signing himself, 'George Frideric Handel'.

Italian opera continued to be the rage amongst the nobility in London, an almost inevitable outcome of so many English aristocrats embarking on the Grand Tour to visit sites of classical antiquity, there to soak up the culture of the ancient world and the glories of the Renaissance. A group of noblemen created the Royal Academy of Music to ensure regular performances of Italian opera. Some of these gentlemen were amateur players. The King incorporated the Academy in 1719 and gave it £1,000 a year. King George had taken the urgent advice of Sir Robert Walpole, who was to become Prime Minister in 1722, to stay in London as much as possible and to cultivate the affections of aristocrats regularly wintering in the capital by ensuring lavish entertainment to their taste – and that, for the present, was Italian opera. The Lord Chamberlain sent Handel off to the European mainland to recruit famous Italian singers and he returned with the most distinguished of all, Francesco Bernardi, the castrato known as Senesino. Senesino – despite looking somewhat grotesque and standing rather stiffly on stage – had a remarkable resonant voice and an astonishing range. Despite a stormy relationship between the two from the outset, Handel, now Master of the Orchestra, eventually created 17 lead roles for Senesino.

In short, home-grown British opera performers could not even begin to match up to leading imported professionals. Mary Pendarves, the future Mrs Delany, wrote to her sister Anne Granville that 'the stage was never so well served as it is now, there is not one indifferent voice, they are all Italians'.[11] The soprano Francesca Cuzzoni, perhaps the greatest prima donna of her day, was enticed over to London. In 1723 Handel was appointed Composer of Music for His Majesty's Chapel Royal and served as music master to the daughters of George II, Anne and Caroline. In the same year, as a clear indication of his popularity and success, Handel leased a house, 25 Brook Street, in a neighbourhood favoured by the gentry, which became his home for the rest of his life.

'No more th'Italian squalling tribe admit ... 'tis Popery in wit'

Ottone, Re di Germania, Handel's first opera for the 1723 season, was given its première on 12 January. Cuzzoni during rehearsal proved so petulant that Handel cried out (in French): 'Oh! Madame I know well that you are a real she-devil, but I hereby give you notice, me, that I am Beelzebub, the Chief of Devils'.[12] Then he took her by the waist and swore that he would throw her out of the window if she said another word. This opera in which Cuzzoni made her London debut was a triumph from the outset – a courtier who had been brought over from Hanover likened the run on tickets to the South Sea Bubble. During one performance a footman shouted out from the gallery: 'Damme, she has a nest of nightingales in her belly'. John Gay, author of *The Beggar's Opera*, wrote to Swift, now back in his native city of Dublin having taken up his appointment there as the Dean of St Patrick's cathedral:

As for the reigning Amusement of the town, 'tis entirely Musick. Real fiddles, Bass Viols and Haut boys not poetical

Harps, Lyres and reeds. Theres no body allow'd to say I Sing
but an Eunuch or an Italian Woman. Every body is grown now
as great a judge of Musick as they were in your time of Poetry,
and folks that could not distinguish one tune from another now
daily dispute about the different Styles of Hendel, Bononcini and
Attilio. People have now forgot Homer, and Virgil & Caesar, or at
least they have lost their ranks, for in London and Westminster in
all polite conversation's, Senesino is daily voted to be the greatest
man that ever liv'd.[13]

Cuzzoni was joined by another brilliant soprano, Faustina Bordoni
in 1724. The two prima donnas made little attempt to hide their
rivalry. Very soon the opera-goers became passionately – ridiculously –
partisan, and over-excited Cuzzoni and Bordoni fans actually came to
blows in the theatre in the presence of the Princess of Wales in 1727, a
brawl that abruptly closed the season prematurely.

The death of George I occurred in June 1727. For the new monarch,
George II, Handel wrote four coronation anthems, including *Zadok
the Priest* which has been sung at every coronation since. Italian
operas were exceedingly expensive to stage, particularly as the fees
paid to the leading singers were extraordinarily high – for example,
Senesino's fee for his first season was £2,000. The problem was that
the performances were almost exclusively for the aristocracy and
dependent on subscriptions from an élite strictly limited in numbers.
Besides, a growing number of people questioned the dominance of
Italian opera. For Protestant Englishmen to take the Grand Tour and
return to enthuse about Italian opera was seen as a form of cultural
betrayal. While Queen Anne was still on the throne, the journalist and
playwright, Sir Richard Steele, expressed this view in verse:

No more th'Italian squalling tribe admit
In tongues unknown: 'tis Popery in wit,[14]

There seemed to be only one great resident composer, Handel, who,
though he took care to be naturalised, was after all at least as German
as his monarch.

In 1728 John Gay's *The Beggar's Opera* took London by storm. It
incorporated the tunes of popular English ballads with new words to a

plot based on a real-life drama: the escape in 1724 of a condemned man from his cell, his recapture and execution. Gay made sure he included a highly-effective take-off of the rivalry between Cuzzoni and Bordoni, and parodied the coloratura and ornamentation so characteristic of Italian opera. The success of *The Beggar's Opera* undoubtedly brought home to Handel that the public did indeed enjoy hearing English words set to English tunes.

Criticism of the rage for Italian opera (much of it coming, admittedly, from those who could not afford to pay the subscriptions) became more vocal. Protestant sensibilities were offended by the dominance of a variety of musical entertainment which seemed to be besmirched by loose morals from Catholic Europe. Why was it necessary to sing in a foreign language? Why was it necessary to employ men mutilated to become eunuchs? After all, castrati only began to appear after the papacy had refused to allow women to sing in churches. Admiration for Senesino and other castrati seemed a threat to the nation's morals. Earlier the critic John Dennis, Swift's friend, had been certain that Italian opera encouraged sodomy – 'if our Subscriptions go on, at the frantick rate that they have done, I make no doubt but we shall come to see one Beau take another for Better for Worse'.[15]

The poet laureate, Nahum Tate, exhorted readers:

> To cultivate that long-neglected Soil
> Our *English* Language (stor'd with all the Seeds
> Of Eloquence, but Choak'd with Foreign Weeds).[16]

Aaron Hill, one of Handel's librettists, at first had enthusiastically welcomed the arrival of Italian opera in London; now he deplored 'our emasculating present Taste, of the *Italian* Luxury'. 'The Martial Spirit of our Nation,' he continued, 'is effeminated, and gradually relax'd, by the Influence of this softening *Syren*'.[17] It was not the music but the subject matter and words unintelligible to nearly all who heard them that he objected to. In December 1732 Hill wrote a passionate appeal to Handel 'that you would be resolute enough, to deliver us from our *Italian bondage*.' Acknowledging 'your inimitable genius, the establishment of *musick*', he urged the composer to see to it that 'the excellence of the *sound* should be no longer dishonour'd, by the poorness of the *sense* it is chain'd to'.[18]

Criticism of this kind was beginning to alter attitudes in the capital. In a letter to her sister in 1727, Mrs Pendarves gave this bleak assessment:

> I doubt operas will not survive longer than this winter, they are now at their last gasp; the subscription is expired and nobody will renew it. The directors are always squabbling, and they have so many divisions among themselves that I wonder they have not broken up before; Senesino goes away next winter, and I believe Faustina, so you see harmony is almost out of fashion.[19]

Italian opera in London was threatened but it continued to show some vigour on occasion. After a fall-off of subscribers in 1728, which caused a shortening of the season, directors of the Academy decided to fund another five years, sending Handel and his opera house manager to Italy to seek out new singers. The Academy was more dependent than before on the patronage of George II. The problem here was that the Prince of Wales, Frederick, was in protracted conflict with his father and the Whig administration, and championed a rival to The Royal Academy, called the Opera of the Nobility. Senesino, probably upset that his leading role in Handel's new opera, *Orlando*, was insufficiently prominent, left to join the Opera of the Nobility in 1733.

Handel put together a new opera company and found a new castrato, Giovanni Carestini. The Opera of the Nobility took over the King's Theatre, but Handel got two nights a week in John Rich's theatre Theatre Royal in Covent Garden. Handel's output of fresh compositions remained extraordinary but they were not close to being his finest works. His very mixed success at this time caused some to ask whether or not the great composer's talent was running dry. The courtier, Lord Hervey, wrote to his friend Stephen Fox: 'I am just come from a long, dull, and consequently tiresome Opera of Handel's, whose genius seems quite exhausted'.[20]

Meanwhile musical performances on stage in English were growing in popularity. The warm reception given to the opera *Britannia* by John (Johann) Frederick Lampe prompted an anonymous poem in praise published in the *Daily Post* that began:

No more shall Italy its Warblers send
To charm our Ears with Handel's heav'nly Strains;
For dumb his rapt'rous Lyre, their Fame must end.[21]

Handel suffered what seems to have been a minor stroke that led him to visit the spa of Aix-la-Chapelle in September 1737. Joseph Bennett recorded:

> It was thought best for him to have recourse to the vapour baths at Aix-la-Chapelle, over which he sat three times as long as hath ever been the practice. Whoever knows anything of the nature of these baths, will, from this instance, form some idea of his surprising constitution. His sweats were profuse beyond what can well be imagined. His cure, from the manner as well as from the quickness with which it was wrought, passed with the nuns for a miracle. When, but a few hours from the time of his leaving the bath, they heard him at the organ in the principal church, as well as convent, playing in a manner so much beyond what they had ever heard or even imagined, it is not wonderful, that they should suppose the interposition of a higher power.[22]

'THE VOICE OF MANY WATERS AND OF MIGHTY THUNDERS': HANDEL CREATES THE ENGLISH ORATORIO

That autumn Handel returned to find that the Opera of the Nobility had broken up temporarily, and he was able to return to the King's Theatre. A generous contribution to the Fund for the Support of Decay'd Musicians (now the Royal Society of Musicians) did much to restore the composer's reputation with the public. Nevertheless financial difficulties remained, particularly during the 1738-1739 season. Handel, after all, was not just a composer: he was in part a promoter. Contemplation of the huge cost of staging operas was undoubtedly one of the many reasons why Handel turned his attention increasingly to oratorio.

Oratorio was a full-length musical setting of a sacred text. Its origins can be found in medieval mystery plays and the setting of sacred texts to music which told stories from the Bible in dramatic form. During the renaissance and after, oratorios were increasingly influenced by opera music; nevertheless, these entertainments were religious madrigals, concert pieces without scenery, costume or drama and the subject matter was always sacred. Latin dialogues based on Bible stories became popular in Italy in the early seventeenth century, intended to be used alongside motets in a church setting. Operas were growing fast in popularity but such spectacles were strictly forbidden during Lent. Oratorios, however, were permitted and, increasingly, with texts written in the vernacular rather than in Latin. Handel, indeed, had written his own oratorio on the Resurrection when in Rome in 1708. Meanwhile further north in Germany, the 'Oratorium', which placed greater emphasis on chorus than Italian oratorios, was being incorporated more frequently into Lutheran services.

The English oratorio was Handel's creation. Throughout his career the composer had drawn on almost every variety of music he had come across and, he was not only an unrepentant plagiariser of his own work, but also (sometimes to the alarm of his friends) he on occasion looted the compositions of others to weave them in and reinterpret them in his own compositions. When he was creating the English oratorio, Handel was pulling together what he had absorbed from all the parts of Europe he had visited and worked in. That included England and, in particular, the English anthem tradition.[23]

The English public (unlike the Irish public) was to prove itself slow to accept oratorio as a genre. Nevertheless, Handel's oratorios, in spite of the hesitant reception given to the first ones he had performed in England, were to fill a deeply-felt need in eighteenth-century Britain. The Church of England had a passionate belief in the spiritual benefits of beautiful, sublime music if properly directed. 'Musick, when rightly order'd, cannot be prefer'd too much', the essayist Jeremy Collier wrote, because it 'composes the Passions, affords a strong Pleasure, and excited a Nobleness of Thought'. 'Religious Harmony', he continued, is able 'to warm the best Blood within us, and take hold of the finest part of the Affections: To transport us with the *Beauty of Holiness*'.[24] In 1741 Thomas Secker, then the Bishop of Bristol, encouraged choral praise of the Creator. 'All persons indeed who are by nature qualified, ought to learn, and constantly join to glorify Him that made them, in psalms and spiritual songs'. He delighted in 'the harmony of a great chorus', adding that it is something inexpressibly elevating, to hear the voice of a great multitude, as the voice of many waters and of mighty thunders, to speak in the words of Scripture, making a joyful noise to the God of their salvation, and singing His praises with understanding.[25]

The eighteenth century may have been the Age of Reason which treated fanaticism with contempt but it certainly was not a time when passion in high art, particularly in the service of religion, was frowned upon. Anglican churchmen were in the forefront of those who were encouraging the composition of spiritually uplifting, emotionally transporting music. It was widely believed in the early eighteenth century that music possessed enormous, almost irresistible, power. Uncontrolled, music could be dreadfully destructive: in a sermon preached in Oxford on 22 November in 1713, St Cecilia's Day, the saint being the patroness of musicians, William Dingley had declared that 'Musick is almost as Dangerous as 'tis Useful, *it has the Force of Gunpowder, and should be as carefully look'd after, that no unhallow'd Fire give it the power of Destroying'.*[26] The wrong kind of music could wreak appalling havoc, especially amongst the young seeking pleasure. Humphrey Wanley, librarian to the earls of Oxford, thought that a '*Minuet* or *Jigg* ... may go a great way towards enticing a foolish girl to love' but an anthem 'excites the Devotion, moves the Affections, and raises the Passions of those truly religious Souls, who take pleasure in singing Praises to the Honour and Glory of His Name, who lives for ever'.[27] If this music – secular as well as liturgical – is so beautifully crafted that it becomes sublime then it can save souls and give repentant sinners a glimpse of heaven. The poet Joseph Addison contended that this had always been so:

I might shew, from innumerable Passages in Ancient Writers ... that their most favourite Diversions were filled with Songs and Hymns to their respective Deities. Had we frequent Entertainments of this Nature among us, they wou'd not a little purifie and exalt our Passions, give our Thoughts a proper Turn, and cherish those Divine Impulses in the Soul.[28]

In the previous century Puritan attacks on complex sacred music, especially if accompanied by instruments, had often been ferocious and, at times, successful. Many dissenting sects continued to object to anything more complicated than the plain, unaccompanied chanting of psalms in church – well into the nineteenth century, for example, Presbyterian congregations in Ulster resisted the introduction of the organ into their meeting houses, denouncing the instrument as 'a kist o' whistles'. But as the eighteenth century progressed dissenters softened their opinions, especially in later years as the evangelical revival got under way, when congregations were to become enraptured by hymns, those written by Charles Wesley especially – sacred songs they could all sing together to praise their Lord.

The form of praise most favoured by Humphrey Wanley and other leading Anglicans was the anthem. Anthems then were musical settings for soloists and choir of texts generally from the Old Testament, and occasionally from the Apocrypha and New Testament. The requirements of 'full' anthems – such as the Coronation Anthems – were not far short of those needed for Handel's oratorios. Only those venues that had resident choirs of trained vocalists could sing them. These were: Westminster Abbey, St George's in Windsor and the Chapel Royal; the 21 English cathedrals and 6 Oxford and Cambridge colleges with choral foundations; and the London home of one nobleman, the Duke of Chandos. Handel was a regular composer of anthems: he had composed 21 before the first public performance of any of his oratorios in England, in addition to four settings of the *Te Deum* and two of the *Jubilate*. These proved to be enormously popular. After hearing the Dettingen *Te Deum*, Mary Pendarves wrote: 'It is excessively fine, I was all rapture … everybody says it is the finest of his compositions'.[29]

Leading Anglicans would have warmly approved of Mrs Pendarves's use of the word 'rapture'. 'Rapture' was often used in conjunction with 'sublime', a word applied almost reverentially to the very greatest and most moving literature and music. The first-century treatise on rhetoric, *On the Sublime*, attributed to Longinus, was eagerly reread and admired. There was much approval for Longinus's view that 'the Mind is naturally elevated by the true

Sublime' and that 'the Sublime makes near Approaches to the Height of God'. Handel was fast winning recognition for his mastery of the religious sublime, as a composer who wrote music so wonderful that, by giving listeners a foretaste of heavenly bliss, it could be deployed as a formidable weapon against freethinkers and unbelievers. Though he may not have been fully aware of it, Handel was being recruited as an inspiring genius by those in England leading the campaign to defend Christian truths. Certainly Aaron Hill, in his 1733 'Ode on the Occasion of Mr. Handel's Great Te Deum, at the Feast of the Sons of the Clergy', thought so:

> Ah! Give thy *Passport* to the Nation's Prayer,
> Ne'er did Religion's languid Fire
> Burn fainter – never more require
> The Aid of such a fam'd Enliv'ner's Care:
> Thy Pow'r can *force* the stubborn Heart to feel,
> And rouze the Lucke-warm Doubter into *Zeal*.[30]

Handel's credentials as a valiant defender in the faith were reinforced by his fame as a virtuoso organist. In the eighteenth century the organ was regarded as the special instrument of divine worship. Thomas Macro, preaching at Tiverton in 1734, went as far as to describe the organ as 'the most comprehensive of all other, for which Reason it has been appropriated to the Service of the *Sanctuary*, and made the *Instrument of God* in his own House'. The composer went out of his way to perform organ concertos between the acts of his oratorios. Too much showing off with voluntaries in church was considered exhibitionist and unsuitably irreverent; but, without any qualms, audiences felt uplifted by Handel's bravura organ playing when transferred to the theatre and concert hall.[31] Handel's oratorios filled the demand for Scripture drama in music, with words in English, which was profoundly moving, deeply moral, spiritually enriching and which restored choral singing to the central role it had had a century and more before.

'A Religious Farce ... 'tis excessive noisy, a vast number of instruments and voices': an uncertain beginning

The oratorio in Handel's hands was a composition that used soloists but gave a major role to the chorus: an entertainment on a biblical subject to be performed in the theatre rather than in a church. It had three acts and the majority were dramas (always without staging) but a few, including *Messiah*, had nondramatic librettos. All his oratorios, with the exception of *Messiah* and *Theodora*, are based entirely on the Old Testament.

Back in 1716 when the season ended in London Handel left for Germany, apparently to carry out an errand for the Princess of Wales. He took the opportunity to go to Halle to call in on his family. On a visit to Ansbach for the princess he came across the Passion oratorio *Der für die Sünden der Welt gemartete und sterbende Jesus* (Jesus martyred and dying for the sins of the World) by Barthold Heinrich Brockes. Published in 1712, Bach was to include some of it in his *St John Passion*.[32] Undoubtedly this work had an influence on Handel and may have given him added encouragement to consider the sacred oratorio as a form of composition to be well worth attempting again.

Handel's first English oratorio was *Esther: an Oratorio; or Sacred Drama*, composed in 1718. However, Dr Edmund Gibson, Bishop of London, stopped it being performed. Gibson, known as 'Walpole's Pope', not only denounced Sunday racing and operas performed in theatres, which he characterised as 'houses which entertained Sodomitical Clubs', but also condemned representations on stage of scenes from the Bible.[33] Only in 1732 was *Esther* presented in a staged version and, even then, it was only for private performances for the Philharmonic Society and the Academy of Ancient Music. Then, learning of a pirated public performance, Handel made this announcement:

By His MAJESTY'S Command
At the King's Theatre in the Hay-Market, on Tuesday, the 2d of May will be performed, the *Sacred Story* of ESTHER: an *Oratorio* in *English*. Formerly compos'd by Mr. *Handel*, and now revised by him … N.B, There will be no Action on the Stage.[34]

One problem was that while the text was in English the singers were Italian. One member of the audience observed: 'You would have sworn it had been in *Welch*', adding in disappointment that he found 'this Sacred *Drama* a mere Consort, no Scenery, Dress or Action', with Handel 'plac'd in a Pulpit' and soloists 'in their own Habits … a Religious *Farce*'. When *Deborah* was premièred as an oratorio to replace opera at the King's Theatre in 1733, once again advertisements made it clear that there would be no scenery.[35] This performance failed on the very first night, partly because subscribers were angered by a last-minute doubling of ticket prices – later Lord Shaftesbury recalled that 'this Indiscreet Step disgusted the Town, and he had a very thin House'.[36] Again all the solo parts were taken by Italians. The Irish peer, John Perceval, Earl of Egmont, found the oratorio 'very magnificent, near a hundred performers, among whom about twenty-five singers'.[37] No doubt he was impressed by the rich eight-part choral opening but for others in the audience, as Lady Anne Irwin told Lord Carlisle, ''tis excessive noisy, a vast number of instruments and voices, who all perform at a time, and is in music what I fancy a French ordinary in conversation'.[38] *Deborah* suffered also from a clunky libretto and some noticed that Handel had plundered much of the music for it from earlier works.

Athalia, Handel's first great oratorio, was given its première at a degree ceremony in Oxford's Sheldonian Theatre in July 1733. Based on a tragedy by Racine, it told the Old Testament story of Queen Athalia who deserts Jehovah for Baal and eventually pays for this with her life. There is no doubt that the composer's spirits were greatly raised by the warm reception he received there.

HANDELISTS AND ANTI-HANDELISTS

Back in London the potential audience for opera was still limited to aristocrats capable of paying the subscriptions. The rift which led to the formation of the Opera of the Nobility meant that the resources available to entertain this restricted clientele were divided, generally speaking, wastefully divided. Much of London's upper crust became ludicrously partisan being separated into Handelists and anti-Handelists. Lord Hervey recalled:

> The King and Queen … were both Handelists, and sat freezing constantly at his empty Haymarket Opera, whilst the Prince with all the chief of the nobility went as constantly to that of Lincoln's Inn Fields. The affair grew as serious as that of the

Greens and the Blues under Justinian at Constantinople. An anti-Handelist was looked upon as an anti-courtier, and voting against the Court in Parliament was hardly a less remissable or venial sin than speaking against Handel or going to Lincoln's Inn Fields Opera … the king (though he declared he took no other part in this affair than subscribing £1,000 a year to Handel) often added at the same time he did not think setting oneself at the head of a faction of fiddlers a very honourable occupation for people of quality.[39]

After his return from Oxford Handel set about composing music to accompany and celebrate the impending marriage of his former pupil, Anne, the Princess Royal, to the Prince of Orange, Stadtholder of the Netherlands. According to Lord Hervey, for the princess this was 'a miserable match … to this piece of deformity in Holland'.[40] However, royal patronage of this kind was crucial to Handel at a time of deeply divided opinions on his work and of wildly vacillating financial prospects.

A magnificent new theatre, Theatre Royal, had opened in 1732 at the top of Bow Street, Covent Garden, on a site now occupied by the Royal Opera House. Handel got the opportunity to put on his compositions there, including a new opera, *Ariodante*, which had its première in January 1735. Though now regarded as one of his finest operas, *Ariodante* enjoyed only modest success. His second new opera, *Alcina*, was by contrast a great success. Mrs Pendarves was present for a rehearsal in Handel's home. There Handel threw himself into the part of Alcina, the wicked sorceress who on her magic island captivates and imprisons the crusader Ruggiero. Mary Pendarves thought it 'the best he ever made … 'tis so fine I have not words to describe it … While Mr Handel was playing his part, I could not help thinking him a necromancer in the midst of his own enchantments'.[41] Anti-Handelists turned up at the performances, however, to jeer and whistle at the Parisian ballerina, Marie Sallé, who had been brought over to dance the part of Cupid in both of the new operas.

Charles Jennens: the most dedicated Handelian

There is the impression that Handel's loyal friends did not feel that the composer was getting the recognition he deserved. He seemed constantly to move from triumphs to disappointments. Handel did have a habit of alienating some around him with explosive outbursts and, as a bachelor and a foreigner, he at times cut a lonely figure for a man who loved company. There were no more than hints of relationships with women in his youth. One was by the mother of George I who, in a letter to the Queen of Prussia, observed: 'He is a good-looking man and the talk is that he was the lover of Victoria'.[42] She was referring to the soprano Vittoria Tarquini, mistress of Ferdinando de' Medici, prince of Tuscany, known as 'La Bambigia' (cotton wool) possibly because of her full head of blonde hair or rounded figure.

One comforting development for Handel was that there was a steady demand for copies of his music, both printed and in manuscript, not only from the gentry but also from leading musicians and many musical societies, including the Dublin 'Accademy for Vocal Musick'. In addition, members of London's Sephardic Jewish community were fast becoming amongst the most faithful and regular attenders at the composer's oratorios.

The most dedicated Handelian, the most regular subscriber, the most assiduous purchaser of the composer's music, was Charles Jennens of Gopsall Park and Queen's Square, London.

Jennens had travelled to Oxford in the summer of 1733 for the degree ceremony and was present at the well-received première there of Handel's *Athalia* – Jennens, indeed, had lent the composer copies of Scarlatti's music on which this oratorio was partly based. Jennens was to write the libretto for the next oratorio, *Saul*. This tells the story of the jealously of King Saul, of the intensely close friendship of his son David with Jonathan, and ultimately the fulfilment of the prophecy that Israel would fall to the Philistines. The most famous part is the 'Dead March' which accompanies Saul's end.

Handel was always on the look-out for new instruments ever since he had caused a sensation by introducing hunting horns in his *Water Music*. For *Saul* the range of instruments included: flute, oboe, bassoon, trumpet, timpani, harp, theorbo, strings, two organs, harpsichord and – to underscore Saul's jealous rage – a carillon (a keyboard that sounds bells with hammers). Jennens learned that Handel had got himself a carillon while composing *Saul*. Jennens explained to his relative Lord Guernsey in September 1738:

> Mr. Handel's head is more full of maggots than ever. I found yesterday in his room a very queer instrument which he calls carillon (Anglice, a bell) and says some call it a Tubalcain, I suppose because it is both in the make and tone like a set of hammers striking upon anvils. 'Tis played upon with keys like a Harpsichord and with this Cyclopean instrument he designs to make poor Saul stark mad.[43]

Handel's next oratorio, *Israel in Egypt*, with a libretto possibly written by Jennens, had a shaky start when it was first performed in 1739 at the King's Theatre. The audience was not ready for a libretto composed almost entirely from extracts from the Bible. Nevertheless, after the last performance, a letter appeared in the *London Daily Post* defending it, declaring that the 'Entertainment' was the 'noblest Adoration and Homage paid to the Deity that ever was in one'.[44]

This was a difficult time for Handel. Theatre audiences in London no longer delighted in Italian opera and had yet to be won over to the staging of sacred oratorio. In any case, plunging temperatures during the winter of 1739-1740 made them reluctant to venture out of doors. The composer rarely succeeded in filling theatres in the capital in 1740 and 1741 with offerings that included a vocal setting of John Milton's contrasted poems, *L'Allegro* and *Il Penseroso*. In collaboration with his friend, James Harris, Jennens had written the libretto for *L'Allegro*. Jennens had conferred closely with the composer during the time that this musical ode was being put together. In contrast, he seems to have put together the word-book for *Messiah* without consulting a single person. Early in 1741 Jennens sent Handel his libretto for this sacred oratorio. There was no immediate response. Had Handel even opened it and read it?

Chapter 3
Charles Jennens, *Messiah's* Librettist

A NON-JUROR WITH A VERY PARTICULAR FAITH

There would have been no *Messiah* without Charles Jennens. The idea of creating this sacred oratorio was entirely his, and it was he alone who crafted the libretto from Scripture, but because Jennens was uninterested in fame he did not bother to put his name to this 'word-book', let alone ask the composer, George Frideric Handel, for any payment for his labours. Little wonder that, until very recently, few have been familiar with either his name or his achievements.

Wealth and comfort were assured from the moment Jennens was born in 1700 at Gopsall in Leicestershire. At that stage his father was overseeing the production of over 2,000 tons of cast iron a year. The Darbys of Coalbrookdale had discovered the art of smelting ore with coke, but they kept this knowledge to themselves: until the middle of the eighteenth century charcoal was the only fuel that could then produce metal of a quality acceptable to all other ironmasters. Prodigious quantities of wood for charcoal burning were needed to feed the industry now burgeoning in the English west midlands. For a time timber felled in the broadleaved forests of Ireland, shipped across the Irish Sea, had met the requirements of a great many English smelters. By the end of the seventeenth century, however, these forests were no more – heedless exploitation had left Ireland, apart from Iceland, the most treeless country in Europe. Jennens's father, also called Charles, had been assiduously buying up suitably wooded land still remaining in England and Wales to ensure a steady supply for his business: when he died in 1747, his son inherited 736 acres at Gopsall and no fewer than 33 other properties in 6 different counties.[1]

Charles Jennens does not appear to have shown the slightest interest in the source of his immense wealth. His concerns – and, perhaps, his only concerns – were his religious faith, his political conviction, literature, music, and a small circle of like-minded friends. Though not titled, Jennens was well connected and on easy terms with the nobility, having stayed as a guest, for example, with the Duke and Duchess of Devonshire at Chatsworth. At the age of fifteen he entered Balliol College, Oxford. Like most fee-paying 'fellow-commoners' he did not take a degree; but Charles was a dedicated student of the classics and also acquired some knowledge of Hebrew. In 1718 – after being on the waiting list for three months – he became a member of the Oxford Music Club and clearly he acquired a respectable proficiency as a keyboard player. Certainly Jennens was an avid collector of manuscripts of the latest musical compositions to be had from the European mainland.

In time Jennens built up a library of around 10,000 volumes. Of these over 700 were on theological subjects. Jennens had a deep and very particular Protestant faith, a faith which not only inspired him, unprompted and unasked, to write the word-book for *Messiah*, but also ensured that this oratorio would be a fervent expression of his belief in the truth of revealed religion.

Like other members of his family, Charles Jennens was a believer in hereditary monarchy, indeed, in the divine right of kings, and, as a consequence, in the Stuart succession. Parliament had already made its decision: the throne passed, according to the 1701 Act of Settlement, to the next Protestant heir, over the heads of many Catholics with a better hereditary claim. When Queen Anne, a Stuart and a Protestant, died in 1714 dozens of other Stuarts with a legitimate claim to the throne were deemed unacceptable because they were Catholics. Georg Ludwig, Elector of Hanover, was very far down the list of those entitled to succeed Queen Anne, but he was a Protestant. When the Elector was brought to the throne as King George I, Jennens unhesitatingly became a 'non-juror'. Holders of public office had to take the oaths of allegiance and supremacy, acknowledging George I as head of state and of the church. Non-jurors were those who refused to take the prescribed oaths. This meant that they could not be, for example, a clergyman of the Established Church, a Member of Parliament, a magistrate, an army officer, a government servant, or even a director of one of the great chartered trading companies or the Bank of England.

Charles Jennens was so dedicated to the House of Stuart that his seal portrayed the head of the martyred Charles I. He built up one of the most complete collections of paintings of members of the Stuart royal family to be found anywhere. Jennens even had built into the communion table in his chapel at Gopsall a piece of Charles II's oak, wood cut from the tree where, after the Battle of Worcester in 1651, the young Charles had hidden from Oliver Cromwell's men. He crossed out of his copies of the *Book of Common Prayer* the printed names of the Hanoverian royal family. Jennens had a pair of silver gilt cups specially made, bearing the royal arms of France, three fleurs de lys – were these to toast the health of 'the king over the water' with a like-minded friend? There were at least 50 Stuarts with a better hereditary claim than George I, especially the son and grandson of James II sheltering under the protection of the French kings, Louis XIV and then his grandson and successor, Louis XV, in Paris. Yet Jennens had no truck with Jacobites, Protestants as well as Catholics, who were scheming to overthrow the Hanoverian succession.[2]

Jennens's political allegiance meant that he could not join other men of his standing to, for example, seek ordination in holy orders, preside over local courts, be an officer of the yeomanry, or join the jostling bands of those petitioning for positions, pensions and other favours from Sir Robert Walpole's Whig administration at Westminster, which the opposition alleged was becoming increasingly venal. In short, Jennens could devote himself, almost entirely without the distractions of public duties normally expected of a man of his class, to his cultural and religious interests. Jennens was a devoted member of the Established Church. He would be described today as a High Church Anglican, a member of the Church of England who placed the Eucharist at the heart of worship, but nevertheless rejected the Latin liturgy, allegiance to the Pope, and the doctrines of the Catholic Church as defined in the middle of the sixteenth century at the Council of Trent. Like members of most dissenting sects, Jennens regarded the Bible as the rock of his faith – Scripture he viewed without demur as the Word of God. However, the plain forms of worship favoured by Quakers, Baptists, Presbyterians, Congregationalists and other dissenters were not for Jennens: he revered the formality of the prescribed liturgy of the *Book of Common Prayer*.

CHRISTIANITY NOT MYSTERIOUS: THE ADVANCE OF DEISM AND SCEPTICISM

Those like Jennens who regarded the Bible as sacred, as the revealed Word of God, were on the defensive in early eighteenth-century England. To their dismay 'deism' seemed to be gaining ground. Deists accepted that God, or the 'Supreme Being', had created the world but they believed neither in divine intervention nor in biblical revelation. Their philosophy, their 'natural religion', derived the existence and nature of God from reason and personal experience. Deists rejected prophecy, miracles and other supernatural happenings.

The first standard bearer of international importance for deism was, perhaps surprisingly, an Irishman, John Toland. Reputedly the son of a Catholic priest, he was raised in Inishowen as Seán Ó Tuathaláin, until the school he attended at Redcastle near Derry encouraged him to anglicise his name. At the age of sixteen he exchanged his Catholic faith for that of the Church of Ireland and went to Glasgow University (even though this was a Presbyterian foundation) to study theology. After he had obtained his Master's degree at the age of 19 from Edinburgh, to which he had moved, he abandoned Anglicanism for Presbyterianism. In preparation for ordination as a Presbyterian minister, Toland continued his studies at Leiden only to become a freethinker and to give up his training altogether.

In 1696 Toland published *Christianity not mysterious*. In it he argued that the divine revelation of the Bible contains no true mysteries; instead, all the dogmas of the faith can be understood and demonstrated by properly trained reason from natural principles. For this he was chased out of Oxford and a few years later driven out of Dublin – that was in 1697, the very same year Thomas Aikenhead, a student in Edinburgh, was executed for declaring that Christ was an imposter and that his miracles were 'pranks'. The Grand Jury of Middlesex ordered the hangman to burn Toland's heretical volume after which he fled to Dublin. Some Members of the Irish Parliament actually proposed that Toland be burnt at the stake. Since he had fled the country by that stage, it was left to the Dublin grand jury to order that three copies of his tract be consigned publicly to the flames by the common hangman. The author, now in London, compared members of the Irish Parliament to 'Popish Inquisitors who performed an Execution on the Book, when they could not seize the Author, whom they had destined to the Flames'.[3]

Toland thereafter lived a precarious existence in London, managing nevertheless to spend time across the English Channel travelling as far east as Prague. Cantankerous, difficult, quarrelsome and hard-drinking, he was described by one admirer in Oxford as 'a man of excellent parts, but as little share as may be of modesty or conscience'.[4] William Molyneux, the renowned scientist and pamphleteer – who along with a fellow Dubliner, the city developer, Robert, Viscount Molesworth, did his best to defend Toland – informed the philosopher John Locke that he alienated almost everyone by 'his unseasonable way of discoursing, propagating, and maintaining' his views volubly in coffee houses.[5] Nevertheless, Toland's influence on the eighteenth century European Enlightenment was powerful. *Christianity not mysterious* became the handbook of deism, sending shock waves reverberating down the decades. After it, Toland wrote over a 100 more books, most of them dedicated to condemning 'priestcraft' and criticising ecclesiastical institutions. Along with a growing number of Enlightenment figures, Toland argued passionately that political institutions should guarantee freedom and that reason and tolerance were the twin pillars of the good society. Just as he denounced church hierarchy, so he opposed hierarchy in the state. Toland died in 1722 but his republicanism, in addition to his deism, long continued to influence the thinking of many – not to speak of that of Maximilien Robespierre and other members of the Committee of Public Safety who, in addition to unleashing the Reign of Terror, the Jacobin government's bloody suppression of all opposition in revolutionary France, made worship of the Supreme Being the state religion of France in June 1794.[6]

In addition to fostering greater religious toleration, the eighteenth century Enlightenment made scepticism more acceptable and even fashionable, at least in the ranks of the propertied and educated classes. In England there was no shortage of freethinkers eager to continue Toland's questioning of cherished beliefs in the Trinity, the personal nature of God the Father and the divinity of the Son. An extraordinary number of publications appeared to rebut such deist arguments, and especially to challenge the assertion that the Bible, the only source of truth and salvation, was not divine revelation. *Christianity not mysterious* had given the Boyle Lectures, founded by Robert Boyle in 1691, a fresh sense of urgency. Every year the appointed lecturer had to give eight sermons 'proving the Christian Religion against notorious Infidels, viz. Atheists, Deists, Jews and Mahometans'. An abridged version of the sermons published in 1737 filled four large volumes.[7]

'THE BURDEN OF VINDICATING CHRISTIANITY HAS BEEN VERY MUCH INCREASED'

Later on, this time would be dubbed the Age of Reason. This was when the new science was altering perceptions: it was now necessary to show that it was rational to believe in miracles and the fulfilment of prophecies. Sir Isaac Newton had applied his mathematical genius to biblical prophecy and chronology. It was comforting to believers that he had given the assurance that God was essential to the universe: matter was dead, he wrote, and only He could breathe life into it and move it. Newton explained that 'a continual miracle' by God 'is needed to prevent the Sun and fixed stars from rushing together through gravity.'[8] The problem was that deists were able to apply Newton's scientific findings and mathematical calculations to prove the very opposite, in particular to disprove divine revelation. Their opponents had to show that they were reasonable by making *rational* arguments to counter these *rational* attacks. 'Since Divinity has been made a Science', the Reverend Arthur Ashley Sykes wearily observed in 1725, 'and Systematical Opinions have been received, and embraced, in such a manner that it has not been safe to contradict them, the Burden of vindicating Christianity has been very much increased'.[9] Indeed, it had. The Old Testament was becoming the principal focus of this fierce debate. Anthony Collins shocked believers with his book published in 1724, *A Discourse of the Grounds and Reasons of the Christian Religion*. He wrote that 'the chief Proofs of Christianity from the Old Testament are urg'd by the Apostles in the New Testament' and 'if those Proofs are valid, Christianity is invincibly establish'd on its true foundation'. However, 'if those Proofs are invalid is Christianity false'. He argued that the proofs *were* invalid. His book had caused such a stir – Collins reported later with barely-concealed delight – that in just three years after it had been put on sale, there had been no fewer than *35* rebuttals published.[10]

Few freethinkers dared to question Christ's miracles directly. Indeed most deists were not anti-Christian and did not dismiss revelation altogether, preferring to redefine it as allegory. Deists argued that Christ's teaching was based on Mosaic Law and, since their opponents agreed on that point, the outcome was that freethinkers and English Protestants alike scrutinised Old Testament texts over and over again with meticulous care. Deists wanted reasonable, rational explanations for such miracles as the parting of the Red Sea. They also questioned the validity of Old Testament prophecies pointing to the coming of the Messiah. Sykes began his *Essay upon the Truth of the Christian Religion* with these words:

> The Christian Religion having its Origin from JESUS of *Nazareth*, and being manifestly founded upon the Scriptures of the *Old Testament*, there cannot be a more natural Method of examining its Truth, than to compare what was *foretold* with the Consequences and following Events.[11]

Charles Jennens, horrified by the spread of freethinking ideas, became convinced that it was his duty to spring to the defence of traditional Christianity. He did not join the crowded ranks of the devout to add yet another publication to their mounting pile of books and pamphlets. To confront deism Jennens instead picked a unique weapon: he would not write tracts or sermons – he would pen a word-book, a libretto, to have his message about eternal truths, delivered with Handel's sublime music, not from a pulpit but from the stage in a theatre.

'TOO LIABLE TO IRRITATION; FROM WHENCE ARISE VIOLENT PERTURBATIONS AND ANXIETIES OF MIND'

Charles Jennens lived a long life but for much of it he seemed to be lonely, unsettled, ill-at-ease and depressed. He could alienate by being intolerant, overbearing, crabbed, intemperately critical of others and high-handed in the manner typical of a privileged eighteenth-century country gentleman. In many ways he was a tortured soul: even his unshakeable religious conviction did not always bring him comfort. Writing to his closest friend, Edward Holdsworth, he concluded that 'the Doctrine is Stoical: I confess I can draw no solid comfort from it'.[12] Though his father lived to be 85, Jennens lost his mother when he was 7, and his 3 sisters and 2 younger brothers had all died before he reached the age of 30. His youngest brother Robert, who after studying at Oxford, seemed to be doing well preparing for a career in law at the Inns of Court; but he cut his own throat and threw himself out of the window of his rooms in Middle Temple. To men like Charles Jennens those who took their own lives had lost hope of salvation. When Robert's letters were examined afterwards it was revealed that he had been in correspondence with someone who had planted so many doubts about the validity of Christian beliefs in the young man's mind that he had been driven to ultimate despair.

Charles Jennens tended to be shy in mixed company and lived alone. He could be difficult, fussy, opinionated and irascible. Such characteristics, indeed, were referred to by Rev. George Kelly in the eulogy he delivered at Jennens's funeral in 1773:

> If any Part of his Conduct could be deemed exceptionable, it was in the Effects which naturally flow from an Impetuosity of Temper, by which I would be understood to mean some hasty Expressions which escaped him … the rather the Effects of a natural Infirmity than a depraved Habit and Disposition of Mind; and seemed to proceed from a delicate Texture of the nervous System, too liable to Irritation; from whence arise violent Perturbations and Anxieties of Mind, and not infrequently an extreme Lowness and Depression of Spirits … it is well known that he heartily bewailed this his Infirmity, and was frequently angry with himself on this account, much more so than with those he seemed to chide.[13]

Like many men of property, Charles Jennens resided in London during the winter months – indeed, he was usually in the capital for at least half of every year. He chose a part of London favoured by non-jurors and close to their favoured oratories (places where they could meet for private prayer) lodging first in Queen Square and then in Great Ormond Street. In his later life Jennens was to become a distinguished Shakespearean scholar, the first to publish each play as a separate volume, with scrupulous attention to accuracy and – where there was doubt – to provide the reader with the alternative versions available.

In the 1720s and for at least three decades thereafter it was music, new music in particular, which Jennens prioritised in his long list of cultural passions. His collection eventually included the works of over 30 Italian composers. His friend Edward Holdsworth, who had taught Jennens at Balliol, had resigned as a fellow because as a non-juror he could not bring himself to swear allegiance to a Hanoverian monarch. Holdsworth now earned a precarious living by taking young gentlemen on the Grand Tour, and Jennens (subsidising him generously) got him to send music back from Italy. Writing in 1733, Holdsworth assured Jennens that 'Monsr la Cene who has publish'd Vivaldi & Albinoni's works assur'd me that if you have 12 of Vivaldi's op. and 9 of Albinoni, you have all'. Expense was no object: 'Insist on the whole Scores being copy'd', he instructed Holdsworth in 1741. This acquisitiveness was not just a magpie desire to accumulate: Jennens, a man of means, nursed hopes that he could arrange to have some of these works given their London premières. As he wrote to Holdsworth, 'if they deserve we may have them perform'd on the English stage'.[14]

'BROTHER HANDELISTS'

From the outset Jennens was passionate about Handel's music and purchased all of the composer's works since the publication of the opera *Rodelinda* in 1725.[15] For example, he ordered more copies than any other subscriber of a 1738 folio edition of the full score of Handel's setting of John Dryden's St Cecilia ode *Alexander's Feast or The Power of Music*. From the time that he was able to set up house in London, Jennens seems to have attended just about every one of Handel's works put on in the capital. He and his friends described themselves as 'Brother Handelists'. They included James Harris with whom he would later collaborate in writing the libretto for Handel's *L'Allegro*; Lord Radnor, who accumulated a great collection of manuscript copies of works by the composer; Sir Wyndham

Knatchbull, who had been a fellow student at Balliol; and the Earl of Shaftesbury, Harris's cousin and one of Handel's patrons.

In 1733 Handel accepted an invitation to perform several of his works in Oxford. Jennens was there also, primarily to hear his cousin Lord Guernsey (later 3rd Earl of Aylesford) give one of the student orations during the degree celebrations. Clearly Handel and Jennens had become well acquainted before this: the composer's oratorio *Athalia*, given its première on this occasion, was derived in part from manuscript music by Scarlatti lent to Handel by Jennens.[16]

Jennens had succeeded in convincing Handel that, not only did he have a deep appreciation and understanding of contemporary music, he also had the literary prowess to pen librettos closely sympathetic to his compositions. Together they worked on the next oratorio, *Saul*, given its first performance in 1739. No previous oratorio could match the scale of this one. The orchestra, in addition to the usual strings, oboes and bassoons, included flutes, three trombones, two trumpets, a harp, great drums, a carillon and a new organ which, even to Jennens's astonishment, had cost Handel £500. When combined with the voices of soloists and a large chorus, at the several high moments of drama the volume was just too much for some who had come to hear it. Lord Wentworth observed:

> I hear Mr. Handell has borrow'd of the Duke of Argylle a pair of the largest kettledrums in the Tower, so to be sure it will be most excessively noisy with a bad set of singers; I doubt it will not retrieve his former losses.[17]

Though the royal family attended the second night, Wentworth was right to predict that *Saul*, initially at any rate, was not a triumphant success.[18] The next oratorio, *Israel in Egypt*, which may have had its text written by Jennens, flopped at an early stage. Lord Shaftesbury later concluded that as yet 'the Town' had not 'come into a relish for this Species of Musick'.[19] Could it be that the sacred oratorio was not to the taste of the English theatre-going public?

'RELIEVE HIM FROM THE CRUEL PERSECUTION OF THOSE LITTLE VERMIN': HANDEL'S CAREER FALTERS

This was a difficult time for Handel. A long and exceptionally harsh winter – 'the Great Frost' – began in November 1739 causing the Thames to freeze over for weeks. Conflict broke out with Spain – The War of Jenkins's Ear (1739-1748) (which became the War of the Austrian Succession in 1740 and dragged on until 1748) – and admiration for the exploits of Admiral Nicholas Haddock in the Mediterranean combined with the bitter cold immobilised public entertainment in the capital. Horace Walpole, the Prime Minister's son, received a letter from a friend that informed him: 'Plays we have none, or damned ones. Handel has had a concerto this winter. No opera, no nothing. All for war and Admiral Haddock'.[20]

Handel kept himself busy. For the coming season he composed a series of 12 string concerti grossi in just one month. Jennens, meanwhile, heard that one of his 'Brother Handelists', James Harris, had begun a libretto for a new vocal work, a setting of John Milton's *L'Allegro* and *Il Penseroso*. Jennens got Harris to finish the job while the composer was still keen on the idea. 'I have made him impatient to see it in due Form', he wrote, 'for he is so eager that I am afraid, if his demands are not answer'd very soon, he will be diverted to some less agreeable design'. The text was duly delivered, primarily because Jennens had contributed a great deal to the finished product, adding a third part, *Il Moderato*, with his own verse. Handel was not particularly tolerant of competition: finding that Thomas Arne's setting of Milton's *Comus* was playing to packed houses, he eagerly snatched up the Harris-Jennens libretto to compose a riposte.[21]

The freezing weather postponed the first performance until 27 February 1740, with 'the House secur'd against the Cold'.[22] There were five performances and an anonymous poem appeared in the *Gentleman's Magazine* entitled 'To Mr. Handel on hearing 'Alexander's Feast', 'L'Allegro, ed il Penseroso', etc.' and included these lines:

> But *Handel's* harmony affects the soul,
> To sooth by sweetness, or by force controul;
> And with like sounds as tune the rolling spheres,
> So tunes the mind, that ev'ry sense has ears.

When jaundice jealousy, and carking care,
Or tyrant pride, or homicide despair,
The soul as on a rack in torture keep,
These monsters *Handel's* music lulls to sleep.
How, when he strikes the keys, do we rejoice![23]

Nevertheless, real success was eluding Handel in London. He had not abandoned hope that he could revive enthusiasm for his first love, opera, and during the summer of 1740 Handel crossed the English Channel, probably to stay in a German spa, 'having lately found a weakness' in his hand, possibly another minor stroke.[24] He was now 55 years old. On his return he finished *Imeneo*, an opera he had started to compose two years before. Finishing it on 10 October he started another one, *Deidamia*, on 27 October. Even though the King 'and all the St. James royall family' were present on the first night of *Imeneo* on 22 November its reception was at best insipid.[25] *Deidamia* opened early in the new year, but audiences were so thin that it closed after only three performances. Handel had brought over two Italians, a new castrato, Andreoni, and the soprano, Maria Monza. Mrs Pendarves liked her voice well enough, 'strong, but not harsh', but otherwise she found 'her person *miserably bad*, being very low, and *excessively* crooked'.[26] The composer had rented the Theatre Royal in Lincoln's Inn Fields for these operas and so his financial losses must have been considerable. London had tired of Italian operas and Handel was not going to compose any more to re-awaken interest in them in the capital.

The composer's dedicated supporters fretted about his future and felt that the number of his enemies was growing, as an open letter in the *Daily Post* on 4 April 1741 indicated:

I wish I could … persuade the Gentlemen who have taken Offence at any Part of this great Man's Conduct (for a great Man he must be in the Musical World. Whatever his Misfortunes may now too late say to the contrary:) I wish I could persuade them, I say, to take him back into Favour, and relieve him from the cruel Persecution of those little Vermin, who, taking Advantage of his Displeasure, pull down even his Bills as fast as he has them pasted up; and use a thousand other little Arts to injure and distress him.

Was Handel thinking of leaving London? The composer was arranging a concert and his newspaper insertion had a suspicious air of finality about it:

> This being the last Time of performing, many Persons of Quality and others, are pleas'd to make great Demands for Box Tickets, which encourage me (and I hope will give no Offence) to put the Pit and Boxes together, at Half a Guinea each.

The author of the open letter, after appealing to the public 'to take him back into Favour', concluded:

> as this Oratorio of *Wednesday* next in his last for the Season, and if Report be true, probably his last ever in this Country, let them, with a friendly Benevolence, fill this his last House, and shew him on his Departure, that *London*, the greatest and richest City in the World, is great and rich in Virtue, as well as in Money, and can pardon and forget these Failings, or even the faults of a great Genius.

After attending the performance, the Earl of Egmont noted in his diary: 'I went to Lincoln's Inn playhouse to hear Handel's music for the last time, he intending to go to Spa in Germany'.[27]

'I HOPE I WILL PERSWADE HIM TO SET ANOTHER SCRIPTURE COLLECTION … THE SUBJECT IS MESSIAH'

Handel was not the type to be downhearted for long. In July he was found composing a series of Italian duets on texts of an amorous nature. These were just the kind of compositions much in favour in German courts. Was this further evidence that Handel intended to return to his homeland?

Charles Jennens wrote to Edward Holdsworth on 10 July:

> Handel says he will do nothing next Winter, but I hope I will perswade him to set another Scripture Collection I have made for him, & perform it for his own Benefit in Passion week. I hope he will lay out his whole Genius & Skill upon it, that the

Composition may excel all his former Compositions, as the Subject excels every other Subject. The Subject is Messiah.[28]

Just when Jennens had sent Handel the libretto for *Messiah* is not certain. The composer may have had the word-book in his house for as long as 18 months, but it is more likely to have been around 6 weeks. There is no record that Handel had given it his attention or even opened the manuscript until, quite unexpectedly, he got an invitation from Dublin to perform his works there. Handel did not hesitate: he accepted this invitation with alacrity. As well as planning to present a selection of compositions already familiar to London audiences for his visit to Ireland, Handel now turned to Jennens's 'Scripture Collection' and threw himself into the task of putting it to music to have it performed before a new audience which did not include his English critics.

Jennens had observed to Holdsworth that the subject of Messiah 'excels every other Subject', indicating that he was well aware of the perils involved in tackling it. In his search for precedents he studied closely a work by Alexander Pope. This was *Messiah*, a poem written in 1712 which merged the prophecy of Isaiah with a Sybilline prophecy in Virgil's Fourth Eclogue:

> Jam redit et Virgo, redeunt Saturnia regna,
> Jam nova progenies caelo demittitur alto –

Literally translated: 'Now [the cycle of all ages and] the Virgin returns, returns the age of Saturn; now from heaven on high a new generation is sent down'. For many centuries Christian scholars had regarded these lines by Virgil as a prophecy announcing the birth of Christ. Pope certainly did:

> A *Virgin* shall conceive, a *Virgin* bear a Son!
> From *Jesse*'s Root behold a Branch arise,
> Whose sacred Flow'r with Fragrance fills the Skies.

That Jennens believed in this interpretation of Virgil's prophecy is demonstrated by the motto he placed on the title page of his *Messiah* word-book, 'MAJORA CANAMUS'. This was from the fourth eclogue's first line, 'Sicelides Musae, Paulo majora canamus' ('Muses of Sicily, we sing a grander strain').

'Who now reads Cowley?', Pope once asked. Charles Jennens did. Abraham Cowley, born in 1618 the son of a London stationer, may have fallen out of favour by the eighteenth century but his poems had been widely read during his own lifetime. His odes included *Christ's Passion*, *The Resurrection* and *The 34th Chapter of Isaiah*. When writing the word-book for the oratorio *Saul*, Jennens had drawn on *Davideis*, Cowley's unfinished scriptural epic on the history of King David.[29]

Of course adapting extracts from the Bible to create texts to be put to music had been a common practice for centuries. Usually these were for specific episodes such as the Passion of Christ. Until Jennens produced the libretto for *Messiah*, however, nothing so all-encompassing, sweeping across both the Old and the New Testaments, appears to have been written.

REACHING OUT TO SCEPTICS

Since the reign of Elizabeth in the late sixteenth century, the representation of Jesus Christ on stage in England was considered totally inappropriate, unacceptably irreverent. Jennens undoubtedly believed this was right and his libretto in part was shaped by this view. Though there were other powerful reasons why Jennens chose to give such prominence to Old Testament prophecy, the librettist had to keep in mind the sensitivities of the time on the way the Saviour could be portrayed.

The libretto for *Messiah*, like an opera, is divided into three acts. The first act sets out the Old Testament prophesies of God's salvation of mankind, of the Messiah's coming and of his incarnation, and concludes with the announcement of the nativity and assurance of Christ's healing ministry. The second concerns Christ's passion, scourging and crucifixion, his resurrection, ascension, glorification in Heaven, the gift of tongues, preaching the Gospel to the world, the world's rejection of Christianity, divine destruction of the enemies of religion and concludes with Christianity's eternal triumph. The third deals with Christ as Saviour, the promise of eternal life, the Messiah's intercession at the Last Judgement, victory over death and sin and ends with adoration of the Messiah by the blessed in heaven.[30] The libretto for this vast narrative is made up entirely of texts deftly woven together from the Old and the New Testaments: Isaiah, Haggai, Malachi, Luke, Zechariah, Matthew, John, Psalms, Lamentations, Hebrews, Romans, Revelation, Job and Corinthians. Jennens preferred to use the translations in the *Book of Common Prayer* to those in the Authorised Version for excerpts taken from Psalms. Jennens was not particularly original in his choice of texts from Scripture: nearly all of them were to be found in widely-read volumes published as ripostes to deist publications. Jennens's artistry was in the way that he aligned and polished them to create a moving drama, almost devoid of narrative though it was. His daringly original idea was to make this drama on revealed religion a theatrical production.

Some commentators later observed that Jennens had given himself a relatively easy task, that of lifting excerpts from books of the Bible – after all, Jennens had modestly described his word-book as a 'Scripture Collection'. Jennens, however, had already demonstrated just how much meticulous and sustained work he was prepared to put in to the writing of a libretto. For example, the word-book for *Saul*, just over 500 lines, was a distillation of 26 chapters of the Bible and material from the Psalms, and included substantial scenes inspired by non-biblical sources.[31]

The *Messiah* libretto is indeed a kind of scrap book of direct quotations from the Bible, but it is constructed with such artistry that each piece locks tightly together to form a single and powerful narrative. It has to be remembered that this oratorio was intended for the theatre, not a church. *Messiah* was to be an entertainment.

In writing *Messiah* Jennens had an agenda, for this oratorio was not just for the faithful: he was determined to reach out to deists and sceptics. Those with no faith in revealed religion were not likely to be regular church-goers, and even if they were, sermons, homilies and tracts would probably do little to shake their opinions. Such people, however, might well pay to hear an oratorio in the theatre, Jennens hoped, and be so moved by the emotional dynamism of the performance that they would be drawn back from their unscriptural ways. *Messiah* for Jennens was a powerful reassertion of traditional Christianity. Underneath the inscription MAJORA CANAMUS on the libretto title page he had these quotations from Scripture:

*And without Controversy, great is the Mystery of Godliness: God was
manifested in the Flesh, justify'd by the Spirit, seen of Angels, preached
among the Gentiles, believed on in the world, received up in Glory.
In whom are hid all the Treasures of Wisdom and Knowledge.*

This epigraph, drawn from St Paul's epistles to Timothy and the
Colossians, sums up Jennens's message.[32] The oratorio is about
biblical revelation and salvation. The libretto reflected the very
specific beliefs of non-juring Anglicans who, looking on themselves
as the guardians of true orthodoxy, stressed the divinity of Christ
and the importance of Holy Communion and adhered to a strongly
mystical view of Christianity. The dominance of so much of the
word-book by Old Testament prophecies underscores the passionate
belief in revelation. In part Jennens was producing a counterblast,
not only to deists but also to biblical scholars who were beginning
to question whether all of the texts usually quoted from Isaiah
actually referred to the coming of Christ. 'Was Jesus of Nazareth the
Messiah?': this question was being asked again and again. The very
title Jennens chose for his oratorio was an unequivocal statement of
belief: Jesus Christ *was* the redeemer, the Messiah.

CRAFTING THE *MESSIAH* WORD-BOOK
Messiah was a drama destined for the theatre but unlike almost every
other drama before or since, it has no plot. The oratorio *Saul* had
characters, such as David and Jonathan, and Israelite and Philistine
armies in combat. Though there are shepherds guarding their flocks
and there is a scourging mob, *Messiah* is without dramatic action and
has no named characters. Jesus Christ never speaks directly, only in
the third person. And yet the oratorio is a drama which succeeds even
though events are not explicitly presented. Jennens dared to assume
that Handel's intended audience would be completely familiar with
the Bible stories. No direct narrative was necessary, therefore, and the
drama could unfold without the kind of often tedious explanatory
recitative found in eighteenth-century operas.

The core theme of Jennens's word-book is the benevolence of
God the Father in offering to mankind his only Son and the hope of
salvation now that the risen Christ stands at the right hand of God.
Messiah begins with God's promise as spoken by the prophets and

becomes a commentary on the Nativity, Passion, Resurrection and Ascension and concludes with the fulfilment of the divine promise in redemption.

For Jennens the challenge was to mould the *Messiah* libretto to provide Handel with every opportunity to display his genius. The composer's operas were replete with episodes of high drama and intense emotion, emphasised by contrasting interludes of affecting calm. The meditative, almost abstract nature of this oratorio, devoid of plot and with at best a scanty, oblique narrative, made it essential for Jennens to craft his text to allow Handel room to transfix the audience with choruses and solos of appropriate emotion and power. Verses chosen by Jennens, particularly from the Old Testament, gave Handel ample scope for the composition of arresting dramatic pieces to be delivered with operatic force. They include: 'Make straight in the desert a highway for our God'; 'And I will shake the heavens and the earth, the sea and the dry land'; 'And who shall stand when he appeareth? For he is like a refiner's fire'; 'Thou shalt break them with a rod of iron; Thou shalt dash them in pieces like a potter's vessel'; and 'He gave his back to the smiters, and his cheeks to them that plucked off the hair: he hid not his face from shame and spitting'.[33]

The Bible in English from which Jennens drew his libretto (with the exception of Psalms from the *Book of Common Prayer*) was the 1611 Authorised Version (known as the *King James Bible*). The committee appointed by King James I had been instructed to produce a translation to be read aloud in churches as if in performance in order to ensure maximum impact on congregations.[34] Words crafted to be read aloud could be more easily incorporated into a text for singers than those which were not. Since for Jennens the Bible was unquestionably the Word of God, most of the verses he chose to include in his oratorio were as they appear in the Authorised Version. At the same time he was intent on putting together a libretto which was coherent and lucid and form a template to stir the emotions. To accomplish this Jennens did feel it necessary to reorder and prune, and on occasion to recast the words of the 1611 translation by making them more rhythmic and direct. For example:

O Zion, that bringest good tidings, get thee up into the high Mountain; O Jerusalem, that bringest good tidings, lift up thy voice with strength; lift it up, be no afraid; say unto the cities of Judah, Behold your God!

was reshaped by Jennens to become:

O thou that tellest good Tidings to *Zion*, get thee up into the high Mountain: O thou that tellest good Tidings to *Jerusalem*, lift up thy Voice with Strength

Verse 6 in Isaiah chapter 50 begins, 'I gave my back to the smiters' but, to avoid having the 'Man of Sorrows' later on rather suddenly addressing the audience directly, Jennens changed it to 'He gave his back to the Smiters … ' To maintain consistency the past tense had to be substituted for the present tense: Isaiah 53:3 begins: 'He is despised and rejected of men; a man of sorrows, and acquainted with grief'; this was altered to, 'He was despised and rejected of Man, a Man of Sorrows, and acquainted with Grief'. Subtle prunings included the omission of conjunctions and repeated verbs, for example in verse 4 in Isaiah chapter 40: 'Every valley shall be exalted, and every mountain and hill shall be made low; and the crooked shall be made straight, and the rough places plain' was reduced to 'Ev'ry valley shall be exalted, and ev'ry mountain and hill made low, the crooked straight and the rough places plain'.[35]

In condensing and gently reshaping verses from the Bible, Jennens was following the well-established and respected practice of paraphrasing in English anthem composition. Fewer than half the anthems listed in *A Collection of Anthems, as the same are now Performed in His Majesty's Chapels Royal, &c*, first published in 1724, set text from the Bible and the *Book of Common Prayer* without it being changed. The Church of England also respected and adopted recommendations made by the great nonconformist hymn writer, Isaac Watts. Watts – who wrote perhaps as many as 750 hymns, including 'O God, our Help in Ages Past' and 'When I survey the wondrous cross' – advised that for clarity text lifted from Scripture in hymns and versified Psalms should have some obscure similes excised (such as 'Like a crane or a swallow' and 'I have cut off like a weaver my life' Isaiah 8: 12 and 13). Anglicans writing anthems seemed happy to be guided by this dissenter and so, too, was Jennens in his drafting of the word-book for *Messiah*.

Along with those who composed anthems, Jennens liked to apply advice given in *On the Sublime*, the first-century treatise on rhetoric attributed to Dionysius Longinus. The sublime style advocated by Longinus was designed to promote 'Boldness and Grandeur in the Thoughts … the Pathetic, or the Power of raising the Passions to a violent and even enthusiastic degree'. 'The Sublime not only persuades', Longinus continued, 'but even throws an Audience into a Transport'. In his grand design to banish doubt, that was *exactly* what Jennens wanted Handel to be able to do. To promote rhythm and dramatic impact this gave Jennens both approval and encouragement to alter tenses, take verses out of their sequence, substitute the third person for the first person, omit repeated words and conjunctions, incorporate repetition and begin as many sections as possible with an arresting first word such as 'Behold'.[36]

When writing the libretto for the oratorio *Saul*, Jennens had frequent discussions with Handel on what text should be altered, added or dropped, and indeed on whether the composer's draft score was suitable. *Messiah* was written without any of this kind of interchange. When the word-book was finished it was simply delivered to Handel's house in Brook Street. Jennens, worried that Handel's financial position was becoming increasingly precarious, envisaged that the first performance could be a kind of benefit concert for the composer. The right time to put on the oratorio would be the week before Easter when operas and plays could not be staged, but sacred works could be. The right venue for such a benefit performance would, as always, be London.

Jennens was not a little put out to discover that Handel, now working with intense energy on the score for *Messiah*, had made the snap decision to have it performed, not in the capital, but in Dublin.

Chapter 4
Music in Dublin

A VICTORIOUS PEACE

'*Le jour est à nous*, the day is ours, *mes enfants*', the French
commander Charles Chaumont, the Marquis de Saint-Ruth
shouted to his men. But at that moment a cannon ball, fired at
extreme range, took off his head. Total confusion followed in the
ranks of the Jacobite Irish and Louis XIV's veterans he had been
commanding. Seizing the opportunity presented by the ensuing
disarray to make use of a causeway around a treacherous bog in
front of them, their opponents, the forces of William of Orange
commanded by Baron de Ginkel of Utrecht, made a devastating and
decisive assault.

Fought on the limestone plain of east Galway at Aughrim on 12
July 1691, that battle was the bloodiest ever fought on Irish soil. In
one afternoon, the French commander Marquis de Saint-Ruth, three
major-generals, seven brigadiers, twenty-two colonels, seventeen
lieutenant colonels and over seven thousand other ranks were killed.
That battle ended the attempt of James II to recover his throne
with the help of Louis XIV and the Catholic Irish, and secured
the position of the Prince of Orange who had deposed him and
now, along with his wife Mary, was ruling England, Scotland and
Ireland as William III. Aughrim certainly decided the political future
of Ireland for the next two centuries and more. For much of the
preceding hundred years the island's soil had been drenched in blood.
Now Ireland, indisputably back under the rule of its larger neighbour,
was to experience a century of peace, the longest in its history.

In the years that followed the Williamite victory, a fresh bout
of land confiscation and a succession of laws, later collectively
known as the Penal Code, deprived the Catholic gentry of the
means and the will to renew resistance. All important decisions

affecting Ireland were being taken in London. This reality ensured the domination of a Protestant élite in Ireland for decades to come. And the long victorious peace was to make possible the spectacular development of Ireland's principal city.

DUBLIN: A PROTESTANT STRONGHOLD

In *A Description of the City of Dublin*, published in 1732, Edward Lloyd – 'a silk thrower of London who has lived near twenty years in Ireland' – accurately informed his readers that the 'city of Dublin is the metropolis of the most ancient and valuable kingdom of Ireland and is the largest and most populous city in the Imperial Dominions of Great Britain, excepting the city of London'. Dublin's population was estimated at 62,000 in 1706 and by 1740 it was at least 110,000. It was probably the ninth largest city in Europe, the fifth largest north of the Alps, about the same size as Milan, and larger than Madrid or Berlin. Dublin was unique in being the only one of Europe's 10 largest cities which was not the capital of a sovereign state.[1]

During the first decades of the eighteenth century native Gaelic culture appears to have been almost entirely hidden in Ireland's capital city. By this time a pattern of seasonal migration had become well established. After spending the late spring and summer on their country estates, 'the quality' would overwinter in the city. The great town houses, elegant terraces and fashionable squares filled up with the Protestant nobility, gentry, judges and senior clergy together with their families and their guests. Indeed, at all times of the year the city had a Protestant majority: in 1732 Protestants amounted to two-thirds of Dublin's recorded inhabitants, and it is estimated that between 44,000 and 75,000 of them lived there between 1706 and 1760. In short this second city of the empire was as much and more a Protestant stronghold as the heavily colonised province of Ulster.[2]

The years immediately following the ending of the Williamite war in 1691 witnessed a great influx of Scots to Ulster, at least 50,000 and perhaps as many as 80,000, in part driven across the North Channel by a succession of devastating harvest failures remembered in their homeland as 'the seven ill years'.[3] There was also a very considerable migration across the Irish Sea to Dublin. Most of these were English, attracted by opportunities opening up in the city in the wake of assured peaceful conditions. Undoubtedly immigrants were also enticed by legislation to encourage 'Protestant Strangers' to settle in Ireland and a resolution passed in the Irish Parliament in 1692 to grant them freedom of worship 'in their own several rites'. Nearly all of these continental incomers were Huguenots, Protestants expelled from France after Louis XIV had in 1685 revoked the toleration guaranteed to them by the 1598 Edict of Nantes. The earliest arrivals were merchants and their families but in the 1690s skilled craftsmen predominated, largely drawn from southern and western France. Many had served as soldiers with William III and Ginkel. Some travelled on to follow Louis Crommellin to Lisburn where, with the help of a generous grant from the Irish Parliament, he was establishing a colony of Huguenot linen weavers. Henri Massue de Ruvigny, a French commander who had fought in Ireland against the Jacobites, had been ennobled as the Earl of Galway by William of Orange. Granted land in Queen's County (now Laois), the Earl created a Huguenot settlement in Portarlington.[4]

Around half of all Huguenots went no further than Dublin. They numbered about 3,600 in 1720 by which time well over five per cent of Dublin's citizens were of French origin. Some settled in the Liberties where the sophisticated skills they brought with them did much to strengthen and diversify the city's textile industry. However, they were spread across Dublin and they were most numerous in the city's south-east neighbourhoods. The craft most associated with them was silver and goldsmithing – a fifth of all masters of the Goldsmiths' Guild had Huguenot names in 1706.[5] Successful Huguenot entrepreneurs put up attractive town houses with distinctive gables known, somewhat inappropriately, as 'Dutch Billies'. The most prominent Huguenot in Dublin, David Digges La Touche, who had fought on the winning side at the Battle of the Boyne in 1690, set up a cambric and poplin factory in High Street in 1693. He probably recruited silk weavers in London to set up in Dublin; he became a manufacturer of silk and woollen cloth; and he transferred assets and managed funds for his fellow Huguenot exiles. La Touche prospered so well that he founded a bank in Castle Street in 1735 – just about the only bank in a city buffeted on occasion by alarming financial crises to remain solvent – and he became one of the city's most prominent property developers.[6]

THE CULTURE OF A COLONIAL ÉLITE

Dublin's population was also augmented by an influx from the countryside helping to swell the city's large Catholic minority which during the second half of the century would become a majority. Undoubtedly a great many spoke Irish as their first language, sang Gaelic songs and played and listened to and danced to traditional airs in taverns and in their homes. However, the existence of native culture in the city at this time receives scant attention in contemporary written and printed records. Tantalising suggestions that occasional notice was taken of Irish music appear in the city's newspapers. In August 1721 *Harding's Weekly Impartial News-Letter* informed readers:

> We hear that Mr Murphy lately come from London who is the famousest Man in all the World for the Irish Harp, and thought not to be much less on the Violin, is Desired by several Ladies of Quality to perform once before his Grace to shew his Perfections.

The following January the same newspaper had this intriguing report:

> On SATURDAY last Blind Paddy, the Ballad Singer was Married to a young Girl of about fifteen Years of Age. The Supper was very costly, having no less than six several Courses, first an excellent Sir Loin of Beef, the Second a Leg of Mutton and Turnips, the third a curious Dish of butter'd Ling and Plaice, the fourth a Plumb-Pudding, the fifth curious white sausages prepar'd for the Bride-Maids Palates, and the last, Bread, Cheese and Butter. All sorts of Liquors were very Plenty, insomuch that few of the Guests went Sober away.

In 1724 John and William Neal published *A COLLECTION of the most Celebrated Irish Tunes proper for the Violin German Flute or Hautboy Plearak na Rough* to be performed at a subscription concert 'by Senior Loranzo Bocchi'.[7]

Dublin's dominant culture was that of the colonial governing élite and the city's Protestant majority which always looked east for inspiration and for the latest offerings in fashionable entertainment. Musical taste in Dublin reflected that of London. Concert programmes were dominated by the works of baroque composers such as Arcangelo

Corelli, Antonio Vivaldi and, of course, Handel. As in London, concert audiences in the Irish capital were for the most part restricted to the nobility, gentry and upper middle classes. The 'subscription' (the word then for a ticket bought beforehand) was usually a 'British Crown', a sum far beyond the means not only of the skilled artisan but also of the majority of those in the middle ranks of society. Those with more modest means than the gentry might well be able to afford the admission charge of one or two shillings to the theatre or outdoor concerts. A popular venue for inexpensive outdoor concerts in summer was the Bowling Green on the Strand, later known as Marlborough Bowling Green, as this insertion in the *Dublin Weekly Journal* in July 1728 indicates:

> At the Desire of several Persons of Quality. At the Bowling Green on the Strand, will be performed a Concert of Musick, and to continue Tuesdays, Thursdays and Saturdays during the Season. N.B. Every Gentleman to pay a British Shilling at the Door, the Ladies free.

On 24 May 1737 this notice appeared:

> The Marlborough Bowling-Green, near the Ferry-boat Slip… Musick Days … every *Wednesday* and *Saturday* Afternoons, Gentlemen's Subscription … half a guinea, otherwise he is to pay each Music Day, a British Shilling and of other days six-pence of like Money before he enters the *Green*.

Outdoor performances could also be heard at the 'City Bason', a reservoir which supplied most of the city with its water, on a site behind what was to become Guinness's Brewery, and Spring Gardens in St Stephen's Green, as advertisements placed in *Faulkner's Dublin Journal* in June and July 1730 show: 'The Musick designed for the Entertainment of the Ladies, will be continued every Tuesday at the Bason, and every Friday at Stephen's Green during the Season'. Another for June 1737 in the *Dublin News-Letter* informed readers that 'Counsellor Broadsheet intends to have for the Entertainment of Ladies and Gentlemen and fellow Citizens a Band of Musick at the Bason every Monday Night during the Season'.[8]

Indoor concerts were, above all, social occasions where music was an elegant entertainment. Quite often the music was background music. In London those who attended Handel's operas seem to have felt no obligation to stop talking during performances and boisterous chat and card-playing would halt only when a famous castrato or prima donna was singing solo.[9] Musicians and singers in Dublin seem to have had to endure similar performing conditions except, of course, when before a congregation in a church or a cathedral.

STATE MUSIC IN DUBLIN CASTLE

Dublin Castle was the very pinnacle of fashionable society in Ireland. For gentlemen and their spouses, elegant unattached ladies and young beaux, clergy seeking promotion, commissioned officers and other Protestants of fashion, an invitation to a Castle Ball was full of promise. Sure to be present was the Lord Lieutenant, or at least one of the three lord justices acting during his absence, nobles and gentry, bishops and deans, and peers and MPs and others who presented guests at the Castle with the opportunity to become acquainted with those having power and influence. Not only would there be a bewildering succession of fine dishes sumptuously prepared and presented, to be washed down with fine wines including champagne, but also musical entertainment which included the latest offerings by composers in London and Italy.

During the first decades of the eighteenth century the viceroy's court at the Castle rivalled the two cathedrals as the principal provider of music in the city. The Earl of Wharton, arriving as Lord Lieutenant in 1709, had brought with him the composer, Thomas Clayton, as 'director of court festivities'. Though Clayton only stayed for a couple of years it was from his time onwards that a musical consort was permanently based at the Castle. No doubt the musicians had the use of instruments listed in 1716:

Militia Horse; Money spent on Instruments
For 6 trumpets at £6 each £36. 0s. 0d.
Trumpet banners and standards £75. 0s. 0d.
Kettle drum and banners £3. 0s. 0d.
For 7 housings and 6 pairs of bags for trumpets and kettle-drummer £4. 12s. 0d.
7 livery coats for trumpeters and kettle-drummer £62. 0s. 0d.[10]

William Viner, who took Clayton's place, was described in the *Dublin Gazette* as 'Master of the Queen's Music'. After George I had come to the throne, Sigismond Cousser, who took over after Viner's death in 1716, had the official title 'Master of the State Music'. Cousser (baptised Johann Sigismund Kusser) was a musician and composer of distinction. Born in Pressburg (now Bratislava) in 1660, he studied with the great composer Giovanni Lully in Paris and then was employed as Kappelmeister in German opera houses. Cousser had come to Dublin in July 1707 after spending two-and-a-half years in London. He composed the annual Birthday Ode for Queen Anne in 1708 and, even after Viner had taken up his post, Cousser was still asked to write the music for the ode for the monarch every year until his death in 1727. Just why Cousser settled in Dublin is not clear: he was renowned in Stuttgart and Hamburg as a composer, conductor and opera manager who had written 15 operas. Indeed, musical experts consider him to have had a significant influence on German music.

The performance of Cousser's annual ode usually took place in Dublin Castle at noon on the birthday of the reigning monarch preceded by an official procession to the Castle and followed by a banquet, a play at the Smock Alley theatre in the evening and finishing with fireworks over the River Liffey. The ode lavishly praising the monarch generally finished with a chorus expressing continued undeviating loyalty. Between four and ten solo singers portrayed either characters from classical mythology or allegorical figures in costume accompanied by a chorus drawn from Christ Church and St Patrick's cathedrals and an orchestra. The music for court celebrations at the Castle has been lost, but surviving libretti hint that birthday odes were given full stage performances with members of the nobility taking part – just as French aristocrats did at Versailles in the presence of Louis XIV.[11]

Outside the Castle, Dublin had no proper concert hall which could take a sizeable audience until the opening of 'Mr Johnston's Great Room' in Crow Street in 1731. This had been built at the request of the 'Musical Academy for the Practice of Italian Musick', an organisation, signing itself as the 'Musical Accademy', which corresponded with Handel to request the purchase of his scores. The vicars choral from both Christ Church and St Patrick's cathedrals frequently sang together at the Castle and, to supplement their

incomes, they also responded to requests to perform in the theatre
and at charity and private functions. Vicars choral in St Patrick's
Cathedral are first referred to in Dublin as early as 1219. They began
as substitutes for canons to sing the liturgy and in time they became
permanent employees in all cathedrals. Soon they were the most
important professional singers in the city. The Reformation, affecting
Dublin before any other part of Ireland, did not mean that vicars
choral were no longer required: they had to be members of the state
church, of course, and the liturgy they sang was now in English; but
their duties remained much as they had been before. Their numbers
were augmented by other full-time professional singers, paid choir
men known as stipendiaries, those who had ambitions to become
vicars choral later in their careers. In 1680 vicars choral founded
the Hibernian Catch Club as a society for convivial get-togethers
and recreational singing; and this club continued to meet regularly
thereafter, eventually admitting lay members in 1770.[12] Indeed, without
these professionally trained vicars choral and stipendiaries there could
have been no first performance of Handel's *Messiah* in Dublin.

Concert halls, music rooms and visiting artists
Crow Street Music Hall was one of the very first venues anywhere
in Europe outside London specifically built for public concerts. Built
by John Johnston, who for a time was in charge of music provided
by Dublin Corporation, it was opened on Monday 30 November
1731 with a *ridotto*, a form of public entertainment very popular in
London which consisted of singing and instrumental music followed
by supper and dancing, very often with masks. Two years later the
violinist and lute player, Carlo Arrigoni, played to packed audiences
there. On 17 December 1733 Francesco Geminiani made his Irish
début in this music hall. On 1 May 1734 Handel's *Acis and Galatea*
received its first Dublin performance in Crow Street 'with all the
chorus's as it was perform'd in the Opera House in London'. There
were frequent benefit concerts for and by musicians and charitable
musical organisations held weekly concerts in this concert hall.[13]

Geminiani was the most distinguished musician to reside in
Dublin in these years. Born in Lucca in 1687, he was a pupil of
Arcangelo Corelli and Alessandro Scarlatti. A professional violinist
in Naples and Lucca, he moved to London in 1714, working there

until 1732 when he moved to Dublin, brought over by his patron
Baron Charles Moore of Tullamore. On 6 December 1733 he
performed 'several Solo's and Concerto's of His own Composition' in
Crow Street Theatre.[14] This virtuoso violinist and composer opened a
concert hall that became known as 'Geminiani's Great Musick Room'
in Spring Gardens off Dame Street. There he also pursued his interest
in the printing of music and dealing in works of art. He was the most
famous foreign composer to have lived in Ireland. Geminiani was the
author of the earliest treatises on baroque performance practice and
he seems to have been responsible for establishing the high standard
of instrumental playing remarked on by Handel after he had returned
from his visit to Dublin in 1742.[15] According to Oliver Goldsmith, it
was after listening to Geminiani 'in the house of an Irish nobleman'
that the great blind harper, Turlough Carolan, composed his famous
'Carolan's Concerto':

> Carolan immediately challenged him to a trial of skill …
> The musician accordingly played over on his fiddle the fifth
> concerto of Vivaldi. Carolan, immediately taking his harp,
> played over the whole piece after him without missing a note…
> but their astonishment increased when he assured them he
> could make a concerto in the same taste himself, which he
> instantly composed, and that with such spirit and elegance
> that it may compare (for we have it still) with the finest
> compositions of Italy.[16]

The Beggar's Opera, a satirical play by John Gay with music arranged
by J C Pepusch predominantly from English ballads, had its
première in London on 29 January 1728. Less than two months
later, this ballad opera, featuring beggars, criminals and prostitutes,
crossed the Irish Sea to be staged for the first time in Dublin's Smock
Alley Theatre. It was hugely popular from the outset. During the
remainder of the year there were no fewer than 40 performances,
almost always to packed houses. The second performance, on 16
March, the *Dublin Intelligence* reported, was received:

with great applause, his Excellency, the Lord Carteret being present; the boxes were so crowded with ladies and the stage and pit with gentlemen, that 'twas remarked above half the people in the gallery, were persons of distinction in disguise.

After this performance, *Dickson's Dublin Intelligencer* informed its readers: 'All boxes bespoke for 16 or 18 nights to come'. Mrs Sterling, who played the part of Polly Peachum, got £105 14s 0d from a benefit performance on 11 April in addition to an estimated £30 thrown onto the stage. A version was put on in 1731 with a cast made up entirely of children, including Peg Woffington, who won instant stardom in the role of Polly Peachum. The daughter of a bricklayer, she went on to become the most famous actress of her day. Woffington became an overnight success in London in 1740, and she continued to captivate audiences there for the ensuing 17 years.[17]

In short, a wide variety of musical tastes were being catered for in Dublin. Francesco Scarlatti and Francesco Geminiani were by no means the only foreign performers to settle in Ireland's capital. 'Madame Violante' arrived in the city 'after a tedious and dangerous passage of six weeks' in December 1729 and converted a large house in Fownes Court off Dame Street into a 'commodious booth'.[18] Here, with the help of tumblers and dancers she had brought over with her, she entranced her audiences by displays of strength and by walking on a rope from the stage to the upper gallery, and then 'by flapping down the rope on her breast without being fastened thereto'.[19] One lady thought that she was too daring in the showing of her limbs and that her acts were shockingly indecent and 'masculinely indelicate'.[20] It was Madame Violante who formed a company of child actors, putting them on the stage in *The Beggar's Opera* and giving Peg Woffington her big break. Madame Violante moved to another venue in George's Lane in 1731, and her entertainments proved such a draw that it led to a fall in audiences for Smock Alley theatre nearby. The Lord Mayor, Nathaniel Pearson, objected so strongly to her practice of 'showing her brawny parts' that she had to move to a new theatre in Rainsfort Street (in the liberties) outside his jurisdiction. Dr Bartholomew Mosse bought Madame Violante's 'booth' in George's Lane and opened it as a lying-in hospital in March 1745 while the much larger Rotunda Hospital was being built.[21]

MATTHEW DUBOURG

The tempo of musical life in Dublin quickened in the 1730s. In part this was due to the energy, commitment and talent of Matthew Dubourg. The illegitimate son of a court dancing master, he was a child prodigy who had played Corelli's music in 1712 while standing on a stool in Thomas Britton's Music Room in London. Handel had been present on that occasion, and very soon after got to know the boy. The composer gave Dubourg frequent employment and was to remain his very good friend for the rest of his life. Dubourg became a pupil of Geminiani while he was still in London in 1714. By 1719 he was performing his own compositions in the Theatre Royal in Drury Lane and in 1721, when he first led an orchestra, he moved to Dublin. In 1723 Dubourg accepted an invitation to become a member of the Irish State Music. He returned to London in 1727 but was enticed back to Dublin. He accepted the post of 'Chief Composer and Master of the Music attending his Majesty's State in Ireland' in 1728.[22] This had been first offered to Geminiani but he turned it down. Why did Dubourg choose Dublin rather than London? Undoubtedly he was pleased to be given a prestigious and a well-paid position in a glittering court. Dubourg had often been engaged by Handel but at the time there were anxieties about the composer's future career. In May 1736 his friend Benjamin Victor wrote to him: 'As to the Operas, they must tumble, for the King's presence could hardly hold them up, and even that prop is denied them, for his Majesty will not admit his royal ears to be tickled this season'.[23] A few months later Dubourg got another letter from Victor containing this gloomy prediction: 'It is the confirmed opinion that this winter will compleat your fried *Handel's* destruction, as far as loss of money can destroy him'.[24]

Apart from regular visits to London, Dubourg remained in Ireland until 1752. Not only did he compose no fewer than 31 birthday odes (of which the music of just 4 survives) but he also acted as leader of the orchestra at most public concerts, including the first benefit concert for Mercer's Hospital on 8 April 1736. No wonder that, six years later, Handel had no hesitation in choosing Dubourg to lead the orchestra for the première of his oratorio *Messiah*.[25]

THE MUSIC TRADE

During the early eighteenth century the Neal family dominated the music trade in Dublin. From 1721 John Neal was selling sheet music imported from England: he placed advertisements in *Harding's Weekly Impartial News-Letter* that year informing readers that he had for sale 'Newest Musick just imported', 'Direction-Books for all Sorts of Instruments; Likewise Choise FIDLES of all-Sorts...N.B. the old OPARA's may be had at the same Place as well as the New', and, in the *Dublin Courant* on 20 December:

> Just Arriv'd from LONDON: A parcel of the newest MUSICK, Compos'd by the most famous Masters in *Europe*, and are Sold by John Neale Instrument-Maker in Christ-Church-Yard, Dublin; where all Gentlemen may be furnish'd with New Musick as it comes out of *London*. Note, there is FIDLES to be had, with Direction-Books for all Sort of Instruments.

The Neals were by no means the only music vendors in town. 'S. Button in Anglesey Street in Dublin' advertised in *Harding's Weekly* in December 1722:

> Lately imported from Leghorn, a Great parcel of Right Venus Catlin Strings for Violins, and base Vialls etc. also Silver Thirds and Fourths for Violins, the best Strings that have been in this Kingdom. And are to be Sold for three Pence per Knot the Caitlin Strings, or for six Shillings per Bundel, the Silver Strings will be Sold for five Pence per Ring, which is one Penny Chaper in Each, than they were Sold for here

Nathaniel Cross, a musical instrument maker in Bow Church Yard in Cheapside, found it worth his while to travel from London in 1729 and rent rooms in the Flying Horse in Temple Bar. He advertised that he had for sale at premises next door to The Three Tons and Crown in Dame Street 'choice Musical Instruments, as Base Violins and Violins, etc., Flutes of all sorts, 4 Valuable Cremone Violins, one above 100 Years old, and wonderfully preserved: Likewise Music Books, and the best of Strings'.[26]

Renatus Harris, originally from Brittany, got contracts to build and supply organs to Christ Church and St Patrick's cathedrals in 1696-7. These were installed and maintained by his assistant, John Baptiste Cuvillie, who was subsequently paid £10 a year to tune and maintain the organ in Christ Church. Cuvillie soon established himself as Ireland's leading organ-builder. He built organs for Trinity College Dublin, and the city's Church of Ireland parish churches of St Mary's, St Peter's, St Michan's and St Werburgh's between 1701 and 1725. He may have added what could have been the earliest tremulant stop (a device which varies the wind supply to organ pipes to produce a tremolo and vibrato effect) in England or Ireland while making tonal alterations to Harris's organ in Christ Church. Cuvillie explained that he had:

> removed the vox humaine which was on the choir organ before now to the great organ and for to adorn that stop and to make it appear like a humane voice, I added a Tramblen stop to it…which no organ in England can show the like.[27]

During the early eighteenth century the main plucked keyboard instrument, the spinet, was primarily for domestic use. Every concert venue of any importance had to have the larger harpsichord on the premises. In 1702 Christ Church acquired a harpsichord to teach the choir boys, and there was one in Dublin Castle in 1705, if not before. It was not until later in the century that Dublin became a noted centre for the making of harpsichords and spinets.

BENEFIT PERFORMANCES

A striking feature of the musical scene in Dublin was that a very high proportion of performances took place to raise money for charitable purposes. There were numerous 'benefit' concerts, for example, to support ageing musicians, to reward artists who had brought special delight to audiences and to help out others in difficulties. *Harding's Weekly Impartial News-Letter*, for example, had this insertion on 20 March 1723:

Tomorrow … Will be perform'd a Consort of Vocal and
Instrumental MUSICK. For the Benefit of JACKY CLEGG, a
BOY of about Nine Years of Age. Who is very much improv'd
on the Violin. The Master Pieces by the BOY.[28]

On 20 October 1733 there was a benefit concert in Crow Street
for 'Signior Arrigoni' – 'The Songs are all compos'd and to be
performed by himself'.[29] On 22 December 1736 *The Provok'd
Husband* was performed at Smock Alley for the benefit of prisoners,
by order of the Charitable Musical Society and by permission of
the Lord Mayor, George Forbes. The Charitable Musical Society
had a benefit concert at Smock Alley on 4 February 1738 at which
'the famous MR. MURPHY will perform on Irish Harp'.[30] And
in December 1738 a ball was organised in the 'Great Room in
Fishamble-street' for the benefit of 'a Vintner in Distress.[31] After
spending the years 1719 to 1724 in London, the composer and
violinist, Francesco Scarlatti (brother of Alessandro and uncle of
Domenico Scarlatti) settled in Dublin. An insertion in *Faulkner's
Dublin Journal* in 1733 revealed that he was having some problems:

> Whereas JANE SCARLATTI, wife of FRANCIS
> SCARLATTI, Master of Music hath eloped from her said
> Husband. This is to desire that no Body may give any Credit to
> the said Jane Scarlatti on account of her said Husband; for he
> will not pay any Debts that she shall contract; nor answer any
> Bills she may draw on him. April 7th 1733. Francis Scarlatti.

Shortly before he died a benefit concert was put on for Scarlatti in
Geminiani's Room on 13 February 1741.[32] Those who organised
benefit performances and balls were almost certainly members of
a wide range of musical societies in Dublin who in turn would be
regular customers of retailers supplying both amateur and professional
musicians with their needs.

Instrument makers, printers of sheet music and music shop
proprietors played a leading role in founding and sustaining musical
societies in the city. Keeping track of them is not easy, since they
often merged and changed their names. The most venerable was the
Hibernian Catch Club – which still exists – and others included:

The Musical Society which arranged concerts at the City Bason and St Stephen's Green; The Honourable Musical Society, also called The Old Musical Society; The Musical Academy for the Practice of Italian Music, founded in 1729, which was instrumental in building Crow Street Music Hall, and later became The Philharmonick Society; and what eventually became The Charitable Musical Society – the society which built the Musick Hall in Fishamble Street and, committed to giving aid to debtors crowding the prisons in the wake of a terrible famine, made the momentous decision to join forces with other charities in the city to invite Handel to Dublin.

Chapter 5
Significant Encounters: 'An Acquaintance Among the Wits'

HANDEL'S FRIEND VISITS DUBLIN

In 1724 Mrs Mary Pendarves arrived from Cornwall to begin a new life in London, moving into the home of her mother's relatives, the Stanleys, in Brook Street. She was delighted to find that, a few months before, Handel had leased a new house just a few doors away. It was not long before these neighbours became well acquainted. Mary had first heard the composer play when she was ten years old and now, a passionate admirer of his music she rarely missed any of his public performances. Her brother, Bernard ('Bunny') Granville, became a dedicated 'Handelist', a close friend of the composer and an assiduous collector of his manuscript music. Handel accepted invitations to stay at Bernard Granville's Staffordshire home, Calwich Abbey, there to compose in peace in the rococo 'fishing temple' on an island in the middle of a lake.[1] Handel seems to have had very few really close friends but clearly Mary, in addition to her brother, was one of them. The composer was a frequent guest in her house and, being a very competent harpsichord player herself, she was always welcome back in his home, especially when she was accompanied by her close companion Anne Donnellan (Handel was to leave Anne 50 guineas in his will).

In the spring of 1734, Mary Pendarves was entertaining Handel and one of his favourite Italian prima donnas, Anna Strada, along with a group of amateur musician friends, when there was a knock on the door. She described the scene to her sister Anne:

> I must tell you of a little entertainment of music I had last week … Lord Shaftesbury begged of Mr. Percival to bring him, and being a *profess'd friend* of Mr. Handel (who was here also) *was admitted*; I never was so *well* entertained at *an opera*! Mr. Handel was in the

best humour in the world, and played lessons and accompanied
Strada and all the ladies that sang from seven o'clock till eleven.
I gave them tea and coffee, and about half an hour after nine had
a salver brought in of chocolate, mulled white wine and biscuits.
Everybody was easy and seemed pleased. Bunny staid with me
after the company had gone, eat a cold chick with me, and we
chatted to one o' the clock.[2]

Married at 17 to an elderly Cornish squire, Alexander Pendarves,
at the behest of her paternal uncle Lord Lansdowne, Mary had
become a widow when she was only 24. Since she had taken 'an
invincible aversion' to her 'ugly and disagreeable' husband, his
sudden death released her from unhappy isolation in the West
Country. Thereafter Mary relished all that London society could
offer her.

Then, in September 1731, Anne Donnellan took her to stay with
relatives in Dublin. The city so delighted Mrs Pendarves that she
extended her visit from the six months previously planned to a year
and a half. There is little doubt that on her return to London, she often
spoke to Handel about the many attractions she had found in Dublin.

'I MEET WITH GREAT CIVILITIES'

In Dublin the two young ladies were the guests of Dr Robert
Clayton, Bishop of Killala, and his wife Katherine, Anne
Donnellan's sister. Mary found the Claytons' town house
'magnifique'. The house was a newly-completed mansion in St
Stephen's Green designed by Richard Cassels who, a decade later,
would be the architect of the Musick Hall in Fishamble Street.
Today it forms part of Iveagh House, the home of the department
of Foreign Affairs. It was in just about the most fashionable part
of the city: 'I think this square may be preferred justly to any in
London … it is a great deal larger than Lincoln's Inn Fields'.[3]

The wealthy and well-connected Claytons made sure their visitors
from London were able to enjoy the best that Dublin society could
offer. 'I meet with great civilities', Mrs Pendarves wrote. Vivacious,
witty and intelligent, Mary was a welcome guest at a continuous
round of card-parties, suppers, ridottos and balls. Her hosts took
her in their splendid coach, drawn by six horses, to a military review

in Phoenix Park. 'Nobody's equipage out-looked ours, except my Lord Lieutenant's', and as for the park, 'I never saw a spot of ground more to my taste, it is far beyond St James or Hyde Park'.[4] On many occasions she was invited to be a guest of the current viceroy, Lionel Sackville, Duke of Dorset, at social gatherings in Dublin Castle. In a letter to her brother Bernard, Mary described a ball she attended in the Castle in March 1732:

> The ball was in the old beef-eaters hall, a room that holds seven hundred people seated: it was as well it did, for never did I behold a greater crowd. We were all placed in rows one above another, so much raised that the last row almost *touched the ceiling*! The gentlemen say we looked very handsome, and compared us to Cupid's Paradise in the puppet-show. At eleven o'clock minuets were finished, and the Duke, Duchess, and nobility, marched into the supper room, which was the council chamber … When the doors were *first* opened the hurly-burly is not to be described; squawling, shrieking, all sorts of noises; some ladies lost their lappets, others were trod upon. Poor Lady Santry almost lost her breath in the scuffle, and fanned herself two hours before she could recover herself enough to know if she was dead or alive. I and my company were more discreet than to go with the torrent; we staid till people had satisfied their curiosity and their hunger.[5]

'Our parliament was dismissed yesterday', she wrote on 11 March 1732. 'The town will now grow idle – most people talk of going into the country. The Duke goes to England the 27th of April'.[6] There were still many attractions, however, to keep the two young ladies pleasantly occupied in the city.

Mrs Pendarves heard Francesco Geminiani play at the new Crow Street concert room. She also went to a concert at St Patrick's cathedral on St Cecilia's Day, when Matthew Dubourg led the orchestra in a performance of Corelli's concertos and Purcell's *Te Deum* and *Jubilate*. She attended a concert in Christ Church: 'I cannot say they have much reason to brag of the architecture of it, but they have good voices and a very sweet organ'. The party also visited puppet-shows and Smock-Alley Theatre and was taken to the

Parliament House in College Green to hear an election determined.

In June the Claytons moved to Killala where she was almost overwhelmed by the hospitality of the bishop's Co. Mayo neighbours. 'I have not seen less than fourteen dishes of meat for dinner, and seven for supper, during my peregrination … *no people can be more hospitable or obliging*'. Only a chosen few could enjoy such abundance: 'The poverty of the people as I have passed through the country has made my heart ache – I never saw greater appearance of *misery*; they live in great extremes, either *profusely* or *wretchedly*'.[7]

When Mary Pendarves came back to Dublin it was thought that she could not possibly return to England without an introduction to the most renowned living Irishman, Jonathan Swift.

DEAN SWIFT THE 'DRAPIER'

A dramatic change in the political climate had brought Jonathan Swift back to his native city. In London this clergyman had made his name as a brilliant and caustic Tory satirist, but on Queen Anne's death in 1714, the Tory tide fast retreated and the Whig tide surged in. All hopes of being made a bishop dashed, Swift was left with little choice other than to accept appointment as Dean of St Patrick's cathedral in Dublin.

This cathedral, only a few hundred yards south of Christ Church, stands in the Liberties, so called because these enclaves just beyond the old city walls then lay outside the jurisdiction of Dublin Corporation. The Liberty of St Patrick abutted the Earl of Meath's Liberty. This was Dublin's industrial heartland: here on land confiscated by Henry VIII from the Augustinian monks of St Thomas's Abbey, immigrant craftsmen had made this place, the Coombe, a vibrant centre of cloth production. Just beyond the congested warren of streets echoing with the rhythmic clacking of looms, on the south-western edge of the city, stood the tenterfields. Here weavers had erected wooden frames to dry out and clean their cloth, fixed to the timber by tenterhooks, by stretching them between posts in the open air.

Swift, almost despite himself, came to enjoy his responsibilities as Dean. And, in his carefully-timed and vigorous daily walks, he became acutely aware that these skilled artisans – like *sans-culottes* in Paris – were vulnerable not only to periodic bread shortages but also to alarming fluctuations in the trade cycle. The downturn of 1720-21, for example, had left around 7,000 idle in the Liberties. Dr William King, Archbishop of Dublin, had reported that in just one parish, St Catherine's, 1,300 men were utterly destitute, 'besides wives and children, out of employment, having sold everything to get bread'.[8] Swift became an eloquent champion of this community of cloth workers.

Like other European colonial powers, Britain controlled its trade with mercantilist laws designed to ensure that the mother country remained the focus of its imperial trade. The fiendishly complex regulatory system devised at Westminster had Ireland categorised as a colony. This provoked outrage from the Irish Protestant élite. In particular they were incensed by the Woollen Act of 1699 which banned the export of woollen goods from Ireland to any destination other than England, where they already faced prohibitive import duties.

Swift's understanding of economics was at best rudimentary. He blamed the distress he observed in the Liberties, not on such factors as bad harvests overseas or interruptions to international commerce brought about by war, but solely on what he regarded as Westminster's vindictive, punitive legislation. In 1720 he wrote, anonymously, an angry pamphlet entitled *A Proposal for the Universal Use of* Irish *Manufacture ... utterly Rejecting and Renouncing Everything Wearable that comes from England*. In vivid and forceful language he made this recommendation:

> Upon the whole, and to crown all the rest, let a firm Resolution be taken, by *Male* and *Female*, never to appear with one single *Shred* that comes from *England*; and let all the People say, Amen ... I could wish our Shopkeepers would immediately think on this *Proposal*.

Swift quoted without disapproving comment 'a pleasant Observation of some Body's; *that* Ireland *would never be happy 'till a Law were made for* burning *every Thing that came from* England, *except their* People *and their Coals*'.

Then in 1722 the London government gave William Wood, a Wolverhampton ironmaster, a patent for the minting of a great quantity of halfpennies and farthings for Ireland. Since Wood had given George I's mistress, the Duchess of Kendal, £10,000 in return for using her influence, he was clearly expecting to make a handsome profit. With good reason the Irish were certain they were going to be ruined by having debased coinage foisted on them. Swift joined the fray, even though he was in the middle of writing his masterpiece, *Gulliver's Travels*:

> But Mr Wood made his HALF-PENCE of such *Base Metal*, and so much smaller than the *English* ones, that the *Brazier* would hardly give you above a *Penny* of good Money for a *Shilling* of his; so that this sum of £108,000 in Gold and Silver, must be given for TRASH that will not be worth above Eight or Nine Thousand Pounds real Value … THEREFORE, my Friends, stand to it One and All: Refuse this *Filthy Trash*.

He signed himself 'M.B. Drapier', posing as a draper dealing in woollen cloth. But – to use a phrase widely used in Ireland – even the dogs in the street knew that the author was Jonathan Swift. Not one person could be found to identify Swift before the authorities as the author. The Dean became a national hero overnight. Under this pseudonym he published seven 'Drapier's Letters' in all. The fourth letter was considered his best: in it he declared 'that by the laws of God, of nature, of nations, and of your own country, you are and ought to be as free a people as your brethren in England'. Irish MPs buried their differences to support a motion to reject the new coinage; and in 1725 the humiliated government had no choice but to withdraw Wood's patent and his notorious halfpence.[9]

The publication of *Gulliver's Travels* in 1726 established Swift's fame in England and beyond. This vivid, inventive, astonishingly imaginative allegory, replete with irony, and alternatively teasing and satirical, was impossible to categorise: because nothing like it had been published before, it certainly was new and therefore a novel in the literal meaning of the word. This work quickly found a huge audience not only because it could be read simply as an intriguing, diverting and engrossing tale, but also by the many who relished it as a hard-hitting critique of contemporary politics and society.[10] However, when Mary Pendarves arrived in Dublin she found that it was *not* primarily as author of *Gulliver's Travels*, then being avidly read in her native England, but as the brilliantly satirical pamphleteer who had saved his country from ruin that he had become, unquestionably, the most famous man in Ireland. Here it was as the 'Drapier' that Swift was revered, and revered for years to come.

'A CONSTANT SERAGLIO OF VERY VIRTUOUS WOMEN'

Swift loved to entertain and his deanery became renowned as one of Dublin's liveliest centres for stimulating conversation, witty exchanges, convivial dinners, poetry readings and for the host's speciality, 'raillery', a combination of clever word play, badinage, mock insults and practical jokes. His closest male Irish friends were two fellow clergymen, Dr Thomas Sheridan and Dr Patrick Delany. Sheridan was the grandson of Donnchadh Ó Sioradáin (anglicised as Dennis Sheridan), a native Irish convert to Protestantism in Co. Cavan. Ó Sioradáin had taught Irish to William Bedell, the Bishop of Kilmore, and who, in time of rebellion and massacre, had kept safe for posterity the bishop's translation, the first ever, of the Old Testament into Gaelic. Dr Sheridan was, in Swift's words, 'of a weak constitution, in an employment precarious and tiresome, loaden with children ... a man of intent and abstracted thinking, enslaved by Mathematiks'.[11] Swift would often help Sheridan out in the boys' school he kept in Capel Street. The two men delighted in exchanging jocular riddles and playful verses. Almost certainly Sheridan had a hand in the composition of the Drapier's Letters.[12] His son, also called Thomas – in time the father of the playwright Richard Brinsley Sheridan – was to accompany Dr Delany to the Musick Hall in Fishamble Street to be present at the first performance of Handel's *Messiah*.

Well-known across the city as a compelling preacher, an inspiring lecturer, an author, an art collector, a *bon viveur* and a good-hearted host, Patrick Delany had come a long way. Brought up on a modest farm near Athy, he had been a 'sizar' – that is, a servant to fellow students – when at Trinity College Dublin. After graduation he had become a senior fellow of the college, with a chair in oratory and history, and he was such an engaging teacher that in the 1720s it was thought that he was earning as much as £700 a year giving additional tuition to students. Now he was rector of the fashionable parish church of St Werburgh's, close to both of Dublin's cathedrals. Swift described Dr Delany to Alexander Pope as 'a man of the easiest and best conversation I ever met with in this Island, a very good list'ner, a right reasoner, neither too silent, nor talkative, and never positive'.[13]

It was Patrick Delany who introduced Mrs Pendarves to Swift. In January 1733 Delany invited Mary and Anne to his country villa of Delville near Glasnevin, north of the city. The Dean was one of the guests. 'In such company', Mary wrote afterwards, 'you may believe time passed away very pleasantly'. 'Swift is a very *odd companion* (if that expression is not too familiar for so extraordinary a genius); he talks a great deal and does not require many answers; he has infinite spirits, and says abundance of good things in his common way of discourse'. They dined again at Dr Delany's a couple of months later where Swift 'corrects me when I speak bad English, or do not pronounce my words distinctly. I wish he lived in England, I should not only have a great deal of entertainment from him, but improvement'.

Roger Boyle, Earl of Orrery, a regular guest at Dr Delany's table, had no doubt Swift was at his happiest in the company of women. He likened the Dean to the 'Grand Seignor', the Sultan of Turkey. 'A constant seraglio of very virtuous women', he observed, 'attended him from morning to night, with an obedience, an awe, an assiduity that are seldom paid to the richest or the most powerful lovers; no, not even to the Grand Seignor'.[14] Swift had been left bereft when 'Stella', his closest and dearest female friend Hester Johnson, had died in 1728.[15] The Dean was well ahead of his time in his treatment of women as intellectual equals. In his essay, *Of the Education of Ladies*, he wanted women to be 'able to read and relish history, books of travels, moral or entertaining discourses, and be a tolerable judge of the beauties in poetry'.[16]

Indeed, Mary Pendarves was an exception in Swift's 'constant seraglio': the others were all aspiring writers. 'I have just began an acquaintance among the wits', she wrote.[17] This group included Constantia Grierson, Mary Barber and Laetitia Pilkington – Swift called them his 'triumfeminate'. The Dean did all he could to help his protégés. Constantia Grierson, as well as being a mother and helping her husband in his print house, managed to publish a three-volume edition of Tacitus. Mary Barber, a wool draper's wife with four children, saw herself as:

> A Wretch, in smoaky Dublin pent,
> Who rarely sees the Firmament.

She felt 'Doomed by inexorable Fate' to drudgery:

> Sick of Smells, and dirty Streets,
> Stifl'd with Smoke, and stunn'd with Noise[18]

Swift admired her work and did much to ensure that a volume of her poems was published in London in 1734. Mary Barber abused his friendship, however, by forging his signature on a testimonial to the Queen. He forgave her.

LAETITIA PILKINGTON'S 'LONG AND MOURNFUL STORY'

Dr Delany introduced the Pilkingtons to Dean Swift, something he was later to regret. Matthew Pilkington, a young curate in St Anne's parish, was beginning to make his name as a writer, having composed an ode for the King's birthday celebration in 1728 that was set to music by Matthew Dubourg and performed in Dublin Castle. But it was his wife Laetitia who was to prove the most talented and liveliest member of Swift's literary circle. Charmed by her witty responses to his playful insults, Swift took her to his study in the deanery and got her to read to him from his unpublished manuscripts. He dined in their home in Lazar's Hill (renamed Townsend Street) and became firm friends of this diminutive pair, describing Matthew as 'mighty Thomas Thumb' and Laetitia as 'her serene Highness of Lillyput'. Taken to dine with members of the Grattan family at their country home at Belcamp, five miles north of Dublin, Laetitia found that she was the only woman in the company. Heavily pregnant with her third child, she could eat nothing and declared that she wished she was a man in order to get less of their polite attention. This gave Swift the opportunity to indulge in some 'raillery'. 'In spite of Petticoats, I was made a Man of after Dinner: I was obliged to put a Tobacco-pipe in my Mouth; but they so far indulged me, as to let it be an empty one, as were the Dean's, Doctor Delany's, and my Husband's'.[19]

For more than five years Laetitia Pilkington was a constant visitor to the deanery. Mrs Pendarves correctly described her as 'a bosom friend of Dean Swift's'.[20] Swift helped Mrs Pilkington to refine her skill as a writer and she appreciated 'the Pains he took to teach me to think and speak with propriety'. The Dean proved 'a very rough sort of tutor', pinching her so hard when she made a mistake that she ended up 'black and blue'.[21] Impressed by her intelligence, wide reading and quick wit, Swift in effect made Mrs Pilkington his secretary. She recalled:

> The Dean running into the Parlour, threw a whole Packet of manuscript Poems into my Lap, and so he did for five or six Times successively, till I had an Apron full of Wit and Novelty, for they were all of his own Writing, and such as had not then been made publick, and many of them, I believe, never will.[22]

To help Matthew Pilkington get his poetry published, Swift obtained for the young curate the post of chaplain to the Lord Mayor of London. He refused to take Laetitia with him, telling her 'plainly he did not want such an Incumbrance as a Wife, that he did not intend to pass there for a married Man, and that in short he could not taste any Pleasure where I was. As this was a Secret I did not know before, I receiv'd it with Astonishment'.[23] In London he not only neglected many of his duties but lived beyond his means and had an affair with an actress. After several months Laetitia made the mistake of going over to London uninvited to see her husband, 'confident he would be pleased'. He was not pleased and sent her back home.[24]

When Pilkington returned to Dublin he started a relationship with a wealthy widow and flaunted the affair. Bishop Clayton's wife, Katherine, actually blamed Laetitia for putting the marriage in danger. Mrs Pilkington was 'both traduced for going to London, and for returning from it', Mrs Clayton using words 'I should have scorned, in respect of my own Gentility, to have given the meanest Servant I was ever Mistress of'.[25] Determined to be rid of his wife, Pilkington introduced her to several compliant men in the desperate hope that she would herself have an affair and be found *in flagrante*. She pitched headlong into her husband's trap. Laetitia fell under the spell of a young surgeon, Robert Adair, who had been giving a series of public lectures in Dr Steeven's Hospital in 1735. His biographer later admitted Adair was a philanderer with 'no enemies but his passions' and 'played the devil with the women'.[26] Laetitia began an affair with him and 'in a moment of giddy rapture' was 'undone'. Assuming her husband was away, she took him to her bed in Lazar's Hill but, around midnight, the door was suddenly broken down and a bunch of armed men burst in. After punching Adair in the face, Pilkington sent for a bottle of wine to celebrate his triumph. At 2 a.m. Laetitia was forced to leave her home without any of her possessions. She could not contest a divorce. Indeed, she was pregnant again, probably by her young surgeon. Adair abandoned Laetitia, giving five guineas to a dissenting minister to pass on to her. From now on this woman of wit would have to live on her wits.

Swift was unforgiving. After describing Dr Delany as a 'very unlucky recommender', he denounced the Pilkington pair: 'he proved the falsest rogue, and she the most profligate whore in either Kingdom'.[27] Matthew Pilkington survived the scandal and, in spite of consorting openly with libertines of the newly-formed Dublin Hellfire Club, managed to be appointed rector of Donabate parish, in north county Dublin.

Laetitia Pilkington in her own words had been 'undone' in a 'tumultuous War of Passion' and was left with 'no Protector, no Friend, no Guardian', with her name 'publickly known through all the Coffee Houses in Dublin'. Some men, including the Earl of Antrim, attempted unsuccessfully to buy her sexual favours. On one occasion the Earl of Rosse 'and several other Persons of Distinction' careered drunkenly through her lodgings intent on having their wicked way with her: 'When those worthy Peers could not find me, they threatened to kick the Landlady'.[28] She described her predicament in her poem, 'Sorrow':

> While sunk in deepest Solitude and Woe,
> My streaming Eyes with ceaseless Sorrow flow,
> While Anguish wears the sleepless Night away,
> And fresher Grief awaits returning Day;
> Encompass'd round with Ruin, want and Shame,
> Undone in Fortune, blasted in my Fame,
> Lost to the endearing Ties of Life,
> And tender Names of Daughter, Mother, Wife;
> Can no Recess from Calumny be found?[29]

Mrs Pilkington fled to London, living precariously by penning poems for gentlemen who would then pass them on to their lady friends, pretending they had written the verses themselves. Her output was extraordinary and she did eventually manage to get her own poetry published. She was befriended by Colley Cibber, the sprightly seventy-year-old poet laureate, whose daughter-in-law, Susannah Cibber, would be a soloist in the première of Handel's *Messiah*. Colley Cibber was good to Laetitia, especially after she had been thrown into the Southwark Marshalsea prison for a debt of 40 shillings she could not pay. Cibber contacted as many of her gentlemen clients as he could and collected enough money to prevent her from starving in her cell, to pay the gaoler and then to have her released. Undoubtedly, he saved her life.

On one occasion Colley Cibber persuaded Laetitia to tell him all of her 'long, and mournful Story'. Next morning she arrived for breakfast at his house in Charles Street and spoke for three hours. They met again to enable her to bring her life story up-to-date. Then 'in flowing Spirits', he shouted out: 'Zounds! Write it out, just as you relate it, and I'll engage it will sell'.[30]

She did and it did sell. When her *Memoirs* were published many a gentleman in Dublin turned pale as he turned the pages to see what she had revealed. One of them was Dr Robert Clayton, Bishop of Killala. She described how this man of the cloth had ravished his wife's maid on a carpet in his Dublin town house, 80 St Stephen's Green. The bishop did not deny the story and later sent her 10 guineas, no doubt in the hope that she would not provide further embarrassing details. For Laetitia Pilkington it was sweet revenge.

EXTOLLING 'THE DIGNITY, THE SUBLIMITY, THE MAJESTY OF THE SACRED WRITINGS'

Dr Robert Clayton, evidently a worldly bishop with a flexible moral code and a taste for the good things in life, was a rather typical Irish Anglican clergyman for his time. But in one important respect he was not: Clayton was a freethinker, a unitarian who denied the existence of the Trinity. Before coming to Ireland he had been influenced by Rev. Samuel Clarke, of St James's, Westminster, who, in the Boyle lectures of 1704-5, had applied Newtonian physics to prove the existence of an interventionist God. This, it seems, had set Clayton on the path of questioning revealed religion.[31] The bishop was outspoken in calling for greater toleration for Quakers and Jews, but – apart from predicting the fall of the papacy in the year 2000 – he remained silent on the condition of Irish Catholics. In 1735 Clayton was translated to the diocese of Cork (he appears to have visited Killala only once) and, ten years later, to the diocese of Clogher. Then, when an anonymous pamphlet was published in 1750, entitled, 'An essay on spirit wherein the doctrine of the Trinity is considered', Bishop Clayton was rightly suspected of being the author. In 1757 he was summoned for trial on a charge of heresy before an ecclesiastical commission of the Church of Ireland. Before it began, however, he died of a fever in his Dublin home.[32] However, nearly all the rest of the Church of Ireland clergy were fierce defenders of orthodoxy. These divines had been following very closely the debate on the other side of the Irish Sea between deists and defenders of traditional Christianity.

The most prominent Irish intellectual to challenge deism was George Berkeley, consecrated Bishop of the diocese of Cloyne in Co. Cork in 1734. Like Swift he was a pungent critic of the careless selfishness of the landlord class in Ireland. He also employed Nicolò Pasquali, the composer and cellist frequently engaged by Handel, lodging him in his bishop's palace to teach his children music. Berkeley would eventually get to know Handel and be associated with him in raising money for the Foundling Hospital in London. One of the eighteenth century's most brilliant philosophers (who ultimately gave his name to Berkeley University in California), he was the first to brand sceptics as 'freethinkers'.

Berkeley had no sympathy for Sir Isaac Newton's view that God was a kind of distant engineer. Nothing separated God and Man, he believed, since matter or nature does not exist as a reality independent of consciousness. 'When in broad daylight I open my eyes', Berkeley wrote in his *Treatise Concerning the Principles of Human Knowledge*:

> it is not in my power to choose where I shall see or no, or to determine what particular objects shall present themselves to my view; and so likewise as to the hearing and other senses, the ideas imprinted on them are not creatures of my will. There is therefore some other Will or Spirit that produces them.

Such reasoning was a bit too cerebral for the average Irish defender of traditional beliefs. Members of the general public seem to have found Berkeley's best-selling little book on the health benefits of tar water much easier to follow.[33]

The man most Irish Protestants regarded as leading the charge against scepticism and infidelity was the rector of St Werburgh's parish church, Dr Patrick Delany. To be sure, Delany lived well and had no difficulty in spending all and more of his considerable income, but he had a very strong sense of what was right and wrong and did his best to act accordingly. It was his duty, he was certain, to do all he could to defend the Bible as the Word of God.

To ensure as wide a readership as possible, Delany travelled to London in order to be published there. The title of his best-known work, first published in 1732, made his intention clear: *REVELATION Examined with CANDOUR, OR A FAIR ENQUIRY into the SENSE* and *USE of the Several Revelations Expresly Declared, or sufficiently Implied, to be given to Mankind from the CREATION as they are found in the BIBLE.* He deplored 'the strange, astonishing contempt, into which the Scriptures (the noblest of all writings this world was ever blessed with) have fallen for some years past'. He was at pains to emphasize 'the wisdom, the dignity, the sublimity, the majesty of the Sacred Writings!' Delany was willing to admire Newtonian physics: 'MATHEMATICAL learning hath, of late years, been greatly and justly in esteem amongst us'. Unfortunately some clergy 'very unhappily mistook their talents; and carried that cold, dry, didactic way, into the pulpit … inasmuch as religion was now considered barely in the light of truth; and was so discussed, like other truths, with a dry cold unconcern'. He bemoaned the failure of so many to contemplate 'their dreadful end'. He continued:

> The terrors of the Lord were things unheard of; hell not once named, or named only to be despised … hence the united ruin of true learning, and true religion! And the triumph of ignorance, infidelity and vice! … Hence a carelessness, and a coldness, in the concerns of religion.

Delany was particularly concerned to exhort those clergy 'as may have forgotten their true character, to return diligently to it', and to beseech them to remember, that the earnest, the instructive preacher, the pathetic, the sublime, the Christian orator, these are the true characters of the ministers of the gospel … to put them in mind, to cry aloud, to lift up their voice like a trumpet, to shew the people their transgressions, and the house of Jacob their sins …[34]

Delany had become one of the most influential shapers of society opinion in Dublin. After all, he was a great admirer of Handel's music, no doubt with the encouragement of Mary Pendarves. It seems very likely that it was Charles Jennens's libretto for the oratorio *Saul* that inspired Delany to write *An Historical Account of the Life and Reign of David, King of Israel*, published in 1740-2. He was in a favourable position to see to it that Handel was warmly received when he came to Dublin. Delany did not think 'it proper' to go to the theatre if the subject was 'a profane story'. It was quite a different matter if the drama was a religious one. Religious truths must be movingly conveyed, he passionately believed, with 'the warmth of piety, the ardour of benevolence, and the zeal of *Christian* charity'.[35] Those words could have been written by Charles Jennens. Some in Dublin's polite society might have been wondering if *Messiah*, an entertainment in a music hall, might be a profanation of God's Name and Word. Their doubts were swept aside when Dr Delany showed no hesitation in becoming a subscriber and when he was seen, accompanied by Dr Sheridan's son Thomas, striding up Fishamble Street to hear the sacred oratorio.

And, as will become plain later, Delany was to have a crucial role in seeing to it that *Messiah* could actually be performed in Dublin. He was the chancellor of both cathedrals in the city; his opinion would be valued on whether or not it was proper for the vicars choral and the choir boys to sing in a music hall at all.

Patrick Delany was the man Mary Pendarves most admired when she was in Ireland. 'His wit and learning were to me his meanest praise'; she explained to her friend the Duchess of Portland, 'the excellence of his heart, his humanity, benevolence, charity and generosity, his tenderness and affection, and friendly zeal, gave me a higher opinion of him than of any other man I had ever conversed with'.[36] Delany became a widower in 1741. It is not surprising that when he asked the widow Pendarves to marry him in 1743, she did not hesitate to ignore the protests of her high-born relatives to become Mrs Delany.

SHARED INTERESTS

Ever since she had returned to London in 1733, Mary Pendarves corresponded regularly with Jonathan Swift. She recalled that at a dinner in Delville he had described Anne Donnellan as 'the syren' and herself as a 'sorceress'. This encouraged her to observe, in a letter she wrote in July 1738, that she should 'set all my charms to work to bring you to England, and should expect a general thanksgiving for employing my spells to so good a purpose'. He wanted her to return to Dublin: 'I wish you were forced over by debts or want' and once back in his city 'I will give you a licence to be as silly as you can possibly afford'. Laetitia Pilkington was not the only woman to be pinched black and blue when being corrected in his deanery. 'Since I have not now an opportunity of receiving your favours of pinching and beating', she continued, 'make me amends by *chiding me* for every *false* spelt, and for my *bad English* … I may in time become worthy of your care'.[37]

When writing to the Dean in the summer of 1738, she had company. 'My Lord Lansdowne is much at your service … and constantly drinks your health in champaign, as clear as your thoughts, and sparkling as your wit. Lord and Lady Carteret, and my Lady Worsley all talk kindly of you'. Lansdowne was her uncle and Carteret was her cousin.[38] It was Carteret who had been Lord Lieutenant of Ireland when the government he headed had been forced into a humiliating climb-down over Wood's Halfpence, precipitated by the *Drapier's Letters*. His lordship held no grudge now.

It was also Lord Carteret who had awarded Matthew Pilkington a premium of £50 for composing the King's birthday ode back in 1728. Pilkington was certainly by any standards a cad, but Laetitia made it obvious in all her writings that he was not stupid and was never a bore. His interest in music was genuine. Mrs Pendarves and the Claytons had dined with the Pilkingtons at their home in Lazar's Hill, and the evening had ended with a sing song. Matthew Dubourg and his wife had been regular guests in the Pilkington household. In pursuit of advancement, and needing to restore his reputation, Matthew Pilkington worked hard to cultivate a friendship with Charles Cobbe, Dean of Christ Church. They shared two strong interests: art and music. Matthew Pilkington was an active member of the Charitable Musical Society in Fishamble Street. He could have been present at the meeting that decided to invite Handel to Dublin, but this will never be known. The final decision on whether or not the Christ Church choristers could take part in the performance of *Messiah* would be made by Dean Cobbe. And Cobbe was also a member of the governing body of Mercer's Hospital, one of the three charitable organisations expecting to benefit from the oratorio's première.

Chapter 6
The Duke of Devonshire Returns

'RECEIVED BY … THE LOUD ACCLAMATIONS OF THE PEOPLE'

On Wednesday 23 September 1741, having sailed through the night from Holyhead across the Irish Sea, the government yacht passed the headland of Howth and steered into the shelter of Dublin Bay. 'About 11 o'clock in the Forenoon the Yacht cast Anchor', *Faulkner's Dublin Journal* reported, 'and was saluted by the Liverpool Man of War'. The report of cannon fired from the warship prompted other vessels to respond in the same way to signal the arrival of the viceroy, the Lord Lieutenant of Ireland, William Cavendish, 3rd Duke of Devonshire. Another seven hours would pass before the viceregal party would disembark. The Duke had been appointed to this post by George II back in 1737. Devonshire was beginning his third official sojourn on this island as head of the government of the Kingdom of Ireland. The Lord Lieutenant had with him his wife Lady Catherine, his son Lord James Cavendish, 'and the two young Ladies, his Grace's daughters, with several other persons of distinction, arrived here from England'.[1] Now it was necessary to wait for full tide to bring the viceregal party directly to the quays rather than put it to the inconvenience of disembarking, as on previous occasions, at the exposed peninsula of Ringsend. From the deck the yacht's passengers had ample time to look across the bay at what was now the second largest city in his majesty's dominions.

From this vantage Dublin's setting certainly was a pleasing one: on the River Liffey below Essex Bridge, a veritable wood made up of masts of colliers, snows, brigs, brigantines, cutters, hookers, fly boats and other vessels tied up at George's Quay or anchored further downstream; directly west and to the north a fertile limestone plain stretching as far as the eye could see, a patchwork of hedged fields of stubble where the last of the harvest – bringing merciful relief to end a terrible famine – had been garnered in, land dotted with residences of the gentry, villages of thatched homes and bristling in places with ruins of the Pale's ancient tower houses; to the south west numerous church spires rising above the pall of smoke from coal burning in countless hearths, and – as a majestic backdrop for the city – a great amphitheatre formed by Three Rock Mountain and, behind it, Two Rock Mountain, both with their distinctive weathered tors, Knockannavea, Corrig Mountain and, the highest, Kippure; to the south – for many, the most romantic view – looking over to the fishing village of Dunleary (later Kingstown and now Dún Laoghaire), Dalkey Island and Killiney Bay, across to Bray Head, and just inland from there, the thrusting quartzite peak of Great Sugar Loaf contrasting with the adjacent rounded peaty heights of Djouce and other broad granite neighbours.

Duly alerted, the authorities were making sure that the Lord Lieutenant would receive a fitting welcome for the Crown's principal representative. Flags were hoisted on the Bermingham Tower at Dublin Castle and the tall parish church of St Werburgh's behind it. On the north side of the River Liffey in the Royal Barracks at Oxmantown Green troops readied themselves: here foot soldiers primed their firelocks and grooms saddled mounts for the cavalry in the Horse Square while field pieces were being drawn up on the nearby Artillery Ground. For a great many citizens the progress of the viceroy from the quays to the Castle was a spectacle not to be missed and now they were gathering to line the route. In the Castle itself Matthew Dubourg, Master of the State Music, gave final instructions to the trumpeters, and 'battleaxes', the quaintly armed and attired viceregal guard, got ready to make sure Devonshire was greeted with appropriate pageantry.

Dignitaries made final preparations before driving down to George's Quay to meet the Lord Lieutenant. The most important of these were the Lords Justices, three men who had responsibility for the government of Ireland during the viceroy's absence. Devonshire had not been in Ireland since parliamentary business had ended in the spring of 1740. As the Irish Parliament then met only every second year, it was not thought necessary for him to be in the country during the recess. On this occasion the Lords Justices were: Hugh Boulter, the Primate and Archbishop of Armagh; Robert

Jocelyn, the Lord Chancellor; and Henry Boyle, Speaker of the Irish House of Commons. William Aldrich, the Lord Mayor, made his way from the Mansion House, his official residence in Dawson Street on the southern outskirts of the city, over to the Tholsel, the civic headquarters next to Christ Church cathedral on Skinners' Row. Here, along with Dublin Corporation's aldermen, he donned his sumptuous robes and put around his neck the livery collar, the heavy gold chain of office adorned with a great medallion on which the likeness of William of Orange had been cast.

The Duke and his family stepped off the government yacht to 'the barge', a tender to take them up the Liffey estuary to George's Quay. Ahead, partly obscured by masts and rigging, Essex Bridge curved gracefully over the Liffey to the fine terraced houses of Capel Street, the city's main thoroughfare north of the river. At this point in his short journey Lord Devonshire, a stalwart supporter of the Hanoverian succession, was left in no doubt about the loyalty of this city to the Crown. Here a large bronze equestrian statue of George I, commissioned by Dublin Corporation in 1722, stood prominently in the middle of the river on a stone pier attached to the bridge. Next to the bridge, the handsome three-storeyed Custom House adorned Essex Quay; built 35 years earlier on an arcade to lift it above spring tides and river floods, it had a particularly attractive double-sloped hipped roof with dormers. *Faulkner's Dublin Journal* described the disembarkation:

> About Six in the Evening their Graces landed at George's Quay (being saluted by the Ships as they came along) where they were received by their Excellencies the Lords Justices, several of the Nobility and Gentry, the Battleax Guards, and Hon Colonel Nevill's Regiment of Horse, and the loud acclamations of the People.

'CONDUCTED TO THE CASTLE IN THE USUAL MANNER'
From the quays the coaches wheeled away from the river into Hawkins Street up to Lazar's Hill. Here 'their Graces were met by the Right Hon. the Lord Mayor, Aldermen, Sheriffs, &c., when the Recorder made a short Speech to his Grace on his Arrival'. From there the procession made its way up College Street into College

Green and, as the Duke looked around him, there can have been no question in his mind but that he was in a capital city. To his right stood Parliament House facing Trinity College, perhaps the finest of its kind in western Europe, certainly more magnificent in every respect than the cramped home of the Commons and the Lords in Westminster (a medieval palace, partly converted by Sir Christopher Wren and accidentally destroyed by fire in 1834). This strikingly original building, the brainchild of a former Speaker of the Irish Commons, William Conolly, had been designed by his young protégé, Edward Lovett Pearce, an unlikely descendant of a principal plotter of the 1641 Rebellion, Rory O'More. Powerfully influenced by what he had seen during a tour of Venice and, dexterously blending imported Portland stone and local granite, Pearce had created a frontage which included elegant arched entrances and, set before a deep corridor, the city's first free-standing colonnade. The foundation stone had been laid in the year of Conolly's death, 1729. Pearce had been appointed Surveyor-General in 1730 and knighted two years later, but he had died suddenly in 1732, still in his thirties. Construction had been uninterrupted from the outset so that MPs and peers of the realm had been able to move in during the year 1733; now, eight years later, skilled craftsmen were still busy adding finishing touches to the interior.

Across the broad sweep of the Green stood Trinity College, founded in 1592 in Elizabeth I's reign. Carrying as much of the college's plate as they could, staff and students, including Jonathan Swift, had fled across the Irish Sea as James II and the French army had approached Dublin in the spring of 1689. Jacobite forces had used the university as a barracks until forced to retreat westwards following their defeat at the Boyne in July 1690. Now the Duke could see, in front of a college park tastefully planted with trees, the tall hexagonal chimneys of the Rubrics, three rows of attached brick houses at right angles to each other. Erected when Queen Anne was still on the throne, these had been designed as residences for the students. The Lord Lieutenant might not have known that the northern terrace of the quadrangle was popularly known as Rotten Row or that, in 1734 at number 25, Edward Ford, a fellow of the college, had been shot dead by some drunken students he was attempting to discipline.

Perhaps the viceroy glanced at the charming Printing House adjacent to the Rubrics: built in 1734, it resembling a miniature Greek temple, complete with Ionic columns, the first independent work in Dublin of Pearce's assistant, Richard Cassels. However, the attention of any newcomer here would first have been drawn to a great rectangular building, by far the largest structure in the college. George Berkeley, by now Bishop of Cloyne, had in Queen Anne's time been the college's librarian. He had convinced the provost and his colleagues that a library fit for the only university in the Kingdom of Ireland should be erected on the southern side of the Rubrics. In 1711 Parliament had voted a substantial sum to build it and Thomas Burgh, Pearce's predecessor as Surveyor-General, was engaged to design it. It proved to be Burgh's greatest achievement, a noble building 270 feet long, three storeys high and the ground floor consisted of an open arcade strengthened with a central wall to keep the books well above the damp rising from marshy ground beneath. When completed in 1732 it was the longest single-chamber library in either Britain or Ireland.

As the escorted train of carriages made its way, the streets were packed with excited citizens cheering their Lord Lieutenant. The city resounded with the ringing of church bells and volleys fired by soldiers drawn up along the route. When the viceregal procession veered right from College Green into Dame Street towards the Castle, the Duke for the second time encountered a bold statement of this city's loyalty: an equestrian statue of William III on a plinth. Made by one of London's most distinguished sculptors, Grinling Gibbons, this had been unveiled in 1701 on the eleventh anniversary of the Battle of the Boyne, 1 July, with great ceremony and marked by a florid speech delivered by the Recorder of the city, 'which being ended the great guns were fired' and then 'several hogsheads of claret being ready placed on stilts, with two large baskets of cakes on each, the claret was set running, and the cakes were thrown about among the crowds of people that were in the streets'.[2] The statue was surrounded by metal railings, an indication even at this early stage that it was in danger of being defaced – if only by high-spirited students returning from an evening's heavy carousing in the taverns.

Trinity College and College Green were just outside the medieval walls of Dublin, and access to the Castle from here in former times had to be through Dame's Gate, named after a dam or mill pond adjacent. The gate had been demolished in 1698 and now the viceregal party drove up a broad fashionable street of elegant brick houses. The most distinctive had curved or stepped front gables and cruciform roof ridges at right angles to the street. Erected in continuous terraces, these Dutch billies tended to share chimney stacks from corner fireplaces with the result that the chimneys were tall and massive structures, dominating much of Dame Street's skyline.[3] 'And then their Graces were conducted to the Castle in the usual manner', *Faulkner's Dublin Journal* continued, 'the Streets being lined with Soldiers, &c. The Barrack Guns were fired, the Streets illuminated, and every other Demonstration of Joy that could be shewn on the Occasion'.[4]

A SAFE PAIR OF HANDS

After seeing at close quarters the sumptuous building newly erected in College Green to accommodate the Lords and Commons of Ireland, Devonshire, on his first arrival in 1737, must have found Dublin Castle, at the top of Dame Street, something of a disappointment. This, after all, was his principal residence during his stay in Ireland. It lacked the splendour which would seem appropriate to his high office. Certainly it was not as magnificent as Devonshire House, his huge Piccadilly mansion completed in 1740. Dublin Castle, begun in 1210 on the orders of King John, until the end of the seventeenth century had been primarily defensive in purpose. Now known as the Record Tower, the original massive round keep largely survived, spasmodically repaired along with the city wall's sole surviving flanker, the Bermingham Tower. Queen Elizabeth's long-serving viceroy, Sir Henry Sidney, finding the castle 'ruinous, foule, filthy, and greatly decayed', had striven to turn it into 'a verie fair house for the lord deputies or the chiefe governor to reside and dwell in'.[5] Accidental fires in 1671 and 1684 had undone most of Sidney's work but this had prompted a rebuilding programme under the direction of the then Surveyor-General, Sir William Robinson. Robinson had also begun the construction of Upper Castle Yard, which at first ensured parking and turning room for carriages, and later provided additional accommodation for personnel.

The upgrading of the castle included the building of a splendid ballroom, admired in 1731 as being 'finely ordered with paintings and obelisks'.[6] Otherwise, accommodation in the scattered buildings of different vintages across the site – expected to house not only the viceregal household and its servants but also the Lord Lieutenant's Chief Secretary, chaplain and other state officials – was extremely cramped and uncomfortable.

Alighting from his carriage in Castle Yard to a fanfare of trumpets, Devonshire was ready to host a dinner which was certain to be lavish. Meanwhile in the streets 'the night concluded with Bonfires and other Rejoicings'. Two days later, *Faulkner's Dublin Journal* reported that Dublin Castle was the occasion of another formal reception:

> Thursday last the Rt. Hon. the Lord Mayor, Recorder, Aldermen, Sheriffs and Common Council, in their Formalities, waited on his Grace at the Castle, to congratulate him on his safe Return, and were received with great Marks of Respect and Distinction.[7]

Such respectful reports may have been routine, but it does seem that Devonshire was proving to be a popular viceroy. George Faulkner, publisher of the city's best-selling newspaper and who had taken many risks by being Jonathan Swift's principal printer, may have been pompous – on occasion, unbearably so – but he was no sycophant. After all he had been cast into the city's most notorious prison, Newgate, in 1735 for breach of privilege, that is, for making an unauthorised report on parliamentary proceedings.

Devonshire did seem to have the qualities required just at that time to maintain political calm and stability. Indeed, he was to be the longest-serving Lord Lieutenant of Ireland in the eighteenth century, remaining in office until 1745. At the same time Devonshire owed his position almost exclusively to his status in society, his wealth and his unswerving loyalty to the Whig cause.

It has to be admitted that he was one of the most unprepossessing and least memorable viceroys of Ireland. Devonshire does not seem ever to have delivered a single stirring speech. Lord Hervey, after attending a dinner at Devonshire House, described the Duke as 'a clown'. Devonshire had served for a time as Lord Privy Seal: Lord Perceval, after seeing him kiss hands during the formalities of taking this office in 1731, observed that he was reminded of Caligula making his horse a consul.[8] The Duke was described as being 'plain in his manners, negligent in his dress' and he was not long in Dublin before being criticised for his dishevelled appearance and hard drinking. As one of his entourage warned, 'the generality of the people of this country … are known to esteem the patrons and the patronised according to the figure they make'.[9] Horace Walpole, the Prime Minister's son, reported that:

> The Duchess of Devonshire was more delightfully vulgar than you can imagine: complained of the wet night and how the men would dirty the room with their shoes, called out at supper to the Duke, 'Good God, my Lord, don't cut the ham – nobody will eat any!'[10]

The Lord Mayor held an important annual formal viceregal reception in Dublin Castle when the Lord Lieutenant was in Ireland. The ritual involved the Lord Mayor making a speech about the city's loyalty to the Crown while at the same time reminding the Lord Lieutenant of the privileges granted to Dublin by previous monarchs. At the end of the speech, a sheathed sword was presented to the viceroy. On one occasion, the Duke, in drawing the sword from the scabbard, used such force that the elderly and rotund Lord Mayor was pulled over and sent tumbling down the steps.[11]

Devonshire, however, had a benign temperament and, for example, took no offence at a dinner hosted by the Lord Mayor when the Dean Jonathan Swift, whose mind was beginning to go, seeing the Lord Lieutenant wearing his Garter ribbon, addressed him as 'You fellow, with the blue string'.[12] The Duke may have had embarrassing limitations but Walpole, with good reason, trusted him completely. Always sociable and invariably unpretentious, he had a flair for sustaining social and political connections, dispensing patronage in a way that caused no alarm to his colleagues in London. Devonshire was considered such a safe pair of hands that, very unusually, he was not replaced when Walpole fell from power in 1742. The Duke remained as Lord Lieutenant after that for another three years. The main reason why the élite was more than content to have Devonshire continue as viceroy was that he seemed almost to be an embodiment of stability. After all, until the very recent past Ireland had been a violently contested island.

A PRIVILEGED ÉLITE

The Irish Parliament met for the first time in 18 months on 6 October 1741. As was customary, the Lord Lieutenant was to address peers of the realm and MPs meeting together in the chamber of the House of Commons. Walpole's cabinet would have carefully vetted this address while Devonshire was still in London. Ireland was just emerging from a terrible famine followed by epidemics of disease that had cut a grim swathe through the population. Devonshire could not but refer to this tragic episode in the speech he was preparing to deliver on behalf of King George II. Indeed he did, describing – what for the Irish was *bliadhain an áir*, 'year of the slaughter' – as 'the sickness':

> The sickness, which hath proved so mortal in several parts of the kingdom, and is thought to have been principally owing to the scarcity of wholesome provision, most very sensibly affect his Majesty, who hath a most tender concern for all his subjects; and cannot but engage your serious attention, to consider of proper measures to prevent the like calamity for the future.[13]

And what did the government propose to do 'to prevent the like calamity' if extreme weather conditions once more destroyed crops and laid low the domestic stock of the island? Members were asked to consider measures to assist 'the encrease of tillage' which would 'usefully employ the industrious poor' and 'whether some further regulations may not be necessary for encreasing and extending the hempen and linen manufactures, which his Majesty is desirous to protect and encourage to the uttermost'.[14]

This was thought to be the limit of what needed to be done in response to another act of God. There was no suggestion, for example, that a compulsory system of poor relief on the English model, based on the parish, should be introduced.

Devonshire addressed an Irish Parliament composed of representatives of a dominant caste, made up principally of those who had gained most from the ruin of the Catholic gentry. The House of Commons in College Green was even more unrepresentative than that in Westminster. Catholics, forming around three-quarters of Ireland's population, could neither vote nor be MPs. Dublin was an exception in having a respectable number of voters by English standards; most of the 234 MPs elected from boroughs (towns with their own councils) had small electorates and a few had none. For example, the 'rotten borough' of Bannow, Co. Wexford, was just a pile of sea sand without a single house, yet it returned two members. It should be remembered, however, that representative institutions were falling out of fashion over most of the rest of Europe: this, after all, was the era of 'enlightened despotism'. And while many representative institutions still existed on the European mainland, it was only in Britain and Ireland that they had a really active part to play in government.

More obviously perhaps than in other parts of western and central Europe, early eighteenth-century Irish society was founded on dispossession and exclusion. The term 'Protestant Ascendancy' only appeared for the first time during parliamentary debates in the 1790s. But it very neatly describes the charmed circle of Church of Ireland (that is Anglican or Episcopalian) aristocrats, squires, clergy and prosperous lawyers, along with their relatives, which formed Ireland's highly privileged élite in the eighteenth century.

Most were descended from the 'New English', Protestant winners who had acquired land and position in the struggle for Ireland during the previous two hundred years. A significant number, nevertheless, were drawn from families that had been on the island for very much longer. Many of these were 'Old English', descendants of Norman colonists and those they had brought over the Irish Sea with them in medieval times. The remainder were the native Gaelic Irish, descended from ruling families able to trace their origins back to pre-Christian times. In 1732 it was reckoned that there were 281,401 Catholic families in Ireland yet only 5,787 Catholic individuals officially 'conformed' (that is, converted) to the Church of Ireland between 1704 and 1800.[15] However, a disproportionate number were drawn from survivors of the once dominant Catholic élite anxious to avoid subdivision of their estates and to find careers for younger sons in the legal profession, open only to Protestants. 'Papists' were not only shut out from political life and from holding public office. They could not buy land and when a Catholic died his estate would be equally divided amongst all his sons; if one son conformed, he could inherit the entire estate. Catholics who converted to the Church of Ireland included: John Bourke and Nehemiah Donnellan. John Bourke (whose ancestor was Richard de Burgo, the thirteenth-century Norman conqueror of Connacht) was the 9th Earl of Clanricarde. Nehemiah Donnellan was a Gaelic landowner from Loughrea who rose to become Baron of the Court of Exchequer. Otherwise known as 'Nemmy', he was the father of Anne Donnellan, who had brought Handel's friend Mary Pendarves, to visit Dublin in 1731. Virtually no Catholic estate of any significance was left in the entire province of Ulster when Alexander MacDonnell, the 5th Earl of Antrim, 'turned' when he reached the age of 21 in 1734 – the same Lord Antrim who unsuccessfully sought to buy sexual favours from Mrs Laetitia Pilkington after her adultery had become public knowledge.

Those who conformed to the state religion for whatever reason, even very late in the day, had no difficulty in being accepted into the élite. Marriage alliances soon blurred any differences and, indeed, were advertised by the custom of giving surnames as first names to male offspring – hence Fitzgerald Aylmer, Beauchamp Bagenal, Rigs Falkiner, Vesey Colcough, Rochfort Mervyn, Crofton Vandeleur, Boyle Roche, Dixie Coddington, and Windham Quin – though what the parents of Barry Barry and St Leger St Leger were thinking of is difficult to explain.[16]

The Church of Ireland, the established state church, now had possession of all of the island's traditional ecclesiastical lands and more – a vast property portfolio. For example, around one fifth of the territory of the six confiscated counties in the early seventeenth-century Plantation of Ulster had been reserved for the upkeep of the state church. To Catholics and Dissenters alike it was particularly galling that all cultivators of the soil were obliged to pay an annual tithe (in theory a tenth of the produce of their land) to support clergymen of a church to which they did not belong. Most Church of Ireland clergy, around a thousand of them at this time, had fairly modest livings but at least they were accounted gentlemen. However, most bishops and archbishops – all of them chosen with scrupulous care by the London government since their votes (as regular attenders) in the Irish House of Lords were highly valued – had incomes enabling them to support extraordinarily lavish lifestyles. Catholic worship was not prohibited as it had been in Cromwell's time; but every one of the island's 1,700 priests and 892 'popish' mass houses (the 1731 enquiry's figures) depended solely on the contributions of the faithful.

In March 1711 Dubliners had gathered in their hundreds in Fishamble Street to attack Henry Oxenard, who had just testified against a number of priests. They pursued this priest-catcher through the streets, hurling 'stones, brick batts and dirt at him in so violent a manner that his life was greatly endangered'.[17] Though the Tholsel, Dublin's municipal headquarters, was just round the corner in Skinners' Row, officials there did not bother to take any action to check this mob. Another priest-catcher, John Garzia, arrested the Catholic Archbishop of Dublin, Edmund Byrne, in 1718; though the law stated that no member of the Catholic hierarchy was permitted to be anywhere in the country, the authorities quietly let him go. Catholics were forbidden to have their own schools, yet a parliamentary enquiry of 1731 revealed that there were 549 of them on the island. There was no rush to close them down.[18] The reality was that active persecution of priests declined sharply after around 1720 – hence the large number present in 1731, more in fact than in the early nineteenth century.

When the Duke of Devonshire returned to Ireland in the autumn of 1741 Ireland had been completely at peace for exactly 50 years. In short, in the absence of violent conflict a certain softening of attitudes could be detected in the ranks of Ireland's ruling caste. By now much of the Penal Code had become a dead letter. However, the élite made sure that those laws designed to withhold political and economic power from Catholics of education and property were *not* relaxed.

COMMAND PERFORMANCES

The long years of peace, despite some alarming trade downturns, ensured rising, dependable returns from Ireland's landed estates. The greatest proprietors were now able to ornament their demesnes with grand Palladian mansions. It is true that close to £300,000 of the rent collected left the country every year to be handed over to absentees, much of it to be spent in London and Bath. Henry Temple, created Viscount Palmerston in 1723, for example, lived permanently in England though he was Chief Remembrancer of the Irish Exchequer and drew on Irish rents worth over £3,000 a year.[19] Nonetheless, most of the income raised from Irish estates remained in Ireland and a great deal of it was spent in Dublin. Nearly all landowners, even 'squireens' with modest resources, endeavoured to arrange an entertaining and comfortable winter season in the Irish capital for their families, friends and dependents.

Each time he returned to Dublin Devonshire could see that the pace of building development here was as hectic as it was around his London mansion. A succession of blockwheel carts each work day brought in limestone from Palmerstown quarry and granite from Dalkey, Kilgobbin, Golden Ball and, above all, from the Woodend and Threecastles freestone quarries at Blessington. Great columns of thick, choking smoke rose from brickfields in Moore Lane, Westland Row and all along the Dodder River from Ballsbridge to Ringsend.[20] The city was expanding outwards, tall terraces of spacious houses rising up in its newest streets with plain, elegant facades in warm red brick, well-proportioned elevations, recessed windows and roofs hidden by parapets. Those settling into them each autumn, seeking entertainment appropriate to their station, were more than content to take a lead from the viceregal court.

Trinity College students, sons of the nobility, gentry and clergy for the most part, were entitled to listen to debates in Parliament just across College Green, provided they were wearing their gowns trimmed with gold or silver according to rank. When night fell they cast their gowns aside to dine at the Eagle Tavern, home of the notorious Hellfire Club, or risk a duel at Lucas's Coffee-House on Cork Hill. Others would eat beefsteaks in the Old Sot's Hole at Essex Bridge or mingle with the humbler classes in the ale shops of Winetavern Street. These bucks were often eager to join fights in the narrow streets, wielding the heavy keys to their rooms as weapons. Others, however, would prefer to join their elders to be entertained from the stage.

Devonshire and his wife, Lady Catherine, adored the theatre and proved themselves generous and enthusiastic patrons of the arts. The Lord Lieutenant gave unflinching support to the Master of State Music, Matthew Dubourg, and the instrumentalists under his charge. When in Dublin the Duke went out of his way to support charitable musical concerts, particularly in St Andrew's 'Round Church' in Suffolk Street.

Devonshire's predecessor as Lord Lieutenant, the Duke of Dorset, had distinguished himself as a supporter of the arts. On his appointment, Lord Hervey observed: 'I am sure he will be happier in that Drury Lane appointment than any man upon earth'.[21] He had commanded no fewer than 30 theatrical performances. Devonshire went even further: he commanded a total of 54 performances in Dublin theatres, a record never beaten by any other viceroy. He had two theatres to choose from, one in Smock Alley and the other in Aungier Street. The theatre in Smock Alley, a narrow lane close to the quays leading off Fishamble Street, had been designed specifically for the viceregal court. To plans drawn up by John Ogilby, 'Master of the King's Revels', it had been built on a cobbled yard with a proscenium arch, itself a statement of allegiance to the monarchy (placed in front of the scenery, through which the audience could view the performance), with an entire gallery of boxes for the 'quality' adjacent to the viceregal box.[22] Simply by attending the theatre with his family, or even better, commissioning performances by his 'command', the Lord Lieutenant attracted the rest of fashionable Dublin. This ensured that the theatre could meet its outgoings by having all its seats filled and that, at the same time, leading members of society had unrivalled opportunities to be noticed and admired. Indeed, the well-lit horseshoe-shaped auditorium placed the audience on display as much as the actors.

'Part of the House' in Smock Alley had fallen down in 1734 and much of the theatre had to be rebuilt. Meanwhile a group of gentlemen had been constructing a second theatre south of Dublin Castle in Aungier Street. It had opened on 9 March 1734, and the Smock Alley company, therefore, had a home while their old venue was being reconstructed. Smock Alley reopened on 11 December 1735: now there were two theatres in the city and it often proved difficult enough to fill them both. Competition encouraged innovation: by 1741 the theatres each had a drum-and-shaft system, with counterweighted lines controlled by a large barrel beneath the stage to move cloudings, drops, borders and other scenic paraphernalia all at once to assist the audience in the suspension of disbelief.

Attending the theatre brought the Lord Lieutenant and his courtiers exceptionally close to ordinary Dubliners. The gentry paid to fill the boxes, which allowed them to bring along their womenfolk free of charge. Fashionable men and women came to be seen and to see each other as much as to view what was being offered on the stage; and ladies, as they are still willing to do today, were prepared to endure extreme discomfort to look their best – it was the Duchess of Devonshire herself who famously observed that 'pride feels no pain'. For six o'clock performances, servants arrived as early as four o'clock to make sure their masters' seats had not been taken by others and then moved to the gods at the price of a couple of pence each to watch the play with the rest of 'the Mob'. Tradesmen occupied the middle gallery while the gentry were cocooned in their boxes above them. Back in 1699 John Dunton, over from London to sell books, had observed of Smock Alley: 'The Playhouse is free to all Comers, and gives Entertainment as well to the Broom man, as the greatest Peer'.[23] The theatre in Dublin was the one place where the humblest servants and artisans could join with the gentry to hiss and cheer in the same enclosed space.

Both George I and George II had appreciated how music could help their subjects to accept the Hanoverian succession and, indeed, the 1707 Union with Scotland. The brilliant success of the innovative performance of Handel's *Water Music* at night by an orchestra seated on a barge on the Thames in 1717 had underscored the importance of music as propaganda. In Dublin, too, the viceroy took care to maintain his position as the island's principal patron of music. Every theatrical performance included music, even between acts of Shakespeare's plays. Instrumentalists were not hidden from view in a pit: Smock Alley theatre had a music loft above the proscenium for its band.

It may well have been the Duke of Devonshire who had seen to it that an invitation was delivered to George Frideric Handel to come to Dublin to perform music of his choice on behalf of three of Dublin's charities.[24] Even if he had not, the Lord Lieutenant had given an unwavering lead to Dublin's fashionable society by constant attendance at public performances both in churches and in theatres. Dubourg, no doubt, would have made Handel aware of this, providing further enticement to the composer to make his way to this great and prospering city.

Chapter 7
'To th'Hibernian Shore'

'To God alone the Glory'

Handel composed *Messiah* in his London home, no. 25 Brook Street, where he had lived for 17 years. The house was modest enough but it was in a fashionable part of the capital, convenient for taking walks in the park and for worship at St George's parish church in Hanover Square. It was big enough to accommodate his servant Peter Le Blond, a cook and one or two maids. There was a room sufficiently spacious for rehearsal, and the house contained a small collection of good paintings, and tasteful walnut furniture – in short, a perfect home not only for entertaining friends but also, above all, the place that clearly provided him with the ideal setting for undisturbed composition.

In 1741 Handel was in his fifty-sixth year. He carefully entered the composition dates in his *Messiah* autograph score. He began work on Saturday, 22 August, finished the drafts of Part One on Friday, 28 August; Part Two on Sunday, 6 September; Part Three on Saturday, 12 September, and the whole score *ausgefüllt*, 'filled up', on 14 September. In all, Handel composed *Messiah* from start to finish in just 24 days. Stories about the composer leaving meals brought in by his servant untouched, of his tears blotting the crotchets and quavers inked on the score and of him declaring, 'I did think I did see all Heaven before me, and the great God himself', are all completely without foundation. However, he *did* write at the very end of his autograph score, 'SDG', *Solo Deo Gloria*, 'To God alone the glory'.

Such a frenetic application to composition was by no means unusual for Handel. The score for his oratorio, *Solomon*, much larger in scale than *Messiah*, was finished in just 20 days in 1748, and the first draft of *Theodora*, another oratorio, took him 19 days in 1750. Indeed, Handel always seems to have composed with intense, at times a fierce, concentration. There is no indication that he was weak from exhaustion when *Messiah* was finished. After relaxing for just a few days, he then set about writing his biggest oratorio, *Samson*, and he had Act I completed by 29 September. The manuscript score of *Messiah* demonstrates on virtually every page the feverish pace with which it was written: blots, smudges, emendations, passages vigorously scored out and evidence of an overturned ink well. At the same time Handel's focused attention to detail is evident throughout the 259 pages of the score. The manuscript, written in a clear, strong hand with an attractive flourish, contains remarkably few errors, no more than the very occasional slip of the pen such as an unfilled bar in the viola part and the odd crotchet surplus to requirements.

Handel notoriously drew extensively on the work of other composers and, particularly when he was under the pressure, he tended to pillage his own earlier compositions. However, considering that it was written so rapidly, there is little evidence of borrowings in the *Messiah* score and virtually all of them were taken from his own work. 'And He shall purify' closely follows Telemann's *Harmonischer Gottes-Dienst*, but it is just about the only detectable borrowing from another composer. Some of his own Italian duets were adapted to become choruses. They include: 'His yoke is easy', taken from '*Quel fior che all'alba ride*'; and 'For unto us a child is born' from '*Nò, di voi non vo fidarmi*' (which results in a somewhat inappropriate emphasis on the first word, '*For unto …* '). The duets had been composed just a few weeks earlier, on 1 and 3 July, respectively.[1]

Charles Jennens had written his *Messiah* word-book to give Handel every opportunity to display his genius. The verses he had selected, particularly from the Old Testament, were intended to provide the composer with ample scope to write a score with as many contrasting colours as could be found in the most dramatic of his Italian operas. This was crucial since *Messiah* – described by Jennens himself as 'a fine Entertainment' – is essentially a meditative oratorio, the libretto being devoid of plot and at best containing a flimsy narrative.[2] Jennens had completed his task so much to Handel's satisfaction that the composer was able to write his score continuously without the structural changes usually considered essential.

What seems certain is that Handel composed *Messiah* specifically to be performed in Dublin. He knew he could depend on his old friend Matthew Dubourg, Master of the State Music in Dublin Castle, to bring together the best instrumentalists and choristers in the city. Handel could call on the services of the cellist Nicolò Pasqualino, who had played in the first performance of *Alexander's Feast* in 1736 at Covent Garden and came over to Ireland to teach music to Bishop Berkeley's children in Cloyne. He could rely on James Baileys, a vicar-choral in both Christ Church and St Patrick's cathedrals, as a soloist – he had been in London in 1737 and had sung the tenor part of the funeral anthem for Queen Caroline.[3] Otherwise, however, Handel had only a very sketchy idea of what the Irish capital could provide. He could not count on selecting talented soloists from a pool of experienced professionals in Dublin as he could in London. No doubt it was appropriate that the theme of this particular oratorio called for some restraint, but Handel also seems to have composed *Messiah* knowing that the musical resources available to him in Ireland were likely to be limited.

Initially there were just four soloists and the orchestration was confined to strings, drums, basso continuo and only one solo instrument, a trumpet. Only when he got back to London did he add bassoons and oboes. At first Handel had four *da capo* arias (major opera-style solos) but, on reflection, he reduced them to just two, 'He was despised' and 'The trumpet shall sound'. He also cut two whole bars of trilling bird-song in 'Every valley' and added the instruction *'da lontano e un poco piano'* ('from a distance and rather softly') for music to accompany the angels at the start of 'Glory to God'.[4]

Tidings of great joy

Messiah is by no means representative of Handel's oratorios. In all his other oratorios, with the exception of *Israel in Egypt*, the role of soloists is more important than that of the chorus. In writing *Messiah* the composer was drawing on all his musical experiences from his childhood in Halle onwards. He had invented the English oratorio, in part to free himself from the financial anxieties of staging his Italian operas, and also to cater for a growing audience eager for sacred music by redeploying in that direction all his genius as a composer of opera. Musical experts have detected a wide range of influences, including: mid-seventeenth-century French overtures; the English anthem tradition; German Passion settings; when introducing the shepherds, the music of the *pifferari*, mountain bagpipers and shawm players he would have heard in Rome 35 years earlier; a popular Italian Christmas song, *'Tu scendi dale stelle'*, in 'He shall feed his flock'; echoes of German chorale in the 'Hallelujah' chorus; the Italian operatic tradition in the airs 'He was despised' and 'The trumpet shall sound'; and the choral music he had composed before ever setting foot in England.[5]

What is absolutely certain is that Handel paid very close attention to interpreting the Old and New Testament words provided in Jennens's word-book – he once declared testily that he knew his Bible as well as any bishop. Part One opens with 'Sinfony', an overture in the French court style, dark and pensive in places, hinting at pain to come. This is followed by 'Comfort ye', the gentle tenor recitative in E major which Judy Tarling notes is 'Handel's favourite key for evoking heaven' and which, she adds, is 'soothing, reassuring in pulsing quavers' until, in a sudden change of tone, 'God speaks in rising crotchets' in 'Saith your God', exclaiming 'The Voice of him that crieth in the wilderness'.[6]

Then the tenor in his aria 'Every valley' paints a musical landscape, the soloist descending into every valley, climbing high with every mountain, and rising gently with every hill; 'crooked' is given different pitches for each syllable and 'straight' has one tone; trilling accompanies 'rough places' and 'plain' has a constant pitch; and the music for 'exalted' is, indeed, exalted. The chorus, 'And the glory of the Lord', ends with solemn gravity because 'the Lord hath spoken it'. The bass recitative beginning 'Thus saith the Lord of hosts', picked by Jennens from the books of Haggai and Malachi, gave Handel the opportunity to let loose his genius for full dramatic operatic power 'to shake the heavens and the earth, the sea and the dry land' and 'all nations'. Handel rose magnificently to the challenge, his emphasis on the word 'shake' giving both the singer and the strings some of the most testing music in the oratorio. The countertenor aria which begins with 'But who may abide the day of his coming?' starts softly only to plunge into music of incendiary force to bring forward the intense heat of 'a refiner's fire'.[7]

'A Virgin shall conceive, and bear a Son', the alto announces with text from Matthew's Gospel before being joined by the chorus to tell 'good tidings to Zion'. The bass warns bleakly that 'darkness shall cover the earth' before his aria which begins with 'The people that walked in darkness …' 'The halting tempo evokes walking in the dark', Ben Finane explains, 'and the music itself seems to grope about, searching (chromatically) for a toehold'. 'For unto us a child is born', the chorus sings with untrammelled joy, all the singers coming together for the climax: here Handel leaves a breathing space for heightened emphasis and dignity to 'Wonderful, Counsellor, The mighty God, The everlasting Father, The Prince of Peace'.[8]

The Incarnation is ushered in with the 'Pifa', a pastoral symphony, introducing the angel's recitative bringing 'tidings of great joy … praising God, and saying,' (here the angelic chorus with trumpet support wafts in) 'Glory to God in the highest. And peace on earth, Good will towards men'. With the aria 'Rejoice greatly, O daughter of Zion', the soprano leads off the section of *Messiah* which is concerned with the miracles of the Saviour. 'Then shall the eyes of the blind be opened. And the ears of the deaf unstopped', the alto predicts, continuing in her aria that 'He shall feed his flock like a shepherd'. Part One is then concluded with a choral rendition of Matthew's words, 'His yoke is easy, his burden is light.'[9]

'A MOST HAPPY AND MARVELLOUS CONCATENATION OF HARMONY, MELODY AND GREAT EFFECTS'

Ever since the early sixteenth century composers had striven to adhere to the principles of classical rhetoric. These had been laid out in *On the Sublime*, attributed to the first-century Greek writer, Longinus. The sublime style was emotionally intense, forceful and elevated, and designed to stir the passions, amaze and transport. In William Smyth's 1740 translation, its elements were defined by Longinus as:

> bold metaphors and those too in good plenty, are very seasonable in a noble Composition, where they are always mitigated and soften'd by the vehement Pathetic and generous Sublime dispersed through the whole. For it is the nature of the Pathetic and generous Sublime to run rapidly along, and carry all before them.[10]

The sublime style permeates *Messiah* throughout. It is particularly evident in Part Two, the emotional heart of the oratorio, which tells of the redeeming power of the Son of God's suffering. It opens with the arresting declamatory invitation: 'Behold the Lamb of God', Handel using alternative long and short notes to depict pathos and (but only after he had returned from Dublin) underscoring tragedy with oboes joining the sopranos. Handel conveys heartfelt grief in 'He was despised', Ben Finane explains,

> by breaking the alto's melody into short phrases, interspersed with replies from the orchestra, e.g. 'He was despised … despised and rejected … rejected of men.' It is as though the alto can hardly bear to tell the story, interspersed with sobs as she catches her breath to continue.

Charles Burney, who at the age of fifteen got his first glimpse of Handel when he was in Chester waiting to sail over to Dublin, and from 1745 was to play regularly for the composer, wrote that this aria 'has impressed me with the highest idea of excellence in pathetic expression, of any expression with which I am acquainted'.[11]

Suddenly, crashing in on this piteous, haltingly-voiced distress, the strings ferociously create an image of flagellation in 'He gave his back to the smiters'. This is followed by the chorus's reminder that all of this agony is for Mankind's redemption: 'Surely' – an emphatic opening – 'he hath born our griefs', and was 'bruised for our iniquities' to ensure that 'with his stripes we are healed'. Then a lighter mood is introduced, if only for a time, by the chorus 'All we like sheep': all voices are together initially but then, when members of the flock veer off this way and that, individual voices show that they 'have gone astray'. As this draws to a close the chorus, by singing in unison 'And the Lord hath laid on him the iniquity of us all', again solemnly stresses the purpose of Christ's suffering.

That suffering on the road to Calvary is made more agonising by the scornful laughter of the crowd. 'They shoot out their lips', the tenor declares with vehemence, the sarcastic taunting 'He trusted in God that he would deliver him', a strident chorus making it all the more heartless in the repeated 'Let him deliver him', with a brutal high note emphasis on the second syllable of 'deliver'. 'He looked for some to have pity on him', but in vain: 'Behold, and see if there be any sorrow like unto his sorrow!', the tenor in this aria being given the lowest note for 'sorrow'. But God has not abandoned his only begotten Son, the soprano providing the assurance that 'thou didst not leave his soul in hell'. Despair is cast aside in 'Lift up your heads, O ye gates'. Handel splits his chorus in two, sopranos and altos asking the question, 'Who is this King of glory?' – certain of a positive reply from the tenors and basses that He is 'The Lord strong and mighty, The Lord mighty in battle'.[12]

After the Resurrection and the gift of tongues, tenors and basses authoritatively announce in unison that that the 'Lord gave the word', followed by the tenor aria telling of messengers bringing 'glad tidings of good things'. But the triumphal choral assurance that the message of redemption 'is gone out into all lands', is halted in its tracks when this good news, the Gospel, is rejected. 'Why do the nations so furiously rage together?' the bass asks, his indignation powerfully beamed out by the insistent quivering of the strings. The mob reappears in the abrasively aggressive 'Let us break their bonds asunder'; its ferocity, Richard Luckett explains, 'is apparent from its abrupt opening, and from the closeness of the entries, which come falling over one another and create a concentrated release of splenetic energy'. The chorus defiantly and ferociously spits out insistently: 'let us – let us – let us – let us', before the grim warning in the tenor aria of the terrible consequences of disobeying God's will by being broken 'with a rod of iron' and dashed 'in pieces like a potter's vessel'.[13]

Part Two is concluded by the 'Hallelujah' chorus – a great anthem of exclamatory praise and triumphal celebration. Jennens had persuaded Handel, with difficulty, not to include a hallelujah in his oratorio *Saul*; now with the three verses he had selected from the Book of Revelation, the librettist gave the composer the scope to write what is arguably the best-recognised and one of the most famous pieces of classical music ever written. This confident message for the future that God is victorious over sin and rules for all eternity is driven home by an extended and exultant dialogue between the instruments and the chorus. Burney made this assessment:

> The last and principal subject proposed, and led off by the bass
> – *And He shall reign for ever and ever*', is the most pleasing and

fertile that has ever been invented since the art of fugue was
first cultivated. It is marked and constantly to be distinguished
throughout all the parts, accompaniments, counter-subjects and
contrivances, with which it is charged. And finally, the words –
'King of Kings, and Lord of Lords', always set to a single sound,
which seems to stand at bay, while the other parts attack it in
every possible manner, in '*Allelujahs – for ever and ever*', is a most
happy and marvellous concatenation of harmony, melody and
great effects.[14]

Audiences hearing *Messiah* for the first time could have been
forgiven for thinking that the 'Hallelujah' chorus was the sacred
oratorio's conclusion. But, now that God's victory over Death
could be celebrated, the librettist was concerned that listeners
should have a preview of the glorious afterlife. Part Three opens
with the sublime soprano aria, 'I know that my Redeemer liveth';
it has a sparse orchestral accompaniment, rising in scale to rejoice
in the certainty of eternal life and descending gently for the words
'from the dead'. Then the chorus slowly begins St Paul's letter to
the Corinthians, 'For as in Adam all die,' increasing tempo with the
happy assurance that 'even so in Christ shall all be made alive'.

The Day of Judgement is introduced by the bass in hushed
tones, 'Behold, I tell you a mystery' before suddenly announcing
the appearance of 'the last trumpet'. A clear trumpet accompanies
the bass as he triumphantly tells how 'the dead shall be raised
incorruptible'. 'Death is swallowed up in victory', the alto assures
us before she is joined by the tenor in an affecting duet to ask the
rhetorical questions, 'O death where is thy sting? O grave, where is
thy victory?' God is glorified in the final aria, the Messiah acclaimed
in 'Worthy is the Lamb that was slain', expressed slowly at first
before the exulting chorus bestows 'Blessing and honour, glory and
power', repeating 'for ever and ever'.[15] John Mainwaring, Handel's
first biographer, found that this chorus filled the ear with 'the glow
of harmony as leaves the mind in a kind of heavenly extasy'.[16] This
leads into the final 'Amen' where Handel 'unembarrassed by words',
Burney observed, 'gave a loose to genius, liberated from all restraints
but those of his own art'. 'Amen' for Richard Luckett 'satisfies every
kind of contrapuntal curiosity with a dazzling display of learning

and inventiveness ... a written out example of the kind of inspired improvisation which made Handel's fame as an organist, here transferred to another medium and made permanent'.[17]

'Handel had been preparing to write this work all his life', Ben Finane, the New York critic and editor, observed in the introduction to his book, *Handel's* Messiah *and his English Oratorios*. He continued:

> *Messiah* is Handel's perfect storm. It was composed as an English oratorio, a genre Handel invented out of necessity to meet the conditions of his market, one that served a sacred music audience while maximising his talents in operatic, instrumental and choral writing. But *Messiah* is unique among Handel's oratorios in that its ethereal narrative freed him from the usual operatic temptations and distractions of plot, action, and character and forced the composer into a meditative corner, where he created a masterpiece which takes on nothing less than Death, Resurrection and Redemption. Handel did so in resplendent fashion and yet – and this is more astounding – he did so modestly and accessibly.[18]

'GONE INTO IRELAND WITH IT'

Handel set off for Ireland at the beginning of November 1741. He took with him his copyist and financial secretary John Christopher Smith, born Schmidt, who was from Ansbach and had been at the University of Halle with Handel. The composer was already on his way when Jennens came to London only to find that Handel was not there:

> I heard with great pleasure at my arrival in Town, that Handel had set the Oratorio of Messiah; but it was some mortification to me to hear that instead of performing it here he was gone into Ireland with it.

Handel had the choice of two ports with a regular cross-channel service to Dublin. The shortest passage was from Holyhead on the Isle of Anglesey but that would entail an additional 60 mile travel along the wretchedly bad roads of north Wales. For centuries Chester had been the principal port for Ireland and had been chosen by William of Orange as the point of embarkation for his great army as he set out to confront the deposed James II in June 1690. Now the port of Chester was silting up and soon would become unsuitable for ships of any size. Cross-channel vessels had already moved downstream of the city to Parkgate, a village on the banks of the Dee, where Handel arranged his passage. It was as he passed through Chester that Charles Burney saw the composer for the first time:

> I was at the Public-School in that city, and very well remember seeing him smoke a pipe, over a dish of coffee, at the Exchange-Coffee-house; for being extremely curious to see so extraordinary a man, I watched him narrowly as long as he remained in Chester; which on account of the wind being unfavourable for his embarking at Parkgate, was several days. During this time, he applied to Mr. Baker, the Organist, my first music-master, to know whether there were any choirmen in the cathedral who could sing *at sight*; as he wished to prove some books that that had been hastily transcribed, by trying the choruses which he intended to perform in Ireland. Mr. Baker mentioned some of the most likely singers then in Chester, and, among the rest, a printer of the name of Janson, who had a good base voice, and was one of the best musicians in the choir.

Though he was not there in person, Burney was told what happened next in a local tavern:

> A time was fixed for this private rehearsal at the Golden Falcon, where HANDEL was quartered; but, alas! on trial of the chorus in the Messiah, '*And with his stripes we are healed*,' – Poor Janson, after repeated attempts, failed so egregiously, that HANDEL let loose his great bear upon him; and after swearing in four languages, cried out in broken English: 'You shcauntrel! Tit not you dell me dat you could sing at soite?' – Yes, sir, says the printer, and so I can; but not at *first sight*'.[19]

Mr and Mrs Maclaine were also in Chester on their way to Dublin. Little is known about them: he was probably the composer, violinist and organist Charles Maclaine (or McLean) from Aberdeen; and his wife (her first name is unknown) would be one of Handel's soloists when *Messiah* was given its first performance.[20] *Faulkner's Dublin Journal* reprinted this extract from a Chester newspaper:

Chester, Nov. 5. – Yesterday arrived here in his way to Dublin, Mr. Maclaine, who was invited to play on our Cathedral Organ, this day, on which he performed so well, to the entire Satisfaction of the whole Congregation, that some of the best Judges in Musick said, They never heard that Organ truly played on before; and his Performance was allowed to be very masterly and in the finest taste.

'TO WAIT ON MR. HANDEL TO ASK THE FAVOUR OF HIM TO PLAY THE ORGAN'

Adverse winds prevented any passenger vessels sailing from Parkgate from 5 November until the 17th of the month. On 18 November Handel eventually stepped ashore in Ireland. *Faulkner's Dublin Journal*, though it gave the wrong port of embarkation and incorrectly awarded the composer a doctorate, reported his arrival:

And last Wednesday, the celebrated Dr. Handell arrived here in the Packet-boat from Holyhead, a Gentleman universally known by his excellent Compositions in all kinds of Musick, and particularly for his *Te Deum, Jubilate, Anthems*, and other Compositions in Church Musick, (of which for some years past have principally consisted the Entertainments in the Round Church, which have so greatly contributed to support the Charity of Mercer's Hospital) to perform his Oratorios, for which Purpose he hath engaged the above Mr. MacLaine, his Wife, and several others of the best Performers in the Musical Way.[21]

Ever since 1736 St Andrew's, the Church of Ireland 'Round Church' at the corner of Suffolk Street and St Andrews Street, had hosted the annual charity concert in aid of Mercer's Hospital. Invariably the core of each performance was made up of Handel's *Te Deum* and *Jubilate*, along with at least one of his anthems. At the beginning of the year 1741, though Ireland was then in the grip of a terrible famine bringing hordes of destitute country people ranging desperately through the streets of Dublin, the governors of the hospital decided nevertheless to go ahead with the annual event. Indeed, the crisis, by increasing the demand for the hospital's services, had made the garnering of charitable contributions all the more imperative. An insertion in the *Dublin News-Letter*, 7-10 February, advertising the concert had emphasised the urgent need for funds:

> The Governors of Mercer's Charitable Hospital, that there will be a Sermon preached at St. Andrew's Church by the Rt Reverend the Lord Bishop of Ferns, on Saturday the 14th of February next, for the Support of that Charity. Divine Service will be performed as formerly with Mr. Handel's Te Deum, Jubilate and two new Anthems ... N.B. The Benefit arising hereby is the main support of the Hospital for the Expense this last year, ending the 1st of November 1740, amounted to £548 10s. 9d. where the annual Subscriptions thereto are but £201. 11s. 9d. 1179 Persons were under the Care of the Hospital in the said Year.

The next issue of this newspaper added: 'Coaches &c. to come to St Andrew's Church by William-street and Trinity Lane, and go off to Suffolk-street, or the Lane leading from the Church to College Green'.[22]

Now, as the year was drawing to a close, the governors decided to take advantage of Handel's presence in the city. The Mercer's Hospital minute book records:

> At a meeting of the Trustees of Mercer's Hospital, Nov. 21st, 1741. Present, - John Putland Esq. Deane Owen. Dr. Wynne. Ld. Bp. Of Cork. Ordered that Messrs. Putland, Owen, and Wynne, be and are desired to wait on Mr. Handel to ask the favour of him to play on the Organ at the Musical Performance in St. Andrews Church. E. J. MATURIN, Secretary.

The trustees attending this meeting included senior Church of Ireland clergy. The Bishop of Cork, Dr Robert Clayton, the former Bishop of Killala who had been host to his sister-in-law, Anne Donnellan, and her companion Mary Pendarves visiting from London a decade earlier; John Wynne was Precentor and Sub-Dean of St Patrick's Cathedral; and John Owen, Dean of Clonmacnoise, who was also a Prebendary (an honorary canon) of Christ Church Cathedral. It is not known whether they persuaded Handel to play the organ for them, but the composer's Utrecht *Te Deum* and *Jubilate* were – as always – included in the programme at the St Andrew's benefit concert on 10 December. In any case, Mercer's Hospital would benefit handsomely from Handel's sojourn in Ireland.

'THE KIND TREATMENT I RECEIVE HERE ... THE POLITENESS OF THIS GENEROUS NATION'

Handel was busy making arrangements. We can only guess at what these were in detail. Certainly Mr and Mrs Maclaine had travelled over at his request: he would act as an organist assistant and she would be one of his soloists. Handel had engaged Christina Maria Avolio, though she had not sung for him before. Between 1731 and 1738 this soprano soloist had been performing in Italy and St Petersburg, the Russian capital. When she came to London in 1741, probably anticipating a place in Lord Middlesex's opera company, Handel sought her out and persuaded to sing for him in Dublin.[23] *Faulkner's Dublin Journal* announced her arrival on 24 November:

> Last Tuesday arrived in the Yatcht from Park-gate, Signiora Avolio, an excellent Singer, who comes to this Kingdom to perform in Mr. Handel's Musical Entertainment.[24]

The Lord Lieutenant, the Duke of Devonshire, who had been in residence in Dublin Castle since October, generally used the Parkgate yacht for crossing the Irish Sea. It is just possible that the viceroy had made special arrangements for the prima donna to obtain a passage over on this vessel.

While Signora Avolio was settling in at her lodgings in Strand Street, Handel had to endure constant distractions from his preparatory work, according to the Earl of Shaftesbury, in a letter dated 10 December 1741:

> His Cloaths & Organ were not yet come but notwithstanding the Speaker forced him to dinner the day he landed & the Master of the Rolls insisted on Handel's doing the same with him the day following. 'Tis thought he will get considerable profit by his Voyage. Some of the Irish people have behaved like true Natives in severall respects towards Handel, which

I have not time to speak of in this. One of These Irishisms
was the asking Handel to Accompany One Mr. Bois's (a
Disciple of Dr. Green's here at London) New Anthem lately
sent them from England. The occasion being a public charity
Handel promis'd to accompany all his own Music which they
perform that day, but beg'd excuse for Mr. Bois's. So they
keep this curious piece for the last. Debourg was enraged at
this proposal & said his own playing should depend on their
behaviour towards Handel. The Town of Dublin in general are
at present strong Handelians.[25]

A letter from Dubourg was probably the source of this information.
Handel certainly brought over a pipe organ but whether or not he had
his carillon with him for *Saul* and *Acis* is impossible to determine.

Interruptions notwithstanding, the composer was turning his
lodgings in Abbey Street into a ticket office for no fewer than six
forthcoming performances. On 15 December *Faulkner's Dublin
Journal* carried this advertisement:

At the New Musick-hall in Fishamble-street, on Wednesday
next, being the 23rd Day of December, Mr. Handel's Musical
Entertainment will be opened; in which will be performed,
L'Allegro, il Penseroso, & il Moderato, with two Concertos for
several Instruments, and a Concerto on the Organ. To begin
at 7 o'clock. Tickets for that Night will be delivered to the
Subscribers (by sending their Subscription Ticket) on Tuesday
and Wednesday next, at the Place of Performance, from 9 o'clock
in the Morning till 3 in the Afternoon. – And Attendance
will be given this Day and on Monday next, at Mr. Handel's
House in Abbey-street, near Lyffey-street, from 9 o'clock in
the Morning till 3 in the Afternoon, in order to receive the
Subscription Money; at which Time each Subscriber will have a
Ticket delivered to him, which entitles him to three tickets each
Night, either for Ladies or Gentlemen. – NB. Subscriptions are
likewise taken in the same Place. Books will be sold at the said
Place, Price a British Six-pence.

Handel's first public concert in Dublin was a triumph. Certainly the correspondent of *Faulkner's Dublin Journal* thought so:

Last Wednesday, Mr. Handel had his first Oratorio at Mr. Neal's Musick Hall in Fishamble-street, which was crowded with a more numerous and polite Audience than ever was seen upon the like Occasion. The Performance was superior to any thing of the kind in the Kingdom before; and our Nobility and Gentry, to shew their Taste for all kinds of Genius, expressed their great Satisfaction, and have already given all imaginable Encouragement to this grand Musick.[26]

Handel was so delighted with this reception that he wrote a long letter to Charles Jennens, indeed, the longest letter he ever penned to his gentleman librettist. He, no doubt, was aware that he should have explained his seemingly precipitate departure from London to show that it had been very worth his while to come to Dublin:

Dublin Decembr. 29 1741
Sr,
It was with the greatest Pleasure I saw the Continuation of Your Kindness by the Lines You was pleased to send me, in Order to be prefix'd to Your Oratorio Messiah, which I set to Musick before I left England. I am enboldned, Sir, by the generous Concern You please to take in relation to my affairs, to give You an Account of the Success I have met here. The Nobility did me the Honour to make amongst themselves a Subscription for 6 Nights, which did fill a Room of 600 Persons, so that I needed not sell one single Ticket at the door, and without Vanity the Performance was received with a general approbation. Sigra Avolio, which I brought with me from London pleases extraordinary, I have form'd an other Tenor Voice which gives great satisfaction, the Basses and Counter Tenors are very good, and the rest of the Chorus Singers (by my Direction) do exceeding well, as for the Instruments they are really excellent. Mr. Dubourgh being at the head of them and the Musick sounds delightfully in this charming Room, which puts me in such spirits (and my Health

being so good) that I exert my self on my Organ whit more
then usual success.[27]

Handel went out of his way to tell him how much the audience
enjoyed *il Moderato*, the text of which had been rather daringly
written by Jennens to follow on from Milton's immortal words in
l'Allegro and *il Penseroso*:

I opened with Allegro, Penseroso, & Moderato, and I assure
you that the Words of the Moderato are vastly admired. The
Audience being composed (besides the Flower of Ladies of
Distinction and other people of the greatest quality) of so many
Bishops, Deans, Heads of the Colledge, the most eminents
People in the Law as the Chancellor, Auditor general &tc.
all which are very much taken with the Poëtry. So that I am
desired to perform it again the next time. I cannot sufficiently
express the kind treatment I receive here, but the Politeness of
this generous Nation cannot be unknown to You, so I let you
judge of the satisfaction I enjoy, passing my time with Honnour,
profit, and pleasure. They propose already to have some more
Performances, when the 6 Nights of the Subscription are over,
and My Lord Duc the Lord Lieutenant (who is allways present
with all his Family on those Nights) will easily obtain a longer
Permission for me by His Majesty, so that I shall be obliged to
make my stay here longer than I thought. [28]

The 'Tenor Voice which gives great Satisfaction', the singer Handel
told Jennens he had 'form'd', was probably John Church who
would be one of his male soloists in *Messiah*.[29] The Musick Hall in
Fishamble Street did not yet possess an organ and it seems certain
that Handel's reference to 'my Organ' indicates that he brought his
own over with him. This is thought to have been a bureau organ,
with carrying handles and a key board that folded out, made to look
like a piece of furniture – whether or not it was the one he had paid
£500 for in London is impossible to say.

Just before leaving London for Ireland, Handel had attended the
opening night of *Alessandro in Persia*, part of Lord Middlesex's new
extravagant opera venture in the King's Theatre. The composer had

been invited to become involved but he rightly suspected that it was headed for financial disaster, partly because 'the men of penetration give hints that his Lordship's sole aim is to make his mistress, the Muscovita, appear to great advantage on the stage'. Handel concluded his letter to Jennens to tell him how the poor performance he had been at had put him in good spirits:

> I expect with Impatience of your News concerning your Health and welfare, of which I take a real share, as for the News of Your Opera's, I need not trouble you for all this Town is full of their ill success, by a number of Letters from your quarters to the people of Quality here, and I can't help saying that it furnishes great Diversion and laughter. The first Opera I heard myself before I left London, and it made me very merry all a long my journey, and of the second opera, called Penelope, a certain nobleman writes very jocosly, il faut que je dise avec Harlequin: nôtre Penelôpe n'est qu'une Sallôpe, but I think I have trespassed too much on your Patience.
> I beg you to be persuaded of the sincere veneration and Esteem with which I have the hounour to be
> > Sr
> > > Your most obliged and most humble servant

GEORGE FRIDERIC HANDEL[30]

Indeed, *Faulkner's Dublin Journal* reprinted a damning review of these London operas. The 'prodigious Expense' of putting them on was reaching £16,000. The reviewer observed: 'Is not Britain then in a fine state when, notwithstanding our Taxes, we can fling away such a sum on a Parcel of squeaking, capering, fiddling, Italians, and Foreign Buffoons?'[31]

'LO! GIANT HANDEL STANDS'
While Handel was in Dublin, Alexander Pope published one of his greatest and one of his most controversial poems, *The New Dunciad: As it was Found in the Year 1741*. It was controversial because in the poem he had castigated so many of his prominent contemporaries. In the fourth book, the poet springs to Handel's defence, deriding

the promoters of the recent operas in London as having forced the composer to go to Ireland:

> Strong in new Arms, lo! Giant Handel stands,
> Like bold Briareus, with a hundred hands;
> To stir, to rouze, to shake the Soul he comes,
> And Jove's own Thunders follow Mars's Drums.
> Arrest him, Empress; or you sleep no more' –
> She heard, and drove him to th'Hibernian shore.

Pope, who admitted he did not have much ear for music, decided to ask his friend Dr John Arbuthnot, who had been a physician to Queen Anne, for his opinion of Handel as a composer. Arbuthnot replied: 'Conceive of that you can of his ability and they are much beyond anything you can conceive'. For the poet that banished all doubts about Handel. In footnotes he wrote to his poem, Pope denounced 'the nature and genius of the *Italian* opera; its affected airs, its effeminate sounds, and the patching up of these Operas with favourite Songs, incoherently put together'. He continued:

> Mr. *Handel* had introduced a great number of Hands, and more variety of Instruments into the Orchestra, and employed even Drums and Cannon to make a fuller Chorus; which prov'd so much too manly for the fine Gentlemen of his age, that he was obliged to remove his Music into *Ireland*.

Handel would have had mixed views about Pope's judgements. He, after all, adored good Italian opera and had spent much of his career adding to its canon and in employing fine Italian singers, however effeminate. Handel never gave any indication that he had been *driven* 'to th'Hibernian shore' by the Empress Dulness, Queen of the Philistines – that was only the view of some others. But he would have been pleased by acknowledgement of the way he had introduced new instruments and fresh sounds to the orchestra; and he would have concurred with Pope's judgement on the low quality of the operas on offer in London as he was making his way to Ireland, especially the crude insertion in them of popular songs written by 'a hundred hands'.[32]

Dublin was so delighting Handel that, immediately after the very

KILLINEY OBELISK,

Obelisk on the top of Killiney Hill in south County Dublin erected as part of a relief scheme funded by John Mapas, a Catholic landlord from Rochestown, to provide work for the starving during *Bliadhain an Áir*, 'Year of the Slaughter', in 1741. A higher proportion of Irish people died in that one year than during five years of famine in the 1840s. Beyond is Bray Head and the Sugarloaf mountains. (*Courtesy of the National Library of Ireland*)

A Prospect of the Parliament House, in College Green, DUBLIN. | *Veüe de l'hôtel du Parlement ríe du Collége green de DUBLIN.*

RESPECTFULLY DEDICATED TO J. T. GILBERT ESQ. F.S.A. M.R.I.A.
IRISH ARCHIVIST, CHRONICLER AND HISTORIAN OF DUBLIN.
BY HIS HUMBLE SERVANT, PATRICK TRAYNOR.

College Green, with the colonnaded frontage of the Parliament House on the right, looking west up Dame Street and towards Cork Hill. An equestrian statue of William of Orange (later destroyed in a series of hostile attacks) stands in the middle of the entrance to Dame Street in front of a terrace of 'Dutch Billy' houses with their distinctive stepped and curvilinear gables. Engraved by Joseph Tudor in 1753. (*Courtesy of the National Library of Ireland*)

The only surviving representation, sketched around 1850, of the Musick Hall in Fishamble Street. Completed for the Charitable Musical Society in 1741, it was designed by Richard Cassels, the most distinguished architect then working in Dublin. It was here that *Messiah* was given its first performance on 13 April 1742. (© *Hulton Archive/Getty Images*)

The Custom House and Essex Bridge. All goods imported into, and exported out of, Dublin were bound by law to pass through this Custom House where duties had to be paid. Duties on sugar and tobacco imported from the West Indian and North American plantations to Britain and re-exported to Ireland made up more than half of the Irish government's revenue. A bronze equestrian statue of George I stands on a pier against the bridge. Engraved by Joseph Tudor in 1753. (© *Mary Evans Picture Library/Grosvenor Prints*)

A state ball in Dublin Castle in 1731 being opened by the Lord Lieutenant, the Duke of Dorset, and his duchess. A few months after this was painted, Handel's friend and neighbour in London, Mary Pendarves, was invited by the viceroy to a ball here during her stay in Dublin. She wrote to her brother, Bernard Granville: 'We were all placed in rows one above another, so much raised that the last row almost *touched the ceiling*!' Unknown artist. (© The Art Archive/M.L.G. *Stopford Sackville/Eileen Tweedy*)

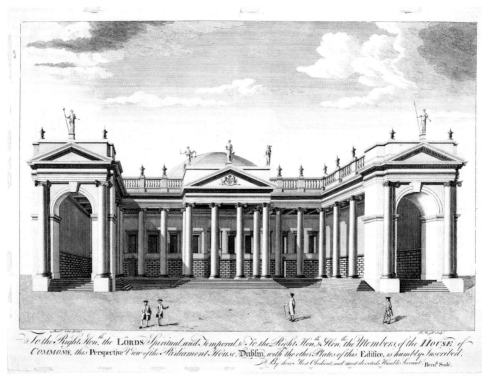

To the Right Hon.ble the LORDS Spiritual and Temporal & To the Right Hon.s & Hon.ble the Members, of the HOUSE of COMMONS, this Perspective View of the Parliament House, Dublin, with the other Plates of this Edifice, is humbly Inscribed. By their Most Obedient, and most devoted, Humble Servant Bern.d Scalé.

The Parliament House in College Green, completed in 1739. Sir Edward Lovett Pearce dexterously blended imported Portland stone and local granite for this building and created a frontage that included elegant arched entrances and, set before a deep corridor, the city's first free-standing colonnade. The Irish Lords and Commons, representing only a narrow élite, met here every second year. Engraved by Peter Mazell. (*Courtesy of the National Library of Ireland*)

THE CHARITABLE INFIRMARY on y² Inns Quay

Founded by six Catholic doctors in 1718, the Charitable Infirmary could claim to be the oldest voluntary hospital in either Ireland or Great Britain. Starting out in Cook Street with just four beds, it moved in 1728 to the building depicted here with 36 beds on King's Inns Quay. It received one-third of the takings from the first performance of *Messiah*. Since Inns Quay was chosen as the site for the new Four Courts in 1786, the Infirmary moved to the Earl of Charlemont's former mansion at 14 Jervis Street and continued to serve the citizens of Dublin there until 1987. (*Courtesy of the National Library of Ireland*)

When Mrs Mary Mercer died in 1734 she left a substantial house in Stephen Street to be turned into a hospital for the reception of 'lunatics and persons afflicted with the King's evil [scrofula], cancer, leprosy, falling sickness, etc.' With the help of Dublin Corporation and generous donors, the institution was able to increase the number of its beds to 62. By 1742 Mercer's Hospital had become the city's most prominent charity. It received one third of the takings from the first performance of *Messiah*. (*Courtesy of the National Library of Ireland*)

A view from Phoenix Park on the north-western outskirts of Dublin city, engraved by Joseph Tudor in 1752. Flanked by trees, the Royal Hospital Kilmainham, Ireland's finest seventeenth-century building, is prominent; it had been erected by Charles II for the care of retired soldiers. Behind it (from right to left) are the spires of St Patrick's and Christ Church cathedrals and St Werburgh's parish church. The Musick Hall in Fishamble Street was next the eastern side of Christ Church. (*Courtesy of the National Library of Ireland*)

Portrait of Handel about 1728 attributed to Balthasar Denner. Then in his early forties, shortly after he had been naturalised as an Englishman, he was at the height of his fame in London as a composer of Italian operas. Only from 1733, when *Athalia* was staged in Oxford, did Handel become a regular composer of oratorios. (© *Heritage Image Partnership Ltd/Alamy*)

For much of his time in London, Handel had to endure sustained and cruel attacks from a rival company, 'The Opera of the Nobility'. His opponents, known as 'Anti-Handelists', were delighted to publish this caricature of the composer portrayed as a greedy porker playing the organ draped with dead fowls and hams. Joseph Goupy, once his friend, had etched this engraving after Handel had failed to invite the artist to share his dinner with him. (*The Charming Brute (colour etching), English School, (18th century)/Private Collection/ Bridgeman Images*)

Without Charles Jennens there would have been no *Messiah*: the idea of creating this sacred oratorio was entirely his, and it was he alone who crafted the libretto from extracts from the Bible. His purpose was to win back deists and atheists from their unscriptural ways by having *Messiah* performed where they were very likely to meet, in the theatre. When this portrait by Mason Chamberlin was painted, Jennens was in his early seventies, and had become a leading Shakespearean scholar. (© The Art Archive/Private *Collection/Eileen Tweedy*)

Jonathan Swift was fifty-one when this portrait by Charles Jervas was painted in 1718. Disappointed not to have been appointed to an English bishopric, he had taken up his post as Dean of St Patrick's Cathedral in 1714. There he strove to improve the quality of his cathedral choir but, in his dotage, he very nearly succeeded in refusing to make his choristers available to Handel. Internationally famous after the publication of *Gulliver's Travels* in 1726, in Dublin he was mainly revered as the 'Drapier', the pamphleteer who was a fearless champion of citizens' rights. (© *National Portrait Gallery, London, UK/Getty Images*)

A neighbour of Handel in Brook Street in London, Mary Pendarves became a close friend of the composer and, after a visit to Dublin in 1731-32, she almost certainly spoke to him warmly about the city's many attractions. In the company of Dean Jonathan Swift, she became acquainted with Rev. Patrick Delany, rector of St Werburgh's and a noted biblical scholar, and married him in 1743. Her correspondence reveals much about Handel's time in both London and Dublin. (© *Mary Evans Picture Library*)

Portrait of Dr Robert Clayton and his wife Katherine painted by James Latham about 1740. Then Bishop of Cork, he was just about the only prominent Protestant clergyman in Ireland to question the doctrine of the Trinity. In 1757 Clayton was about to be tried on a charge of heresy when he died of fever in his St Stephen's Green home, now Iveagh House, the headquarters of the Department of Foreign Affairs. Katherine invited Handel's friends, her sister Anne Donnellan and Mary Pendarves to Dublin. Clayton, as a governor of Mercer's Hospital, helped to ensure the services of cathedral choirs for the first performance of Messiah. (*Double Portrait of Bishop Robert Clayton (1695-1758) and his Wife Katherine (née Donnellan) (d.1766), c.1740, Artist: James Latham, 1697-1747, Oil on canvas. Photo © National Gallery of Ireland*)

On the left 'Senesino' (so called because he came from Sienna), the renowned castrato, Francesco Bernardi, given many title roles in Handel's operas. He was paid the huge fee of £2,000 a year. The prima donna, Francesca Cuzzoni, in the centre, was an equally famous import from Italy. 'Damme, she has a nest of nightingales in her belly', a member of the audience once shouted out at the conclusion of one of her solo performances – but during a rehearsal Handel threatened to throw the diva out of the window unless she brought her petulant antics to an end. (© *The Print Collector/Alamy*)

Laetitia Pilkington was almost certainly the most talented and liveliest member of Dean Jonathan Swift's literary circle. 'A bosom friend of Dean Swift's', according to Mary Pendarves, Laetitia acted as his unofficial secretary for several years. She was 'undone' in a 'tumultuous War of Passion' when her husband Matthew found her in bed with a young surgeon. Forced to flee to London, this woman of wit henceforth lived on her wits. Her *Memoirs* provide a remarkably vivid picture of life in early eighteenth-century Dublin. (*Mrs Laetitia Pilkington/British Library, London, UK/© British Library Board. All Rights Reserved/ Bridgeman Images*)

Francesco Geminiani, born in Lucca in 1687, was the most famous foreign composer to have lived in Ireland. He arrived in London in 1714 where he taught the violin to Matthew Dubourg who would become Master of the State Music in Dublin Castle and conducted the orchestra at the first performance of *Messiah*. He made Dublin his home in 1732 and opened 'Geminiani's Great Music Room' in Dame Street where he printed music, sold paintings and wrote critiques of contemporary baroque music. (*Portrait of Francesco Geminiani (1687-1762), Italian violinist, Soldi, Andrea (1703-71)/Gerald Coke Handel Collection, Foundling Museum, London/Bridgeman Images*)

Susannah Maria Cibber delighted audiences from the moment she first appeared on the London stage at the age of 17. But a very public court case brought by her husband against her lover for 'criminal conversation' forced her to flee the capital. She came to Dublin in December 1741 to rebuild her theatrical career. Though her voice was soft and untrained, it was deeply affecting. Handel, already in the city, did not hesitate to engage her as the contralto soloist in *Messiah*. (© *Derek Bayes/ Lebrecht Music & Arts/Lebrecht Music & Arts/Corbis*)

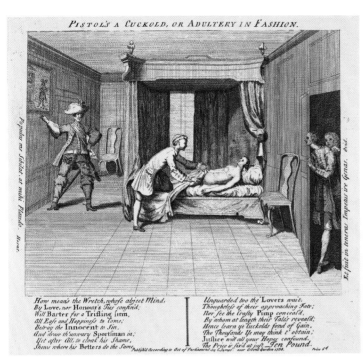

PISTOL'S A CUCKOLD, OR ADULTERY IN FASHION.

How mean's the Wretch, whose abject Mind,
By Love, nor Honour's Ties confin'd;
Will Barter for a Trifling Sum,
All Ease and Happiness to Come;
Betray the Innocent to Sin,
And draw th'unwary Sportsman in;
Yet after all, to cloak his Shame,
Shews where his Betters do the Same.

Unguarded too the Lovers wait,
Thoughtless of their approaching Fate;
Nor see the Crafty Pimp conceal'd,
By whom at length their Tale's reveal'd;
Hence learn ye Cuckolds fond of Gain,
The Thousands Ye may think t'obtain;
Justice will all your Hopes confound,
The Price is fix'd at just Ten Pound.

Published According to Act of Parliament by Edward near Covent Garden 1738.   Price 6d.

The scandal that drove Susannah Cibber from the London stage and brought her eventually to Dublin. In return for money, her husband Theophilus (dressed to play the part of Pistol) looks on to approve her affair with William Sloper, here lowering the bedclothes. Mr Hayes, peeping round the door, gave evidence at the trial that actually he saw the lovers through holes he bored through the wainscot. (*Courtesy of the Bodleian Library, University of Oxford*)

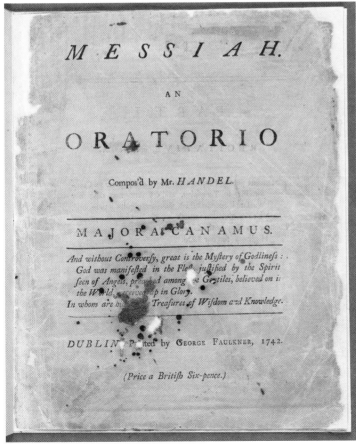

MESSIAH.

AN

ORATORIO

Compos'd by Mr. HANDEL.

MAJORA CANAMUS.

And without Controversy, great is the Mystery of Godliness: God was manifested in the Flesh, justified by the Spirit seen of Angels, preached among the Gentiles, believed on in the World, received up in Glory.
In whom are hid Treasures of Wisdom and Knowledge.

DUBLIN Printed by GEORGE FAULKNER, 1742.

(Price a British Six-pence.)

The cover page of the 'word-book' for the first performance of *Messiah*. With some justification Charles Jennens, the librettist, claimed it was full of 'bulls' or printer's errors. 'MAJORA CANAMUS' ('we sing a grander strain') is taken from a line by Virgil – Jennens believed that the Roman poet was prophesying the birth of Christ. The epigraph is drawn from St Paul's epistles to Timothy and the Colossians.
In the 1970s Donald Burrows, the music historian, discovered a complete copy in the Gilbert Collection at Dublin Public Library. Faulkner published Dublin's most popular newspaper and Jonathan Swift's collected works. (*Courtesy of The Board of Trinity College Dublin*)

Handel's autograph score in Part Two of *Messiah* of the air 'How beautiful are the feet'. The chorus of tenors and basses had just announced authoritatively in unison that the 'Lord gave the word', with messengers spreading the Gospel far and wide. This countertenor aria, pastoral in character, tells how kindly are those 'that preach the gospel of peace, and bring glad tidings of good things'. (© *Lebrecht Music & Arts*)

Handel's autograph score of the Hallelujah Chorus, which is arguably the best-recognised and one of the most famous pieces of classical music ever written. Set to words drawn from three different parts of the Book of Revelation, this is a great anthem of exclamatory praise and triumphal celebration which gives the confident message for the future that God is victorious over sin and rules for all eternity. (© *Lebrecht Music & Arts*)

Handel to Jennens, 29 December 1741. The composer was so delighted with the reception he got during his first month in Dublin that this is a long letter, indeed the longest he ever penned to his gentleman librettist. Handel tells him that the 'Nobility did me the Honour to make amongst themselves a Subscription for 6 nights, which did fill a Room of 600 Persons, so that I needed not sell one single Ticket at the door, and without Vanity the Performance was received with a general approbation'. (© *Lebrecht Music & Arts*)

Later on he writes: 'I cannot sufficiently express the kind treatment I receive here, but the Politeness of this generous Nation cannot be unknown to You, so I let you judge of the satisfaction I enjoy, passing my time with Honour, profit, and pleasure … I shall be obliged to make my stay here longer than I thought …' (© *Lebrecht Music & Arts*)

The Musick Hall in Fishamble Street ceased to be Dublin's premier concert venue after the Rotunda was opened in 1767 in what is now Parnell Square with an audience capacity for 2,000. The Musick Hall was converted into a theatre in 1777 but, as the better off moved out to the suburbs, the area around Fishamble Street became unfashionable and the theatre became the premises of an ironworks company, Kennans. All that remains is the arch shown in this photograph. (© *William Murphy, flickr. com/photos/infomatique/*)

first 'Musical Entertainment' he had put on in the city, he was already contemplating a longer stay. This would allow him the opportunity to offer admiring citizens much more than the six-performance subscription series already arranged.[33]

PACKED HOUSES: 'ALL THE BEST MUSICK BEING ENGAGED TO MR. HANDEL'

By command of the Lord Lieutenant Handel repeated the programme of his first musical entertainment on 13 January 1742. A third concert, once again by special command of the Duke of Devonshire, was advertised for 20 January:

> Acis and Galatea, to which will be added an Ode for St. Cecilia's Day, written by Mr. Dryden, and newly set to Musick by Mr. Handel, with several concertos on the Organ and other Instruments. N.B. – Gentlemen and Ladies are desired to order their Coaches and Chairs to come down Fishamble-street, which will prevent a great deal of inconvenience that happened the Night before; and as there is a good convenient Room hired as an addition to a former place for the Footmen, it is hoped that Ladies will order them to attend there till called for. N.B. – There is another convenient Passage for Chairs made since the last Night.[34]

Handel continued to get enthusiastic support from the Duke, but he probably would have performed to packed houses in any case. His fourth and fifth musical entertainments, on 27 January and 3 February, were given 'by special command of their Excellencies'. Demand for seats was exceeding supply as an advertisement for the fifth concert indicated:

> An Oratorio called ESTHER, with Additions, and several Concertos on the Organ and other instruments. N.B. It is humbly hoped that no Gentlemen or Ladies will take it ill, that none but Subscribers can be admitted, and that no Single Tickets will be delivered, or Money taken at the Door.

The composer was enjoying his status as the darling of Dublin society. This charged him with energy and, for example, on the evening before the fifth public concert, he gave an organ recital in St Patrick's Cathedral, as the *Dublin News-Letter* reported:

> Last Night there was a very numerous congregation at St Patrick's Church, to hear the great Mr. Handel show the best abilities of the best Organist in Europe, upon the fine Organ belonging to that Cathedral.

It had been some considerable time since Handel had played to full houses one after another. Lord Shaftesbury informed Handel's friend, James Harris, 'that the Irish undertakings clear up vastly, & that Handel is like to come home a considerable gainer, if the great hospitality shown him does not kill him with good living'.[35]

The composer did not hesitate to set up a second series of subscription concerts. It was duly advertised in *Faulkner's Dublin Journal* of 2-6 February:

> By the Desire of several Persons of Quality and Distinction, there will be a new Subscription made for Mr. Handel's Musical Entertainments, for Six Nights more, on the same Footing as the last. No more than 150 Subscriptions will be taken in, and no Single Tickets sold, or any money taken at the door. Subscriptions will be taken in at Mr. Handel's House in Abby street near Lyffey street, on Monday next, being the 8th Day of February, from 9 in the Morning, till 3 in the Afternoon. The performances are to continue once a week, till the 6 Nights are over.

It was found necessary to add an additional notice the following week when this advertisement was repeated. Clearly Handel was encountering some problems in getting tickets to his subscribers:

> Whereas several of the Nobility and Gentry have been pleased to desire a second Subscription for Mr. Handel's Musical Entertainments, on the same Terms as the first; Mr. Handel being a Stranger, and not knowing where to wait on every Gentleman who was a Subscriber to his first, to pay his Compliments, hopes

that those who have a mind to Subscribe again, will be pleased to send in their names this Day (being Tuesday, the 9th of February) and To-morrow, at the Musick Hall in Fishamble-street, where Attendance will be given from 10 o'clock in the Morning, till 3 in the Afternoon, and every following Day at his House, in Abbey-street, near Liffey-street.

The first concert of the second series opened with the composer's setting of Dryden's *St Cecilia Ode Alexander's Feast or The Power of Music*, which he had composed in 1736. The narrow and twisting approaches to the Music Hall had changed little since medieval times and Fishamble Street was notoriously steep. Packed houses in consequence resulted in streets around the new Music Hall becoming chaotically congested with sedan chairs and coaches, as insertions in the press made clear, including this one:

> N.B. For the conveniency of the ready emptying of the House, no Chairs will be admitted in waiting but hazard chairs, at the new passage in Copper Alley.[36]

A 'hazard chair' was a sedan chair for hire that would move on after taking on board the first passenger to hail it. The problem was that private sedan chairs waiting for their owners to emerge after a performance made movement in the street almost impossible. For the second concert series the promoters adopted a one-way system pioneered by two ladies, Mrs Hamilton and Mrs Walker, organisers of a popular 'Assembly' held every Saturday evening in the Music Hall.

Dublin's musical resources were being placed at Handel's service to such an extent that other entertainments were being adversely affected. Towards the end of February Monsieur de Rheiner, 'a distressed foreign gentleman', who was to have had a benefit at the Smock Alley Theatre, when he was to have 'attempted the part of Sir Harry Wildair' in Farquhar's *The Constant Couple*, expressed regret for being 'obliged to put off his Day, which was to have been on Tuesday next, on account of all the best Musick being engaged to Mr. Handel's concert'.[37]

Throughout this time, Matthew Dubourg and Handel worked constantly together. Charles Burney later told this story:

One night, while HANDEL was in Dublin, Dubourg having
a solo part in a song, and a close to make, *ad libitum*, he
wandered about in different keys a great while, and seemed
indeed a little bewildered, and uncertain of his original ... but,
at length, coming to the shake, which was to terminate this
long close, HANDEL, to the great delight of the audience, and
augmentation of applause, cried out loud enough to be heard in
the most remote parts of the theatre: 'You are welcome home,
Mr. Dubourg!'[38]

On 15 February the Irish Parliament was prorogued and it would not
meet again for another 18 months. The Lord Lieutenant's presence
was no longer essential and, as was customary, viceregal authority was
handed over to the three Lords Justices. On Tuesday 16 February,
Faulkner's Dublin Journal reported that 'His Grace and Family will
sail for England this day, if the wind be fair'. It was, and 'the Duke of
Devonshire went, with the usual attendance, from Castle to George's-
quay, and there went on board the barge, in order to embark in the
yatch, in his way to Park-gate'. He disembarked on Wednesday
evening, 'from whence he took post, there being sixteen Relais of
Horses on the road for his Grace'.[39] The Duke arrived in London on
Friday 18 February.

Some MPs, bishops and other members of the Irish House of
Lords, freed of any commitment to go to the Parliament House in
College Green, may have left the city. But for most it was far too
early in the year to return to their country seats. The social season
'in Town' was still in full swing.[40] Handel could depend on capacity
attendances at his musical entertainments.

So far, the composer had offered Dublin only those works that
had already been performed and appreciated in London. He had
been in the Irish capital long enough now, however, to be confident
that audiences there were ready to receive the work he had tailored
specifically for them, the sacred oratorio *Messiah*.

Chapter 8
Susannah Cibber's Rocky Road to Dublin

'AN ENGLISH TRADESMAN'S DAUGHTER' RIVALS 'THE SELECTED SINGERS OF ITALY'

During 1741 and 1742 Dublin society was able to enjoy, not only the feast of music being presented by Handel, but also the creative work and performances of some of the other great talents of the London stage. The outcome, it could be said, was that these were the two most exciting theatrical and musical seasons of the entire century in the Irish capital. Peg Woffington, Kitty Clive, David Garrick, James Quin and Dennis Delane appeared at different times at Smock Alley and Aungier Street theatres. Susannah Cibber had also come to Dublin to undertake a punishing schedule of performances. Then in June 1742 she welcomed to her Aungier Street lodgings her brother, the composer and theatre manager Thomas Arne, and his wife Cecilia, the noted soprano. Some of these visitors crossed the Irish Sea after learning of Handel's triumphs in Ireland, hoping that they too would enhance their reputations and fill their pockets. But Susannah Cibber had a very different motive. After all, she had arrived before Handel staged a single performance in Dublin: Susannah had suffered crippling damage to her reputation arising from a notorious scandal, the sensational details of which had been fascinating and shocking Londoners for the past three years. Now she had travelled hundreds of miles to Dublin to distance herself from her critics in an attempt to rebuild her theatrical career.

Back in 1732 Susannah Cibber's father, Thomas Arne senior, an upholsterer and undertaker in London, reckoned he could extricate himself from financial difficulties by putting his seventeen-year-old daughter Susannah on the stage. He was right. Given the star role in Johann Lampe's new English opera *Amelia*, she delighted audiences

at the new Haymarket theatre. An anonymous pamphleteer found
the auditorium so packed that 'I was forced to crowd upon the Stage
and even that was thronged. Is not this odd, I say, for an English
Tradesman's Daughter to spring up all of a Suddain to rival the
selected Singers of Italy'.[1]

In February 1733 London playgoers learned that her brother
'Thomas Arne Junior, Proprietor of English Opera has new set to
Musick … the Opera of Rosamond', and that his sister Susannah
would be the leading soloist.[2] *Rosamond* was a triumphant success.
Of course Handel had to see for himself the work of this young
Englishman, and in doing so he was enchanted by Susannah Arne.
Though her contralto voice was soft and untrained, Handel found
it had such expressive charm that he immediately invited her to be
a principal in his forthcoming new oratorio *Deborah*. Along with
Susannah, Handel also engaged another English singer, Cecilia
Young, soon to become Cecilia Arne. Nine years later both ladies
and both composers would be taking Dublin by storm.

Theophilus Cibber, an actor-manager and son of Colley Cibber,
the Poet Laureate and veteran of the stage, fell for Susannah. She
resisted his advances as long as she could but her father insisted
on the match. In March 1734 they were betrothed. Despite Colley
Cibber's protestations that his son should marry an heiress, this soon
proved to be a financially advantageous marriage for Theophilus.
Susannah was rapidly becoming one of the most sought after actors
in London. This delicate girl, with solemn eyes and a low, sweet
voice was entrancing the city's theatregoers. She was earning £200
a year and another £100 from her benefit performances. However,
Susannah was discovering that Theophilus was a despicable, indeed
a repellent husband. He was more than just a reprobate; he was
malevolently manipulative, mendacious, quarrelsome, vicious, wild,
devious, profligate and heartless. In rapid succession Susannah bore
him two children but both died within days, possibly because her
husband, consorting regularly with other compliant women in Drury
Lane ('Drurian doxies'), had infected her with venereal disease.
Pregnancies only briefly reduced the handsome income Susannah
brought in but the money was dissipated at once by her husband's
reckless extravagance. Indeed his debts were becoming monumental.

Susannah then attempted to put her earnings beyond her husband's grasp. When he learned of this, Theophilus in a drunken fury broke down the door of her theatre dressing room, wrecked the contents, and grabbed her jewellery and costumes, carrying them away to turn them into ready cash as soon as he could. But the debts kept mounting.

The theatrical world was well aware that Theophilus Cibber was a vain and turbulent rakehell but appreciated his undoubted ability to draw in audiences. Susannah in contrast was universally regarded as gentle, demure, serious and upright. A devout Catholic, like her mother Anne and her brother Thomas, Susannah worshipped regularly at the Sardinian embassy's chapel in Lincoln's Inn Fields and was to do so for the remainder of her life.[3] Then as the year 1738 was drawing to a close that image of a virtuous and chaste Susannah was smashed to pieces.

'I BORED HOLES THROUGH THE WAINSCOT': GATHERING EVIDENCE OF 'CRIMINAL CONVERSATION'

Theophilus Cibber brought an action against William Sloper, accusing him of 'Assaulting, Ravishing, and Carnally Knowing Susannah Maria Cibber, the Plaintiff's wife'.[4] He was demanding damages of five thousand pounds. When the trial began at the Court of the King's Bench on Thursday, 5 December 1738 the Right Hon. Sir William Lee, Lord Chief Justice, presiding, ruled that in view of the special nature of the case no report should be made of the proceedings. But in the packed courtroom an anonymous clerk, using his own shorthand, secretly recorded all that was said for future publication.

Evidence of an illicit affair – in legal terms 'criminal conversation' – between William Sloper and Susannah Cibber presented by the prosecution team, led by the Solicitor General, John Strange, was both irrefutable and sensational. An upper floor had been rented a year before by Sloper in Blue Cross Street in Leicester Fields from a certain Mrs Hayes.[5] Her husband provided the 'special jury of gentlemen' with graphic details of the pair's secret trysts:

I have a closet on the same floor, adjoining to the room where they used to sit. I bored holes through the wainscot and could see them very plain. He used to kiss her and take her on his lap. On 22nd day of December I was looking through. He took her on his knees, lifted up her clothes and took down his breeches and took his privy member and put it between her legs.[6]

On another occasion, Mr Hayes continued:

I stayed there longer ... He let down the turn up bed softly, she laid herself upon it, upon her back, and pulled up her clothes. Her body was bare. He unbuttoned his clothes, hung up his bag wig upon a sconce, let down his breeches, took his privy member in his hand and lay down upon her.[7]

'Enough!' For the judge this was definitely too much information. 'There is no occasion to be more particular. We are not trying a rape!'[8]

William Sloper's father, also called William, was a distinguished member of England's élite. A friend of Sir Robert Walpole, he was an admired philanthropist who had in the past been one of the four founders of Georgia Colony, the Westminster government's agent for the colony of New York, and paymaster of His Majesty's army in Scotland. Though his son was already married with two young children, old William Sloper was determined to engage for him the finest legal defence team London could supply. In court it was junior counsel, William Murray, who with devastating effect proved that Theophilus Cibber had engineered the whole affair in return for ready cash.

From evidence given by a succession of witnesses, it emerged that Cibber not only had full knowledge of the affair, he also had introduced Sloper to his wife. Initially, Sloper did no more than teach Susannah to play backgammon. During the summer of 1737 Sloper rented a villa for the three of them at Kingston-on-Thames; and with Cibber's full compliance, Susannah and William became lovers. Anne Hopson, a maidservant, told the court:

Mr. Cibber's bedchamber and Mr. Sloper's had a door opened between them. Mrs. Cibber used to undress herself in my master's room and leave her clothes there, and put on a bedgown, and take away one of the pillows from my master's bed, and go away to Mr. Sloper's room. My master used to shut the door after her, and say 'Good night, my dear,' and sometimes he used to knock at their door in the morning to call them up to breakfast.[9]

Back in the city during the autumn elaborate arrangements had to be made to hide the affair from prying eyes. Mr Hayes, however, was able to keep track of their movements – 'I dogged them both home in their chairs'.[10]

This arrangement had broken down when Sloper decided to detach Susannah permanently from her husband. The pair moved to a rented house in Burnham near Slough in Buckinghamshire, but Theophilus – already planning to raise more cash from 'Mr. Benefit' Sloper by going to court – decided to prove to the world that he was a heartsick husband. On 8 September 1738, with the assistance of two hired and well-armed men, he burst into the house at Burnham. Susannah, terrified of her husband, agreed to go back with him to London. Sloper, after following Cibber's coach to no avail, then sought the help of Susannah's brother, Thomas Arne. Cibber kept her trapped in a locked room near Clare Market, closely guarded by a Mr Stint, a theatre candle-snuffer armed with a case of pistols. Then her brother came to the rescue, accompanied by 'at least a hundred', according to Stint. Susannah 'cried out murder' to identify exactly where she was, Arne's posse broke down the door and, Stint later told the court, 'beat me severely and tore all the clothes off my back and took Mrs. Cibber away with them'.[11]

Theophilus soon after fled his creditors by walking over rooftops in the dark, and then crossed the Channel to Calais. This brought him no nearer to a solution to his problems. He returned to London, there to make arrangements for taking legal action against Sloper.

SUSANNAH CIBBER INVITED TO DUBLIN

The gentlemen of the jury had no choice but to find in favour of the plaintiff. However, they made their opinion very plain by only awarding Theophilus Cibber a paltry £10 in damages. This may have been a satisfying outcome for William Sloper, but the wide dissemination of salacious details revealed during this court case, the talk of the town, was a disaster for Susannah. Some other women in London's colourful theatrical world could have ridden out such a storm with no difficulty, but not Susannah. Her reputation was in tatters. Besides, she was still married to Theophilus who now – as a husband was then entitled to do – vindictively refused to allow her to appear again on the stage.

Susannah and William disappeared into the country and for three years only a few trusted individuals knew where they were. By the time of the trial she was already pregnant by Sloper. Susannah gave birth to a daughter, Molly, who survived. They remained together, she giving birth to a son, Charles, ten years later; the couple were only to be parted by Susannah's death in 1766.

During their time in the country Theophilus Cibber returned to court and this time the jury instructed William Sloper to pay him £500 – after all, his wife had not returned to him. Meanwhile, there were many in London who longed to have Susannah return to the stage. They included Kitty Clive and James Quin. Daughter of William Raftor, an Irish officer who had served in Louis XIV's army, Mrs Clive was a talented singer and for long the city's best loved comedienne, especially in her role as Polly in Gay's *The Beggar's Opera*. Quin, though born in London, had Irish parents and had been sent over to Dublin to complete his education. He first appeared in Smock Alley theatre before moving back to London. For many years Quin was just about the most distinguished actor in the metropolis, a bear of a man with an extraordinarily resonant voice. His great girth fitted him well to be any theatre manager's first choice as Falstaff. By 1741, however, both of these stars felt that they were being outshone on the London stage by another two actors, Charles Macklin and Peg Woffington, both of them Irish and both captivating audiences in the capital.

Born Cathal Mac Lochlainn in Culdaff, Co. Donegal, around 1699, Macklin had been brought up in Dublin. In 1725 he arrived in London where he anglicised his name for the stage. There he pioneered a more natural and passionate style of acting, breaking away from the old declamatory style that long had been the norm. In his most famous role Macklin played Shylock in *The Merchant of Venice*, not as a comic character with a large red nose but as an intelligent, scheming and villainous man. James Quin, the great exponent of the old portentous and rather static style, and often sharing the stage with Macklin, was finding himself increasingly upstaged.

Peg Woffington had been born into poverty in Dublin, and as a child sold watercress from door to door in the city. At the age of ten she was discovered by Madame Violante, the tightrope performer and promoter, and starred as Polly in a juvenile performance of *The Beggar's Opera*. She made her name as Ophelia in Shakespeare's *Hamlet* in Aungier Street theatre in 1737; and then, in 1740, she travelled with her lover across the Irish Sea to further her career. Audiences in London were immediately enraptured by this beautiful young woman with an inimitable deep voice, expressive arched eyebrows, a slightly aquiline nose, dark and lustrous eyes, and black tresses falling luxuriantly on her neck and shoulders. Peg particularly enjoyed playing male parts as this gave her the opportunity to wear breeches to show off her shapely legs.[12]

Peg had a fiery temperament and soon was quarrelling with fellow thespians, none more so than her greatest rival, Kitty Clive, who defended herself against the abrasive taunts of this young interloper with matching pugnacity. Indeed, their shared loathing was so permanent as to preclude any reconciliation. Meanwhile, Quin had received a handsome offer from the Aungier Street theatre. When he suggested that Kitty join him to do a season together in Dublin, she did not hesitate to accept. They arrived in Ireland early in June 1741.

All the actors at Drury Lane were appalled by what had happened to Susannah Cibber, but none took her disgrace to heart more than James Quin. He had admired her talents ever since he had first played opposite her in Sir Richard Steele's *The Conscious Lovers* in 1736. Quin remained a bachelor all his life, but he seems to have had deeper feelings for Susannah than for any other woman. A few months after the trial he had demonstrated his loathing for Theophilus Cibber by dragging him out of the Bedford Tavern and forcing him to fight a duel in the street. Both men had drawn blood with their swords before being separated. Then in the late summer of 1741 Quin wrote to Susannah from Dublin inviting her to join him there.

'THE ELOQUENCE OF MR. QUIN AND THE HARMONY OF MRS. CLIVE'
Why did Susannah Cibber decide to accept the invitation and
attempt a return to the stage? After all, William Sloper, always true
to her, was ensuring that she and their child, Molly, were being well
provided for in what many would have regarded as a rural idyll. By
returning to public performance she risked, if not vilification – at
the very least – sniggering chatter behind her back, embarrassing
catcalls from the pit, and the contempt of polite society. Did she
really want to go back to the jealousies and violent brawls which
then almost constantly convulsed the performing community?
Susannah knew well, for example, that in his youth James Quin
had been convicted of manslaughter after killing a fellow actor in a
duel; he had been fortunate to avoid condign punishment. Not long
after, in a drunken brawl, Quin had killed another actor. Then in
May 1735 Charles Macklin, in an argument over a wig backstage
with the actor, Thomas Hallam, in a rage – in front of dressers,
stagehands and performers – had plunged a fire poker into his eye,
killing him. Thanks to the intervention of his manager and James
Quin, the charge had been reduced to manslaughter and Macklin
was freed after just being lightly branded on the hand. Whereas, the
11 other defendants at the Old Bailey that day had been capitally
convicted, some of them merely for petty theft: one had taken a
guinea and another had just stolen a hood.

There was probably no more complicated reason for Susannah
to risk resuming her theatrical career than a burning desire to act
and to sing again before appreciative audiences. And by emerging
from obscurity far away in Ireland she would make it difficult, if
not impossible, for her husband to stop her stepping onto a stage.
Susannah could trust James Quin's assurances in his letters to her
that he and Kitty Clive had been enthusiastically received in Ireland.
Surely she could expect an equally warm reception there.

On 5 June 1741, the packet *The Pearl Galley* sailed into Dublin, and
Quin stepped ashore, tightly corseted and sporting a periwig, followed
by his valet and great trunks of costumes. Mrs Clive, also finding it
necessary to be carefully corseted, accompanied him, managing to
attract as much, if not more, admiring attention from journalists.[13]
Aungier Street theatre had set up a very demanding schedule for
her but she rose to the challenge magnificently. Mrs Clive did not

look back after her first Dublin appearance on 16 June in the part of Lappet in a comedy, called *The Miser*, 'in which will be introduced a Song call'd the Life of a Beau'.[14] Six days later Mrs Clive was Nell in *The Devil to Pay or The Wives Metamorphosed*, part of a benefit for Mr Quin during which he made his Dublin debut in *Othello*.

The summer season, when the landed gentry returned to their country estates, usually resulted in a much reduced programme of stage offerings in the city. This did not happen in 1741, nor, indeed, in 1742. Kitty Clive, in particular, can hardly have been idle for a moment. During June, July and the beginning of August she appeared in *The Provok'd Husband*, a repeat of *The Devil to Pay*, *The Double Dealer* and *The Virgin Unmasked*, along with songs between acts. Arne's stage masque *Comus* was given its first performance in Aungier Street on 6 August with Charles Quin as Comus and Mrs Clive as Euphrosyne. The *Dublin Journal* reported that the performance was acted:

> to a crowded Audience of Persons of the best Quality now in Town; the Dresses, Machines, Flyings, and all the other Decorations were entirely new, and very beautiful; the Orchestra was enlarged, several eminent Hands being added to the Band, for the Occasion, particularly Signor Pasqualino; the Musick was finely performed, having – as we hear – been a long time in Practice under the Inspection of Mr. Dubourg; and the whole Entertainment that Night was executed with a Decorum and Taste so elegant, as has never been attempted in this Kingdom. The Sublimity of the great Milton, the Eloquence of Mr. Quin, and the Harmony of Mrs. Clive, delighted and charmed everyone.

Comus appears to have been performed again four times before the month was out. James Quin and Kitty Clive both appeared in *King Lear* in Aungier Street and, in a benefit concert for her on 19 August, she sang 'the celebrated Song call'd Ellen a Roon'.[15]

Three days later in his home in Brook Street Handel began writing the score of his *Messiah*.

THEIR GRACES TO THE RESCUE

There is no evidence that Handel had given any thought to seeking
the services of Susannah Cibber for any of the performances he
had planned for Dublin, let alone for *Messiah*. The composer may
not even have known how to get in touch with her. He had four
soloists: Mrs Maclaine and Christina Avolio brought over specially
to Ireland; and James Baileys and John Church, already resident
in the city. It is possible that Handel considered Kitty Clive as an
additional principal but she had already returned to London by the
time he had arrived in Ireland.

Kitty Clive had packed Aungier Street theatre every time she
appeared. After 10 weeks, however, she had had enough and she was
anxious to return to London. She did so before the end of August
1741. How was Aungier Street to replace her? Quin recommended
Susannah Cibber to the management. It was probably at this stage
that he wrote to her to invite her to come to Dublin. Quin was able to
inform Susannah that the theatre could offer her £300 for the season.
If Susannah had been entertaining the hope that she could make her
way to Dublin as an unknown, this was immediately dashed when she
stepped ashore on 3 December. The arrival of 'the celebrated actress'
was announced in the city's newspapers.

The risks being taken by Susannah Cibber – and, indeed, by
Aungier Street theatre – were demonstrated all too depressingly
during her first stage appearance in Dublin on 12 December. This
also happened to be her first public performance in three years. She
was playing a role familiar to her, Indiana in Steele's *The Conscious
Lovers*. The audience in the house was so thin that the management
collected only £10 in receipts.

It was obvious that Dublin's theatre-going public was all too well
informed about the intimate details that had been thrown up during
the 'criminal conversation' trial. Clearly members of the city's polite
society hesitated to risk being seen at this theatre when a woman with
such a tarnished reputation – however celebrated – was performing
there. It was at this critical moment that William Cavendish, the 3rd
Duke of Devonshire, Lord Lieutenant of Ireland, and Catherine,
Lady Devonshire, stepped in. They determined to give society
in Dublin a lead. A week after Susannah's calamitous first public
appearance in the city, 'by their Graces special Command' Thomas

Otway's *Venice Preserved* was staged with Mrs Cibber as the innocent but doomed heroine, Bellamira.[16] This time the 'quality' in Dublin had no reason to suppress their curiosity, and subscriptions quickly purchased filled the theatre.

'SHE OFTEN PENETRATED THE HEART, WHEN OTHERS … COULD ONLY REACH THE EAR'

Thereafter, Susannah played to packed houses in the Irish capital.[17] This was not a tentative return to the stage: she subjected herself to an exhausting schedule. On 7 January 1742 she played Euphrosyne in Arne's *Comus* at Aungier Street. This role required her to sing a recitative and three songs, the largo in the last one, 'Ye Fauns and ye Dryads', being perhaps the most moving music in this masque. It is very likely that Handel saw her sing in this role at Aungier Street and that this led him to choose Susannah as the additional female soloist he felt he needed for *Messiah*. On 9 February, as a 'benefit' for the Charitable Infirmary she appeared once more as Indiana in *The Conscious Lovers*. Susannah was also called upon to sing, for example, on 27 February at Aungier Street at a 'Benefit of Mrs. Pasqualino' and on 4 March in the same venue in the second scene of *The Betrayer of his Country*.[18] Handel could well have made a point of attending these performances. In any case, by this stage Susannah had committed herself to taking on a leading role in *Messiah*.

Though right from the start of her career Susannah Cibber had been given singing roles, it was as an actor rather than a vocalist that she had won fame. Her voice, though sweet and exceptionally expressive, was untrained and lacked the power usually required in operas and masques. For example, when *Comus* had opened in Drury Lane in 1738 Susannah played the Lady but 'Sweet Echo, sweetest nymph', which belongs to her part, was performed off-stage by her sister-in-law, Cecilia Arne, while she mimed the song.

Colley Cibber, while giving evidence in the 1738 trial on behalf of the plaintiff, his son, had spoken warmly about Susannah's acting ability. 'I believe I was the person who chiefly instructed her … and took great delight in it, for she was very capable of receiving instruction'. He continued: 'In forty years' experience that I have known the stage, I never knew a woman at the beginning so capable of the business, or improve so fast'. However, he did not have a high opinion of her singing. When Theophilus married Susannah 'she was a singer, but there were better voices. I thought her voice not the best, and if not the best, 'tis nothing'.[19]

Susannah's first engagement with Handel in Dublin was to take the leading role in 'the new Serenata called Hymen', a cut-down version of *Imeneo*, his opera first performed in London in November 1740. This was to be done as a concert performance in the Fishamble Street Music Hall. However, the performance had to be put off because Susannah became ill and was replaced with *L'Allegro, Il Penseroso, ed Il Moderato*. It is possible that she fell victim to an influenza epidemic then sweeping through Dublin. Her continued illness led to another postponement on 17 March, but she had recovered by 24 March when the 'long delayed' *Hymen* was put on in the Music Hall and repeated there on 31 March. This was actually the very last time in his life that Handel gave an Italian opera performance.[20] Susannah had to fulfil her contract with Aungier Street theatre with these performances which seriously reduced the time she had left to prepare for *Messiah*.

The first performance of *Messiah* was scheduled for the following month. Only a fortnight separated the second performance of *Hymen* and the day eventually fixed for the sacred oratorio's première, 13 April. (Originally to have been 12 April but then changed to 13 April.) Susannah's voice was barely strong enough for a solo part but the composer wanted to channel her exceptional ability to capture a particular emotion he sought to evoke at different places in the performance. Others were to testify to the unique quality of Susannah's singing. Thomas Sheridan, the actor-manager and Swift's godson, observed that 'it was not to any extraordinary powers of voice (whereof she has but a very moderate share) nor to a greater degree of skill in musick (wherein many of the Italians must be allowed to exceed her) that she owed her excellencies, but to expression only; her acknowledged superiority in which could proceed from nothing but skill in her profession'.[21]

Charles Burney, the historian of music, who later sang Palestrina's madrigals with Susannah, went so far as to conclude that 'her voice was a thread, and her knowledge of Music very inconsiderable', but at the same time 'by a natural pathos, and perfect conception of the words, she often penetrated the heart, when others, with infinitely greater voice and skill, could only reach the ear'.[22]

Handel had a reputation as something of a martinet, a perfectionist who expected his singers, after receiving copies of his scores, to have thoroughly prepared themselves before daring to appear before him at rehearsal. In the case of Susannah Cibber he had to make an exception for the very simple reason that she had *never learned to read music*. At the outset of her career she depended on her brother Thomas and the composer Johann Lampe to familiarise herself with the songs and airs written down in a notation, which remained incomprehensible to her all her life.

Handel had discovered Susannah's inability to read his scores back in the spring of 1733 when he had asked her to be one of the soloists in his oratorio *Deborah*. Then he had taken her back to his home in Brook Street and, sitting himself down at his harpsichord, patiently taught her the music, phrase by phrase, hour by hour. As Burney observed later, something about that 'voice and manner softened Handel's severity at her want of musicianship'. 'From her intelligence and native feeling', he continued, 'she sang … in a more touching manner than the finest opera singer'. Now in Dublin, having engaged Susannah, he had not only to alter sections of his *Messiah* score to suit her contralto voice but he also had to set aside enough time to sit with her, ensuring that she learned by ear the parts he had assigned to her.[23]

Handel had his soloists and the full cooperation of Matthew Dubourg, Master of the State Music, who could be relied on to gather together for this occasion the finest instrumentalists in the city. He also needed the choirs from both of Dublin's cathedrals. To his horror Handel was hearing that these choristers might well be denied him for the first performance of his *Messiah* and, indeed, for any other performance. The man posing this grave threat was none other than the famous Dean of St Patrick's cathedral, Dr Jonathan Swift.

Chapter 9
'I Remember No Such Licence':
Swift Refuses His Choir

'I AM ABSOLUTE LORD OF THE GREATEST CATHEDRAL IN THE KINGDOM'

In 1742 no one in Dublin was more admired, or more renowned, or more revered by the populace than Jonathan Swift. Across the English-speaking world it was *Gulliver's Travels*, his extraordinary satire on contemporary politics, religion and literature, which had won him fame. In Dublin, however, it was in his guise as the Drapier, the anonymous pamphleteer who had courageously courted prosecution in defence of the ordinary people of the city, that he was loved and esteemed. There was hardly a weaver or a maidservant in Dublin who did not know of this clergyman who had so often reached for his corrosive quill to lampoon with savage wit those in power, especially those who attempted to threaten the rights and livelihood of his fellow citizens.

Nowhere was the Dean more popular than in the warren of densely inhabited streets in the Liberties adjacent to his cathedral. Swift enjoyed this notoriety and wrote to the poet Alexander Pope that he never walked the streets of Dublin 'without a thousand blessings from my friends the Vulgar'.[1] He had played a pivotal role in forcing Walpole's government to withdraw Wood's patent for his suspect copper coinage back in 1725, and the people had not forgotten that. Every year since that great victory, there were celebrations, with bell ringing, bonfires and the firing of small cannon, to mark Swift's birthday on St Andrew's Day, 30 November. In 1741 *Faulkner's Dublin Journal* reported the Dean's birthday celebrations:

> Yesterday being the Anniversary of the Birth of that great and glorious Patriot, the Revd Dr. Swift … when he entered into the

67th Year of his Age; the same was observed here with greater Demonstrations of Joy than have been known. The Morning was ushered in with ringing of Bells. At Noon several Persons of Distinction and Fortune paid their Compliments to him; in the Evening there were Fire Works from St. Patrick's Steeples, and Bonfires and Illuminations in many Parts of the City; and the Night concluded with the greatest chearfulness. Many Poems were writ in Honour of the Day, which shall be inserted in this Paper as Opportunity permits.

More than one ship had been christened *Drapier*, several taverns named themselves The Drapier's Head, with signs showing Swift in clerical garb; medals had been struck in his honour; and he was the subject of many songs and ballads written anonymously in his praise.[2]

As Dean of this cathedral, Swift ruled a tiny fiefdom of nine acres, the Liberty of St Patrick. Here just beyond the ancient limits of the city the rulings of Dublin Corporation did not apply. Even debtors were safe from arrest within this haven. 'It is an infallible maxim', he had written in 1721, 'that not one thing here is done without the Dean's consent'. In 1733 he explained to Pope:

I am Lord Mayor of 120 houses; I am absolute lord of the greatest cathedral in the kingdom; am at peace with the neighbouring princes, the Lord Mayor of the city and the Archbishop of Dublin; only the latter, like the King of France, sometimes attempts encroachments on my dominions.[3]

At its centre was the cathedral, the largest ecclesiastical building in Ireland. It had lost much of its Anglo-Norman splendour since being completed in the middle of the thirteenth century. A storm had toppled its spire in 1316; an accidental fire in 1362 had destroyed its tower; a replacement tower had collapsed in 1394; and at the end of Henry VIII's reign the great stone arch which covered the west isle fell in, destroying many ancient monuments. Then in the sixteenth and seventeenth centuries its stained glass and sculptures had suffered the depredations of Protestant reformers and a second spire had fallen down in 1700 and would not be properly replaced for another half century. The cathedral's condition had suffered from spasmodic neglect and, indeed, parts of the structure were in a state of near dilapidation. Eventually, in 1738, Swift persuaded the chapter to set aside much of the cathedral's income to expend on repairs. These large sums, William Monck Mason observed in his 1820 history of the cathedral, 'testify with what anxious attention Swift regarded this venerable edifice'. But, he added ruefully:

> It is much to be regretted that those measures of improvement should have been rendered ineffectual; the frequency of floods in the Poddle-river, and insufficiency of sewers to carry off the superabundant water, was the occasion of much injury to the building, and, moreover, rendered it, on account of damps, unsafe to assemble in; accordingly, in 1744, the chapter was obliged to solicit the use of the sister cathedral.[4]

'I WOULD NOT GIVE A FARTHING FOR ALL THE MUSIC IN THE UNIVERSE'

Ever since he had taken up his post as Dean in 1714, Swift – unlike so many of his predecessors – had taken his duties very seriously. This included making the cathedral choir the best in Ireland or, at least, as good as that of neighbouring Christ Church cathedral. As he had already made it clear to his friends in London when he was still the brilliant Tory propagandist there, his interest was in the written word, not music. His friend and fellow divine, Dr Patrick Delany, recorded a conversation he had had with Lady Carteret, wife of the Lord Lieutenant at the time, when she had recommended a singer:

> I know nothing of music, madam; I would not give a farthing for all the music in the universe. For my own part, I would rather say my prayers without it. But as long as it is thought by the skilful to contribute to the dignity of the public worship, by the blessing of God it shall never be disgraced by me, nor I hope, by any of my successors.[5]

And, indeed, Swift strove to improve the quality of the music in the cathedral. He had the full support of the Dean's Vicar, Rev. John Worrall, his director of music who skilfully and diplomatically won over the co-operation of the vicars choral and stipendiaries. These adult professional choristers from both Christ Church and St Patrick's cathedrals frequently sang together at Dublin Castle and, to supplement their incomes, they also responded to requests to perform in the theatre and at charity and private functions.

A former Dean, Michael Jephson, had 'Orders and Statutes' for the vicars choral of St Patrick's printed and displayed in 1692, and these were still in force half a century later. 'They are to be men of good repute', these regulations began, 'civil conversations, noe swearers, drunkards or whore-mongers, nor infamous livers, nor ale-house-keepers, players, dancing-masters, or men of any offensive or scandelous imployments'. 'Att the time of performing divine service' the vicars choral were to 'be grave and modest in attire, hayre, gate, and gesture', not to 'use any other posture of body than may beseeme gravity, reverence and attentness to his sacred imployment in which he shall abstaine from all private talkeings, whisperings and laughings'.[6] The Orders and Statutes included an elaborate schedule of fines for misdemeanours, the money collected being assigned to pay for replacing the wainscoting in the vicars' lodging house.

When out and about in town 'every Viccar is soe to demeane himself abroad, as he may in a good example to others and raise no scandal to the church' and no vicar 'is to haunt ale-houses or tavernes or suspicious scandelous places'.[7] This last regulation proved impossible to enforce. Virtually every meeting to arrange concerts – including, almost certainly, that to organise the first performance of Handel's *Messiah* – was held in a tavern. The Hibernian Catch Club, composed of vicars choral and stipendiaries from both cathedrals, always met in alehouses. These men indulged in very secular part singing in the form of a round, usually accompanying racy verse with hidden or double meanings related to sexual seduction and gratification, drink and tobacco.[8]

When Swift had first arrived as Dean it was obvious that the quality of singing at Christ Church by the vicars choral, stipendiaries and the choir boys was significantly higher than it was in St Patrick's. This was probably due to the diligence of Henry Swords, appointed 'Master of the Boys and Pricker of the Anthem Books' at Christ Church in 1709. Swift from the outset was at pains to raise standards in his own cathedral. 'I have the honour to be captain of a band of nineteen musicians (including boys)', he wrote, 'but my quire is so degenerate under the reigns of former Deans of famous memory, that the race of people called Gentleman Lovers of Musick tell me I must be very careful in supplying two vacancies.' During 'this solemn season' of Lent in 1734 he had made these notes in exasperation:

> Mr. Hall: Received lately an admonition for the neglect of his duty … seems careless of performing his duty in the choir. Appears very dirty and indecent in his dress.

> Mr. Smith: Very careless of his attendance, either rambling abroad or idling at home, giving no manner of excuse for his absence, takes a frolic to neglect his attendance for two or three months together … it is high time to animadvert on him and publicly to admonish him.

> Mr. Fox: An infamous sot, who is daily losing his voice by intemperance and will become in a year or two more a burden to the church. Very negligent in his attendance, scandalous in his behaviour and conversation – if he will not endeavour to make himself serviceable … he shall meet with the severity he deserves and be expelled.[9]

One night he asked for the singing of some anthems 'and it was answered that several persons whom I had ordered to perform had all colds. Mr. Phipps, Mr. Mason, Mr. Fox, Mr. Church'. 'There must be some very ill management or carelessness', he continued, 'that at this season the best voices become thus unserviceable when this church is frequented by persons of all ranks'.[10]

Rev. John Worrall, the Dean's Vicar of St Patrick's and 'Master of the Boys' in both cathedrals, had the day-to-day responsibility for ensuring that the city was provided with sacred music sung to a high professional standard. It was a task he carried out most conscientiously in a long career. He and Swift became firm friends and shared an enthusiasm for walking. They would stride out together after divine service and, after some time, return for a meal at the home of one or the other. Since Mrs

Worrall was an excellent cook and an accomplished hostess, the Dean enjoyed dining with the couple, rather curiously paying them an agreed rate on each occasion. Indeed, it was said that Swift used the Worralls' house 'as a tavern'. Swift relied heavily on 'Jack' Worrall to look after matters which had nothing to do with musical direction. When he was staying with Dr Sheridan at Quilca, for example, he fired off letter after letter giving the vicar detailed instructions on a range of petty matters which included caring for the deanery garden (Swift had given it a biblical name, 'Naboth's Vineyard'). Perhaps Worrall enjoyed gardening too much – 'I hear you are ruining me with dung', the Dean scolded.[11]

Worrall's most important function, however, was to be in charge of the vicars choral, stipendiaries and choirboys. Each cathedral generally had six choirboys. Worrall – paid £24 10s. a year to see to their maintenance and 'washing and trimming' – was scrupulous in seeing to the welfare of the choristers. A 'writing master' saw to their education and, assisted by the vicar choral William Lamb in later years, Worrall gave them their musical training. A spinet had been bought in 1708 for £2 10s. 'for the use of the boys' but when it broke Worrall had to repair it himself. Since some choirboys and most vicars choral and stipendiaries were engaged by both cathedrals, it was necessary to stagger religious services, Morning Service, for example, being held at St Patrick's at nine o'clock and then at ten o'clock in Christ Church. Ralph Roseingrave, a prolific composer of anthems as well as an accomplished musician, seems to have played the organ in both cathedrals. Worrall was always on the lookout for choristers of real talent and encouraged Swift to search for them when he was in England. 'I got no voice at Oxford', Swift wrote from London in 1726, 'but am endeavouring for one here'. At least one prospective vicar choral brought across the Irish Sea failed to meet Worrall's rigorous musical standards and was sent back, expenses paid.

Worrall had his work cut out managing the vicars choral and stipendiaries. When he took up his appointment in 1713, the chapter of Christ Church had been finding it virtually impossible to enforce the order requiring their attendance each Saturday at a rehearsal of the following day's music. The 'mulct' or fine for non-attendance had to be raised from 2s. 6d. to five shillings for each offence. John Church, who was to be a soloist for Handel in *Messiah*, was to be involved in disputes with colleagues on more than one occasion. In March 1737 Church registered a complaint against William Lambe for using 'opprobrious language' and threatening 'to beat him in a violent manner in the time of divine service in the church'. Lambe was suspended for a time and then followed a reconciliation, 'both having received the holy communion together'. The Christ Church vicars neglected to look after their lodgings in Christ Church Yard and in 1740 they were ordered 'either to repair the same or pull them down for the safety of the people'. William Taverner was constantly in trouble, getting himself so deeply into debt that he had to surrender his annual salary and have his finances managed by the proctor of St Patrick's.[12]

Without these vicars choral and stipendiaries, occasionally delinquent though some of them may have been, there could have been no first performance of Handel's *Messiah* in Dublin.

'RAGE AND RANCOUR AGAINST PERSONS AND PROCEEDINGS'

Not long after Swift had returned to Dublin to take up his post in 1714, he had made his deanery the most vibrant centre of literary discussion in the city. Friends and visitors were constantly coming through his door, certain of a convivial and stimulating gathering. By the time Handel arrived in Dublin, however, those days were long gone. Swift's birthday was still celebrated enthusiastically every November and any time he stepped out of his deanery he was greeted warmly and respectfully. But with fast failing health and succumbing to melancholia and misanthropy, he had become a lonely and isolated figure.

Back in 1720, when he was fifty-three, Swift was already recognising early indications of dementia. One evening that year Edward Young, secretary to the Lord Lieutenant, had 'found him fixed as a statue, and earnestly gazing upward at a noble elm, which in its uppermost branches was much withered and decayed'. Pointing at it, Swift said, 'I shall be like that tree, I shall die at the top'.[13] In addition, from an early age Swift had suffered vertigo and nausea, and tinnitus like 'the noise of seven watermills in my ears', which eventually made him partially deaf.[14]

On 28 January 1728 Swift was brought news of the death of Stella, Hester Johnson, 'the truest, most virtuous and valuable friend that I, or perhaps any other person, ever was blessed with'.[15] He was so heartbroken that he took time off to travel by horseback to the south and the west. In *A Proposal for the Universal Use of Irish Manufacture* he had referred disparagingly to:

> our Country Landlords; who, by unmeasurable *screwing* and *racking* their Tenants all over the Kingdom, have already reduced the miserable *People* to a worse *Condition* than the *Peasants* in *France*, or the *Vassals* in *Germany* and *Poland*.

That was written in 1720. Now he returned to Dublin appalled by the miserable condition of so many of the wretched inhabitants he had seen deep in the Irish countryside. In 1729 he launched a savage attack on the landlords. It was entitled *A Modest Proposal for Preventing the Children of Ireland, from Being a Burden to their Parents or Country; and for Making them Beneficial to the Publick*. Since he believed that the landlords treated their domestic stock better than the poor people who worked for them, he set out to shock his readers with terrible irony; he suggested that the peasantry should raise their babies to be served for dinner at the tables of the rich.

> I have been assured by a very knowing American of my Acquaintance in *London*; that a young healthy Child, well nursed, is at a Year old, a most delicious, nourishing, and wholesome Food; whether *Stewed, Roasted, Baked* or *Boiled*; and I make no doubt that it will serve in a *Fricassée* or a *Ragoût*. I do therefore humbly offer it to *publick Consideration*, that of the Hundred and Twenty Thousand Children, already computed, Twenty thousand may be reserved for Breed…the remaining Hundred thousand may, at a Year old, be offered in Sale to Persons of Quality and *Fortune*, through the Kingdom, always advising the Mother to let them suck plentifully in the last Month, so as to render them plump, and fat for a good Table…
> I grant this Food will be somewhat dear, and therefore very *proper for Landlords*, who, as they have already devoured most of the Parents, seem to have the best Title to the Children … It will have one other Collateral Advantage, by lessening the Number of *Papists* among us.

As to our City of Dublin; Shambles may be appointed for this Purpose ... and Butchers may be assured will not be wanting; although I rather recommend buying the Children alive, and dressing them hot from the Knife, as we do *roasting Pigs*.[16]

Swift's *Modest Proposal* is almost certainly the most ferocious and uncomfortable pamphlet ever to have been written in the English language. When it was published, *A Modest Proposal* had nothing like the impact of his earlier *Drapier's Letters*. Undoubtedly many of those who read it did not know what to make of it. Some may have concluded that the great Dean was becoming unhinged. One way of looking at *A Modest Proposal* is that it is an indicator of Swift's growing misanthropy and deepening despair. Death had deprived the Dean of many of his closest friends and now he was losing the remainder by his increasing irascibility. In 1734 Swift – aware that he was unlikely to write anything important again – had authorised George Faulkner to publish his collected works in four handsome volumes. Mrs Pendarves was an early subscriber. Dr Patrick Delany, his dinner companion for many years, in his enthusiasm bought no fewer than *nine* sets. Then for some unexplained reason, Swift fell out with him and they never saw each other again. Delany held no grudge and remained fiercely loyal to his old friend. When Lord Orrery published the first biography of Swift with many caustic observations on the Dean's behaviour, Delany rushed into print in defence of his deceased companion. Dr Thomas Sheridan had been Swift's closest male friend in Dublin for very many years, and had been at Stella's bedside as she died. But just as Swift's health was failing and he was finding himself in financial difficulties, Sheridan found inexplicably that he was no longer welcome at the deanery.

By 1736 Swift was very ill. 'My giddiness is more or less constant', he informed Pope, 'I have not an ounce of flesh between skin and bone ... I can as easily write a poem in the Chinese language as my own'. Two years later he told Lord Orrery: 'I have been many months the shadow of the shadow of the shadow, of etc. etc. etc. of Dr. Swift – age, giddiness, deafness, loss of memory, rage and rancour against persons and proceedings'. He longed for death. When parting from a friend he was given to saying, 'Well, God bless you; good night to you, but I hope I shall never see you again'.[17]

By 1742 Swift was severely incapacitated – but he was still Dean of St Patrick's cathedral.

FINDING CHORISTERS

The first public concert given by Handel in Dublin was incorrectly described in the press as an 'Oratorio'. It was not until 3 February 1742 that audiences in the city were given an opportunity to hear one of the composer's oratorios; this was *Esther* 'with Additions', which probably meant a truncated version, performed in the Fishamble Street Music Hall. One reason why Handel had not yet given *Messiah* its first performance was that he needed to be sure that he had a full complement of musicians and singers before presenting it. Matthew Dubourg, Master of the State Music, saw to it that from the very first public concert accomplished instrumentalists were put at his disposal. Ensuring an adequate choir proved to be more difficult. At one stage it looked as if it might be impossible.

Handel needed the choirs of both Christ Church and St Patrick's cathedrals. For this he had to seek and obtain permission from the deans and chapters. For its charitable concerts Mercer's Hospital generally had the assistance of the amateur instrumentalists of the Musical Academy in Crow Street; in 1741 it had changed its name to the Philharmonick Society, and, like the Charitable Musical Society, it had new premises in Fishamble Street. On occasion the hospital governors also got permission to use the cathedral choirs. Minutes of meetings in January 1742 indicate that there was a problem: the Dean and Chapter of Christ Church had approved the use of its choristers for this charity but would St Patrick's follow suit?

Extracts from the minutes of meetings of the Governors of Mercer's Hospital

At a meeting of Governors, Jan 4, 1742. Present – John Rochfort, Esq., in the chair; Richd. Balwin, Esq., John Putland, Esq., Rev. Dean Owen, Dr. Hutchinson, Archdn. Congreve, Mr. Stone, Mr. Daunt, Dr. Anderson.

Ordered – That John Rochfort, John Putland, and Richd. Baldwin Esqs., be desired to apply in the name of the Governors of Mercer's Hospital, to the Revd. The Dean of St. Patrick's, Dublin, for their leave that such of the choir as shall be willing may assist at the Philharmonick Society Performances, which are principally intended for the benefit of the sd. Hospital. And to notifie to them that the Dean and Chapter of Christ Church have been pleased to grant them the same request.

Jan 23, 1742...The Dean and Chapter of St. Patrick's are ready to concur with the Dean and Chapter of Christ Church, in permitting the Choir to assist at the Musical Performance of the Philharmonick Society, - if the Dean and Chapter of Christ Church will concure with them in permitting the Choir to assist at Mr. Handel's. They think that every argument in favour of the one, may be urged with equal strength at least in favour of the other. Particularly that which with them is of the greatest weight, the advantage of Mercer's Hospital. Mr Handel having offer'd, and being still ready, in return for such a favour, to give the Governors some of his choicest Musick, and to direct and assist at the performance of it for the benefit of the hospital, which will in one night raise a considerable sum for their use, without lessening the annual Contribution of the Philharmonic Society, or any of their other funds; and in order to prevent this permission to be brought into a precedent, which some time or other may be of evil consequence, the Dean and Chapter of St Patricks will concur with the Dean and Chapter of Christ Church, in any proper rule to hinder their voices or other members of the Choir from performing at any public musical performance excepting in Churches, without the joint permission of both Deans and Chapters first had and obtained.

At a meeting of Governors, March 4, 1742. Present:- John Putland, Esq.; Mr. Baldwin, Dean Owen, Dean Hutchinson, Dean Maturine.

Whereas Mr. Putland reported from a Committee appointed to consider of a Performance designed for the benefit of this Hospital, the Infirmary, and the Prisoners of the Marshalseas, That it was the desire of the Gentlemen of that Committee, that a Deputation from the Trustees for those several Charities should Attend the Deans and Chapters of Christ Church and St. Patrick, to desire their leave that the Choir of both Cathedrals may assist at the said Performance.

Ordered – That the Trustees of this Hospital do concur with the Committee provide that the whole Benefit of the said Performance, and of all Rehearsals previous to it, shall be entirely applied to the Support of the said Charities, and that Tickets be given out for whatever Rehearsals shall be necessary, at such prices as shall be thought most Convenient by the Trustees of said Charities.

Mercer's Hospital was not only the most important charity in Dublin but it was also the most prestigious in the whole island of Ireland. Funds were raised principally by holding charity concerts. The first had been in the 'Round Church' of St Andrew's in Suffolk Street on 8 April 1736, also the first occasion on which Handel's music had been performed in Dublin – as reported in *Pue's Occurrences*, 'a grand Te Deum, Jubilate, and an Anthem composed by the famous Mr Handel'. The then Lord Lieutenant, the Duke of Dorset, had attended what was to become an annual event in that church.

The governors of Mercer's Hospital met on 4 January 1742 to consider musical events to raise funds over the coming year. The most important would be the performance Handel had agreed to give in Fishamble Street Music Hall for the benefit of three charities: Mercer's Hospital, the Charitable Infirmary and the Charitable Musical Society for the Release of Imprisoned Debtors. A date for that event had yet to be fixed. More immediately the Mercer's Hospital Governors were concerned to finalise the Philharmonick Society performances regularly put on specifically to raise money for the hospital. For these the governors need the cathedral choirs of both Christ Church and St Patrick's. The Dean and Chapter of Christ Church had readily agreed to make their choristers available. It was by no means certain, however, that permission would be granted by St Patrick's. Swift continued to preside over meetings of his Chapter, though, due to his infirmity, these were now held in the deanery rather than the chapterhouse. The hospital governors decided to send a delegation to talk to the Dean of St Patrick's in person. The chairman, John Rochford, with fellow governors John Putland and Richard Baldwin, went to call on Swift to seek 'leave that such of the choir as shall be willing may assist at the Philharmonick Society Performances, which are principally intended for the benefit of the sd. Hospital'.[18]

There is no account of this meeting but it is evident that the delegation did not get the kind of approval it was seeking. It must be remembered that the Dean's decision could not be overruled – as he had said himself in 1721, 'not one thing here is done without the Dean's consent'.[19] The Governors met again on 23 January. They had before them a long reply from the Dean and Chapter of St Patrick's. No doubt the committee had to spend time attempting to interpret the meaning of the letter's convoluted and tortuous prose, duly transcribed into the minutes. The letter was almost certainly not written by Swift but by a member of his Chapter given the unwelcome task of committing his ruling to paper. The response from St Patrick's did begin in a positive tone:

> The Dean and Chapter of St. Patrick's are ready to concur with
> the Dean and Chapter of Christ Church, in permitting the Choir
> to assist at the Musical Performance of the Philharmonick Society,
> - if the Dean and Chapter of Christ Church will concure with
> them in permitting the Choir to assist at Mr. Handel's.

Further down the letter, however, the blow fell: St Patrick's would *not* allow its choristers to sing 'at any public musical performance excepting in Churches' in aid of these charitable causes, very worthy though they might be. This restriction was 'in order to prevent this permission to be brought into a precedent, which some time or other may be of evil consequence'.[20] The Dean and Chapter of St Patrick's hoped that their counterparts in Christ Church would also approve of this restriction.

It might be thought that Mercer's Hospital and the composer himself could manage somehow with the vocalists from just one cathedral. However, permission obtained from Christ Church but not from St Patrick's created an insuperable problem: the majority of the vicars choral were employed by *both* cathedrals. A licence granted by the dean of one cathedral only would therefore be practically useless. The governors therefore rejected the suggestion made by the Dean and Chapter of St Patrick's. In any case the invitation to Handel to come to Dublin had originated – and very possibly actually delivered in person by the Duke of Devonshire – with the Charitable Musical Society, which had a magnificent new music hall in Fishamble Street capable of holding an audience large enough to yield a generous sum to be shared by the three charities. And what would Swift's response have been had he known that the librettist, Charles Jennens, described *Messiah* as a 'fine Entertainment'?

Handel was so busy at this time that he does not seem to have entered into correspondence of any kind since he had written his long letter to Jennens on 29 December 1741, the one describing how warmly he had been received in Dublin. The composer, unfailingly cheerful, always looking on the bright side, must nevertheless have been a worried man. He could not contemplate giving his new oratorio its première without the cathedral choirs. And then, after that, he had his anxieties about Susannah Cibber being struck down by a fever causing her appearance on stage to be either repeatedly postponed or cancelled.

Any hope that Swift would change his mind was dashed by an intemperate order to the Sub-Dean and Chapter of St Patrick's that he issued on 28 January:

> I do hereby require and request the Very Reverend Sub-Dean, not to permit any of the Vicar Chorals, choristers, or organists, to attende or assist at any public musical performances, without my consent, or his consent, with the consent of the Chapter first obtained.
> And whereas it hath been reported that I gave a licence to certain vicars to assist at a club of fiddlers in Fishamble Street, I do hereby declare that I remember no such licence to have been ever signed or sealed by me; and that if ever such pretended licence should be produced, I do hereby annul and vacate the said licence; intreating my said Sub-Dean and Chapter to punish such vicars as shall ever appear there, as songsters, fiddlers, pipers, trumpeters, drummers, drum-majors, or in any sonal quality, according to the flagitious aggravations of their respective disobedience, rebellion, perfidy and ingratitude.
> I require my said Sub-Dean to the proceed to the extremity of expulsion, if said vicars should be found ungovernable, impenitent, or self-sufficient, especially Taverner, Phipps, and Church, who, as I am informed, have, in violation of my Sub-Dean's and Chapter's order in December last, at the instance of some obscure persons unknown, presumed to sing and fiddle at the club above mentioned.[21]

John Phipps and John Church were vicars choral of both cathedrals, and the Rev. William Taverner of St Patrick's only.

Actually, Swift had forgotten that he had granted permission *just the day before*. The Mercer's Hospital minutes record that, on 27 January, the Governors had received a communication from the Dean of St Patrick's granting his permission to six of the vicars-choral and to two of the choristers, to assist at the weekly performances of the Philharmonick Society, 'upon account of their being chiefly intended for the benefit of this Hospital'.[22] Swift's furious missive must have been decisive: the church authorities concluded that the time had come to remove their famous Dean from his position as 'absolute lord' of St Patrick's.

Exactly how Swift had been persuaded, on 27 January, to agree to allow his vicars choral and boy choristers to sing outside the walls of a cathedral or a church is not documented. For some years his duties as Dean had been almost entirely taken over by Dr John Wynne, the Sub-Dean, who also just happened to be both a governor of Mercer's Hospital and a member of the Charitable Musical Society for the Release of Imprisoned Debtors. The role of Dr Charles Cobbe, the Dean of Christ Church with an official residence in Fishamble Street, was also crucial. He would become Archbishop of Dublin the following year, in 1743. Cobbe, too, was a governor of the hospital, and so the Dean of one cathedral and the Sub-Dean of the other sat around the same table and devised ways of either persuading Swift to alter his original unworkable decision or to how best to get round him.

Had Swift been able to enforce his ruling on 28 January 1742, *Messiah* could not have been performed in Dublin. It must not be forgotten, however, that had the not the Dean in earlier times striven tenaciously to raise the quality of the singing of sacred music in his cathedral, the choristers of St Patrick's might not have reached the standard Handel required to ensure that they be asked to take part in his new oratorio.

Chapter 10
'A Species of Musick Different From Any Other': The First Performance of *Messiah*

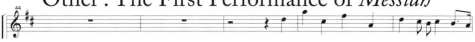

'THE FINEST COMPOSITION OF MUSICK THAT WAS EVER HEARD'
It was actually Susannah Cibber who caused Handel to alter the date set for the rehearsal of *Messiah*. It clashed with a performance she was due to give in Aungier Street theatre on 8 April – she had no choice but to do so 'at the Desire of several Persons of Distinction' since her recent illness had kept her off the stage for so long she was in arrears to the management.[1] During the last week of March *Faulkner's Dublin Journal* carried this advertisement:

> For relief of the Prisoners in the several Gaols, and for the Support of Mercer's Hospital in Stephen's Green, and of the Charitable Infirmary on the Inns Quay, on Monday 12th April, will be performed at the Musick Hall in Fishamble Street, *Mr. Handel's new Grand Oratorio, call'd the* MESSIAH, in which the Gentlemen of the Choirs of both Cathedrals will assist, with some Concertoes on the Organ by Mr. Handell. Tickets to be had at the Musick Hall, and at Mr. Neal's in Christ-Church-Yard, at half a Guinea each. N.B. No Person will be admitted to the Rehearsal without a Rehearsal Ticket, which will be given gratis with the Ticket for the Performance when pay'd for.

The same advertisement (regarded by many as the most famous music advertisement of all time) was repeated in the *Dublin News-Letter*, except that it described *Messiah* as a 'New Grand Sacred Oratorio' and added that 'Books are also to be had at a British Sixpence each'.

When he was in Dublin Handel returned to his *Messiah* score to make a few adjustments. Perhaps to avoid any loss of momentum, he edited down sections he thought too long, particularly at points where he wanted to maximise the emotional impact. Other changes, however, were clearly made to suit the musicians and singers immediately available to him in the Fishamble Street Music Hall. To underscore the dramatic effect of 'Thus saith the Lord, the Lord of Hosts' he shortened the opening from three bars of instrumental introduction to an accompanied recitative with a single bar of introduction. He altered and shortened 'Rejoice greatly, O daughter of Zion'. To suit Susannah Cibber's voice he transposed the recitative 'Then shall the eyes of the blind be open'd' and its air 'He shall feed His flock like a shepherd' from the soprano to the alto voice; and also for her he transposed 'If God be for us' from G minor into C minor. He shortened 'Why do the nations' to heighten tension and reduced the alto solo 'O death, where is they sting' by almost half.[2]

According to the records of the Bishop's Visitations of 1743, there were sixteen boy choristers from the two cathedrals, those from St Patrick's identified as William Cooley, William Williams, George Magee, Samuel Murphy, George Betts and John Marsh. But it is by no means certain that any choirboys from either cathedral sang in the first performance or, indeed, in the second. It is possible that, instead, the top line was sung by female sopranos.[3] The names of all but one of the sixteen adult male singers have been recorded: Rev. William Taverner, John Phipps, James Bayley, John Church, John Mason, Rev. John Eusebius Smyth, Rev. John Worrall, Rev. William Jones, William Lambe, Robert Hall, Ralph Roseingrave, Robert Woffington, Joseph Ward, John Griffith and John Hill. A 'Mr. Carter' and a 'Mr. Colgan' or 'Calloghan' have also been included in some lists. The names of the alto, tenor and bass soloists are all present in the lists of the vicars choral. The usual number of soloists in modern performances of *Messiah* is four; and Handel generally engaged five (two being sopranos) in his London performances. Musicologists reckon that on 13 April 1742 in the Fishamble Street Musick Hall that there were no fewer than *eight* soloists and there may have been nine. Five of them were members of both the choirs of St Patrick's and Christ Church: William Lambe and Joseph Ward, altos or countertenors; James Bayley (or Baileys), tenor; and John Hill and John Mason, basses. Hill sang just one number as a solo, 'Why do the nations so furiously rage together?' It seems very unlikely that Handel would not have engaged John Church also as a tenor soloist – when Handel wrote to Jennens in December 1791 he explained that 'I have form'd another Tenor Voice which gives great Satisfaction', he was probably referring to Church.[4] Along with Susannah Cibber, alto, there were two other female soloists, the sopranos Signora Christina Maria Avolio and Mrs Maclaine.

Lack of documentation prevents absolute certainty about the names and numbers of participants. Musicologists are dependent on Handel's autograph score, on John Christopher Smith's fair copy, which is what the composer used to conduct from in Dublin. There is, in addition, an annotated copy of the word-book (whether it is from the first or second performance is not clear), in which an unknown member of the audience attempted to write singers' names alongside some of the items, but this contains at least one definite mistake: Susannah Cibber did not sing the chorus 'Behold the Lamb of God' at the start of Part Two.[5]

On 30 June 1922, as the Irish Civil War got under way, Commandant Ernie O'Malley ordered his men, besieged in the Four Courts, to pour paraffin on documents and set them alight. The outcome was the total destruction of the public records stored there; more than likely the loss included information about players and their instruments Handel had available to him for *Messiah*'s première. We know that Matthew Dubourg led the orchestra which was largely made up of the state band of which he was master. There seems to have been no harp or lute and only one trumpet. In short, not only was the complement of vocalists a great deal smaller than in virtually all modern performances but also the orchestra was much more limited in size and range.[6]

Choral societies today would be startled to learn that there was *only one* full rehearsal. That took place at 11 a.m. on 9 April. The Music Hall was packed. Judging by the press reports, the reception was rapturous. *Faulkner's Dublin Journal* gave this opinion:

> Yesterday, Mr. Handel's new Grand Sacred Oratorio, called The MESSIAH, was rehearsed at the Musick Hall in Fishamble-street, to a Most Grand, Polite, and Crowded Audience; and was performed so well, that it gave universal

Satisfaction to all present; and was allowed by the greatest Judges, to be the finest Composition of Musick that ever was heard, and the sacred Words as properly adapted for the occasion.

The view of the *Dublin News-Letter* was little different: the new sacred oratorio 'in the opinion of the best Judges, far surpasses anything of that Nature, which has been performed in this or any other Kingdom. This elegant Entertainment was conducted in the most regular Manner, and to the entire satisfaction of the most crowded and polite Assembly'. It added that for 'the benefit of three very important Charities, there will be a grand Performance of this Oratorio on Tuesday next' – the date had been changed to 13 April at 'the desire of several persons of Distinction, Monday being Cathedral Day'. *Faulkner's Dublin Journal* added this request:

Many Ladies and Gentlemen who are well-wishers to this Noble and Grand Charity, for which this Oratorio was composed, request it as a Favour, that the Ladies who honour this Performance with their Presence, would be pleased to come without Hoops, as it will greatly increase the Charity, by making Room for more company.

The *Dublin News-Letter* also informed readers that the 'Stewards of the Charitable Musical Society' not only made this request of the ladies but also added: 'The Gentlemen are desired to come without their swords'.[7]

The fullest press account of the reception given to the première of this sacred oratorio is in *Faulkner's Dublin Journal*, the reporter demonstrating that he was able to draw from an even deeper well of hyperbole than in his report of the rehearsal:

On Tuesday last, Mr. Handel's Sacred Grand Oratorio, the MESSIAH, was performed in the New Musick Hall in Fishamble-street; the best Judges allowed it to be the most finished piece of Musick. Words are wanting to express the exquisite Delight it afforded to the admiring crowded Audience. The Sublime, the Grand, and the Tender, adapted to the most elevated, majestic and moving Words, conspired to transport and charm the ravished Heart and Ear. It is but Justice to Mr. Handel that the World should know he generously gave the Money arising from this Grand Performance, to be equally shared by the Society for relieving Prisoners, the Charitable Infirmary, and Mercer's Hospital, for which they will ever gratefully remember his Name: and that the Gentlemen of the two Choirs, Mr. Dubourg, Mrs. Avolio, and Mrs. Cibber, who all performed their Parts to Admiration, acted on the same disinterested Principle, satisfied with the deserved Applause of the Publick, and the conscious Pleasure of promoting such useful and extensive Charity. There were above 700 People in the Room, and the Sum collected for that Noble and Pious Charity, amounted to about £400, out of which £127 goes to each of the three great and pious charities.

Laurence Whyte, the mathematics teacher who was a member of the Charitable Musical Society, promptly penned a long poem to celebrate the première. It was published in the *Dublin Journal* a week after *Messiah*'s first performance:

> What can we offer more in Handel's praise?
> Since his Messiah gain'd him groves of bays;
> Groves that can never wither nor decay,
> Whose Vistos his Ability display:
> Here Nature smiles, when grac'd with Handel's art,
> Transports the ear, and ravishes the heart;
> To all the nobler Passions we are mov'd
> When various strains repeated and improv'd,
> Express each different Circumstance and State,
> As if each sound became articulate.
> None, but the great Messiah could inflame,
> And raise his Soul to so Sublime a Theme,
> Profound the Thoughts, the subject all divine,
> Not like the tales of Pindus and the Nine:
> Or Heathen Deities, those Sons of Fiction,
> Sprung from old Fables, stuff'd with contradiction;
> But our Messiah, blessed be his name!
> Both Heaven and Earth his Miracles proclaim.

His birth, his Pasion, and his Resurrection,
With his ascension have a strong connection;
What Prophets spoke, or Sybils could relate,
In him were all their Prophecies compleat.
The Word made Flesh, both God and Man became;
Then let all nations glorify his name!
Let Halleluiahs round the Globe be sung,
To our Messiah, from a virgin sprung.[8]

'THE HARMONY IS SO GREAT AND OPEN, AS TO PLEASE ALL WHO HAVE EARS'

Press reports apart, only one account by a member of the audience survives. This is a letter to Handel, written immediately after the performance, by Dr Edward Synge, who had been appointed Bishop of Elphin in 1740. Since the Protestant population in this western diocese was distinctly sparse, Synge's duties were not particularly onerous, thus giving him ample time to pursue his literary and musical interests. Like most members of the Church of Ireland hierarchy, he liked to spend the winter months in Dublin. In any case, Synge was obliged to be in the capital during the parliamentary sittings of 1741-1742 since his presence in the Irish House of Lords was required; and, after the Lord Lieutenant had returned to England, the bishop evidently stayed on in the city long enough to be present at the first performance of *Messiah*.

Very soon afterwards Synge wrote to Handel, offering him a libretto for an oratorio intended as a sequel to *Messiah* to be called *The Penitent*. Along with his letter to the composer, the bishop included his own eyewitness account of the first performance of *Messiah*, a testimonial, written in the form of a review. It is full of perspicacious observation:

As Mr. Handel in his oratorio's greatly excells all other
Composers I am acquainted with, So in the famous one, called
The Messiah he seems to have excell'd himself. The whole is
beyond any thing I had a notion of till I Read and heard it.
It Seems to be a Species of Musick different from any other,
and this is particularly of it. That tho' the Composition is very
Masterly & artificial, yet the harmony is so great and open, as

to please all who have Ears & will hear, learned and unlearn'd. without doubt this Superior Excellence is owing in some measure to the great care & exactness which Mr Handel seems to have us'd in preparing this Piece. But Some reasons may be given why He has Succeeded better in this than perhaps He could with all his skill, fully exerted, have done in any other.
1 one is the Subject, which is the greatest & most interesting. It Seems to have inspir'd him.
2 Another is the Words, which are all Sublime, or affecting in the greatest degree.

The word 'interesting' had a much stronger, a more positive meaning in the eighteenth century than it does today. Synge's testimonial describes how the audience responded, warmly, respectfully, and on occasion rather too enthusiastically, to this new sacred oratorio. He continued:

3 a Third reason for the Superior Excellence of this piece, 'Tis this there is no Dialogue. In every Drame there must be a great deal & often broken into very Short Speeches & Answers. If these be flat, & insipid, they move laughter or Contempt.
Whereas in this Piece the attention of the Audience is Engag'd from one end to the other: and the Parts Set in Recitativo, being Continu'd Sentences, & Some times adorn'd with too much applause, by the audience as the rest.-
They Seem'd indeed thoroughly engag'd from one end to the other. And, to their great honour, tho' the young & gay of both Sexes were present in great numbers, their behaviour was uniformly grave & decent, which Show'd that they were not only pleas'd but affected with the performance. Many, I hope, were instructed by it, and had proper Sentiments inspir'd in a Stronger Manner on their Minds.

Handel sent Synge's testimonial on to Jennens with this annotation: 'I send you this Sr only to show how zealous they are in Ireland for Oratorio's. I could send you a number of Instances more from others in Print and in writing'. This was included in the first letter he wrote to Jennens after he had come back to London. Dated 9

September, it began with an apology for not calling on him on his return journey:

> It was indeed Your humble Servant which intended You a visit in my way from Ireland to London, for I certainly could have given You a better account by word of mouth, as by writing, how well Your Messiah was received in that Country, yet as a Noble Lord, and no less then the Bishop of Elphim (a Nobleman very learned in Musick) has given his Observation in writing of this Oratorio, I send you here annexed the Contents of it in his own words.

Handel added: 'As for my success in general in that generous and polite Nation, I reserve the account of it till I have the Honour to see you in London'.[9]

Journalists a century later would not only have provided readers with a list of the most distinguished members of audiences attending notable musical and theatrical events but also in addition would have described what many of the ladies were wearing. Regrettably, no record survives of those who had paid half a guinea each to be in the Fishamble Street Music Hall on 13 April 1742. It is known that Dr Patrick Delany, rector of St Werburgh's Parish Church, once a member of Swift's literary circle and subsequently appointed Dean of Down, was in the audience. As the chancellor both of St Patrick's and Christ Church, no doubt Delany felt it was his duty to hear the cathedral choristers perform – indeed, it is more than likely that he had used his considerable influence to see that Swift's prohibition on their participation had been overruled. His wife, Margaret, had died only a few months before and he was still in first mourning. Stone masons had just arrived at the cemetery to raise the inscribed gravestone over her remains. That very day, 13 April, *Faulkner's Dublin Journal* contained a long paid insertion providing the words he proposed to have inscribed on this tombstone which Delany hoped would not be 'unacceptable to the Publick, as it may be a useful lesson to the Living'. It included the words: 'A truly virtuous, and valuable Woman ... Giving no Offence, and remitting Injuries of every kind. *Not overcome of Evil, but overcoming Evil with Good*'.[10] Delany's attendance was an act of piety: he did not think it appropriate for a clergyman to be in a theatre or concert hall for a 'profane' performance, especially during Passion Week. But *Messiah* after all was a sacred oratorio and the librettist, Charles Jennens, had always intended this work to be performed at such a solemn time. Clearly Dr Delany was aware of Susannah Cibber's colourful past. He had come to the Musick Hall with Swift's twenty-three-year-old godson, Thomas Sheridan, who would later make his career as a theatre manager. A passionate admirer of Susannah Cibber, Sheridan would have kept Delany fully informed of her colourful past. According to an account based on Sheridan's memory of that day, Delany was so deeply moved as Susannah Cibber sang the oratorio's most tragic air, 'He was despised' that – no doubt full of compassion for this frail, lost sinner – he could not remain silent:

> Mrs. Cibber, in *The Messiah*, in Dublin, executed her airs so pathetically, that Dr. Delany, the great friend and companion of Swift, exclaimed, as he sat in the boxes, 'Woman, for this, be all thy sins forgiven'.[11]

'A PANE OF GLASS WILL BE REMOVED FROM THE TOP OF EACH OF THE WINDOWS'

Handel did not perform to the public again for some weeks, but a fortnight after the first performance of *Messiah* more of his work was being presented to Dublin audiences. There were 12 items in 'Mr. Charles's Grand Concert' in the Fishamble Street Music Hall on 12 May, which included: 'Mr. Handel's Water Musick with the March in *Scipio* and the Grand Chorus in *Atalanta*' and 'The Overture in *Saul* with the Dead March compos'd by Mr. Handel but never performed here before'. Mr Charles was Hungarian and at his concert gave a solo on the French Horn 'to show the Beauty of that Instrument' and another on the 'Hautbois de Amour'. Meanwhile, Susannah Cibber was kept busy at Aungier Street Theatre, starring there as Polly in *The Beggar's Opera* on 10 May.

The warm reception given to *Messiah* encouraged Handel to present his oratorio, *Saul*, to his admiring Dublin public. First performed in the King's Theatre, Haymarket, in January 1739, this oratorio with its great range of contrasting airs and its opulent orchestration would have stretched vocalists and instrumentalists to an even greater extent than

Messiah. Those who had paid half a guinea for a ticket were entitled to attend the rehearsal. *Faulkner's Dublin Journal* reported:

> Yesterday there was a Rehearsal of the Oratorio of Saul, at the Musick Hall in Fishamble-street, at which there was a most grand polite and numerous Audience, which gave such universal Satisfaction, that it was agreed by all the Judges present to have been the finest Performance that hath been heard in this Kingdom.

In the same issue, word-books could be purchased at the Music Hall, 'Price a British Sixpence'. *Saul* was performed at seven o'clock on Tuesday, 25 May. Though it was clearly well received, no detailed account has survived.

Demand, meanwhile, was mounting for a repetition of the performance of *Messiah*. On Saturday, 29 May this notice appeared in *Faulkner's Dublin Journal*:

> At the Particular Desire of several of the Nobility and Gentry. On Thursday next, being the 3d day of June, at the new Musick Hall in Fishamble-street, will be performed Mr. Handel's new Grand Sacred Oratorio, called MESSIAH, with Concertos on the Organ. Tickets will be delivered at Mr. Handel's house in Abbey-street, and at Mr. Neal's in Christ-church-yard, at Half a guinea each. A Rehearsal will be given with the ticket for the Performance. The Rehearsal will be on Tuesday the 1st of June, at Twelve, and the Performance at Seven in the Evening. In order to keep the Room as cool as possible, a Pane of Glass will be removed from the top of each of the Windows.
> N.B. This will be the last Performance of Mr. Handel's during his stay in this Kingdom.[12]

'OH! A GERMAN, AND A GENIUS! A PRODIGY! ADMIT HIM.'
Susannah Cibber had a benefit concert at Aungier Street on 31 May. Christina Avolio, the soprano, who would be engaged by Handel in London on many future occasions, was scheduled to have her own benefit concert on 16 June. This was advertised in the *Dublin Journal* as 'a Concert of Vocal and Instrumental Musick, at the Musick-Hall in

Fishamble-street'. Tickets were 'a British Crown each', and the notice of this benefit for Signora Avolio ended:

> N.B. As she is a Stranger in this Kingdom, she most humbly hopes, that our Nobility and Gentry, who are so remarkable for their Humanity and Generosity to Strangers, will be pleased to countenance her at this Affair.

This 'affair' had to be postponed because of the 'Players arrival from England, who perform that Evening'. This certainly was a star-studded cast, which included: Peg Woffington, David Garrick, the dancer Signora Barbarini and Theophilus Cibber. Woffington, who had entranced London audiences and was now returning to her native city. Garrick was arguably the most famous English actor of the eighteenth century. Cibber's arrival in Dublin, no doubt alarmed his estranged wife, Susannah.

Susannah Cibber did not flee Dublin, however. On 30 June, her brother, Thomas Arne, arrived in the city with his wife, Cecilia. A 'Grand ENTERTAINMENT of MUSICK' was put on in the 'Great Room' in Fishamble Street Music Hall on 21 July for the benefit of Mrs Arne. Several 'favourite Songs and Duetto's will be performed by Mrs. ARNE and Mrs. CIBBER … O beauteous Queen, from Mr. Handel's Oratorio of Esther by Mrs. Cibber … And a Duetto of Mr. Handel's in Saul, by Mrs. Arne and Mrs. Cibber … Un Guardo solo, from Mr. Handel's Opera of Hymen, by Mrs. Cibber'. Originally intended for Aungier Street theatre, this entertainment was in such demand that it was transferred 'at the Request of Several Gentlemen and Ladies to the Great Room above mentioned'. This concert was so successful that it was repeated a week later. Thomas and Cecilia Arne returned to London, but they were back in Dublin before the end of the year and they spent almost the next two years in that city.[13]

When he first arrived in Dublin, Handel had planned no more than a charity concert in the Fishamble Street Musick Hall and a six-performance subscription series. By the end of his visit he had given two six-concert subscriptions and three further performances. Indeed, he found the company of his patrons and admirers so appealing that he stayed on in Ireland for another two months after his last performance on 3 June 1742.[14] It is more than likely that 'the quality' vied with one another to have the composer as a guest. A certain Dr Quin, a medical practitioner in Dublin at the time, later told Charles Burney that 'Handel was received in Ireland by people of the first distinction with all possible marks of esteem'. He added that the composer was a guest of the Vernons, owners of an estate on the north side of Dublin Bay at Clontarf:

> There were many noble families here with whom Mr. Handel lived in the utmost degree of friendship and familiarity. Mrs. Vernon, a German lady, who came over with King George I., was particularly intimate with him; and at her house I had the pleasure of seeing and conversing with Mr. Handel; who, with his other excellencies, was possessed of a great stock of humour: no man ever told a story with more. But it was requisite for the hearer to have a competent knowledge of at least four or five languages; English, French, Italian, and German; for in his narratives, he made use of them all.[15]

On one occasion Dr Quin had to give Handel emergency treatment, as Redmond Simpson, Matthew Dubourg's son-in-law, later explained:

> When Handel was in Dublin, he was attacked by another Paraletic stroke, while he was at dinner with my father Dubourg. It was violent and universal. It happened luckily, that Doctors Barry & Quin, and Mr. Nichols, Surgeon General, were present: all extremely fond of Music, consequently adorers of Handel, by violent bleedings & other evacuations, & by the immediate assistance he received he was soon perfectly recovered, & never had any return to it, tho' very apprehensive.[16]

Handel was preparing to return to London. Before departing he decided to call on Jonathan Swift. Letitia Pilkington recorded in her *Memoirs*:

> I was told the last sensible Words he uttered, were on this Occasion … The Servant was a considerable Time, e'er he

could make the Dean understand him; which, when he did, he cry'd, 'Oh! A *German*, and a Genius! A Prodigy! admit him.' The Servant did so, just to let Mr. Handel behold the Ruins of the greatest Wit that ever lived along the Tide of Time, where all at length are lost.[17]

On 13 August 1742, *Faulkner's Dublin Journal* informed its readers, 'the celebrated Mr. Handel, so famous for his excellent Compositions and fine Performance with which he entertained this Town in the most agreeable Manner, embarked for England'. The *Dublin News-Letter* added that he 'embarked on board one of the Chester Traders, in order to go to Parkgate'.[18] In the letter he wrote to Jennens on 9 September, when back in his house in Brook Street, the composer declared his intention to return:

> Whether I shall do some thing in the Oratorio way (as several of my friends desire) I can not determine as yet. Certain it is that this time 12 month I shall continue my Oratorio's in Ireland, where they are going to make a large Subscription already for that Purpose.[19]

Handel, however, never returned to Ireland. The nine months he spent there had greatly improved his financial position. At the same time, the first performance of *Messiah* had raised what was then a substantial sum to be divided equally between the three charities. The Charitable Musical Society, responsible for inviting Handel to Dublin in the first place, had its profile raised so impressively after the première of *Messiah* that it was able to hold a succession of fund-raising musical events for the remainder of the year and beyond. The society met on Wednesday, 22 September 'to settle Musick for the ensuing Winter'. Performances to raise funds were held every week, usually in the Fishamble Street Music Hall, but also in the Crow Street Theatre. At its first concert of the season, on 8 October, Mrs Arne sang 'though extremely ill of a cold, with universal Applause'. On 22 October Cecilia Arne was unable to perform at all, as the *Dublin Journal* reported:

Mrs. Arne's absence from the Charitable and Musical Society occasioned by her illness the two last nights of their Musical Meetings, have given great disappointment to a great Number of Lady's and Gentlemen, who attended there in the Expectations of hearing her Sing. We hear she will certainly perform there next Friday night, her Health being something restor'd.

By the close of 1742 the Charitable Musical Society had secured the release from prison of 143 debtors at a cost of £1,225, reported in *Faulkner's Dublin Journal*:

From the Charitable Musical Society. The said Society think themselves obliged to give the Publick an account, that in the year 1742, they released out of the several Marshalseas in and about this City, 142 Prisoners, whose principal Debts and Fees amounted to the sum of £1225 17s. 1d. besides £33 given in Charity to poor creditors and out-going Prisoners.[20]

Chapter 11
London's Initial Verdict: 'What a *Profanation* of *God*'s Name and Word is This?'

'THE ORATORIOS ... GIVE ME AN IDEA OF HEAVEN'

Soon after he had returned to London in August 1742, Handel was offered the very large sum of a thousand pounds if he would write two new operas. This threw the composer into a state of indecision for weeks. In the end, he rejected the offer and spent the rest of the year putting finishing touches to his oratorio, *Samson*. In fact, Handel would never write another opera. 'Certain it is that this time 12 month I shall continue my Oratorio's in Ireland', he had predicted in a letter to Jennens. Actually Handel would never return to Ireland; but the following year he did make a gift of his *Messiah* score to the Charitable Musical Society and also to Mercer's Hospital, which were generous bequests of great recurring value to the city of Dublin. In any case, Handel's visit to Ireland had left him in no doubt that his future lay with oratorio.

Samson had its première at Covent Garden on 18 February 1743. It was warmly received. 'Handel has set up an Oratorio against the Operas, and succeeds', Horace Walpole reported. 'The Oratorios thrive abundantly – ', he observed a few days later, 'for my part, they give me an idea of heaven, where everybody is to sing whether they have voices or not'.[1] *Faulkner's Dublin Journal* reprinted a private letter from London, dated 8 March:

> The new Oratorio (called Samson) which he composed since he left Ireland, has been performed four Times to more crowded Audiences than ever were seen; more people being turned away for want of Room, each Night, than hath been at the Italian Opera. Mr. Dubourg, (lately arrived from Dublin) performed at the last, and met with uncommon applause from the Royal Family and the whole Audience.[2]

But would *Messiah* be as warmly received in the capital? *Samson's* libretto had been drawn from John Milton's *Samson Agonistes*, not from Scripture. It soon emerged that London society was not certain that it liked sacred oratorios staged in theatres which for decades had echoed to arias sung in Italian by Italian castrati and divas.

Christina Avolio had followed Handel to London to be one of his soloists. Then followed 'six Entertainments more' beginning with *L'Allegro ed il Penseroso*. It was only as the season was drawing to a close at the end of March 1743 that the composer felt that the time had come to present *Messiah* to a London audience. Meanwhile, his librettist, Charles Jennens, was doing nothing to boost Handel's confidence in the music he had composed for this sacred oratorio.

'HIS MESSIAH HAS DISAPPOINTED ME'

For months Handel had to endure the protracted and often acrid criticism of the very man who had written *Messiah's* libretto. Jennens may not have forgiven him for taking the oratorio to Dublin rather than giving it its première in London. And Jennens does seem to have been put out by the composer's failure to call in on him at Gopsall on his journey back from Ireland. Then Jennens was furious to discover that, on his return to London, Handel had put on *L'Allegro ed il Penseroso*, composed to Milton's verse, but without *il Moderato*, the final section set to words he had proudly written himself.[3]

It was perhaps just as well that, in his correspondence, Jennens mostly expressed his annoyance and frustration to Edward Holdsworth rather than to Handel himself. He thanked Holdsworth, who was abroad collecting music for him, for the box of scores he had just received and then accused Handel of plagiarism:

Handel has borrow'd a dozen of the pieces & I dare say I shall catch him stealing from them ... His Messiah has disappointed me, being set in great hast, tho' he said he would be a year about it, & make it the best of all his Compositions, I shall put no more Sacred Words into his hands, to be thus abus'd.

Holdsworth, meanwhile, had been getting uncomplimentary reports on *Messiah* from those who had been reading the score prior to the oratorio being given its first performance in the capital. This was evident in his reply:

> I am sorry to hear yr. friend Handel is such a jew. His negligence, to say no worse, has been a great disappointment to others as well as yr.self, for I hear there was great expectation of his composition, I hope the words, tho murther'd are still to be seen, and yt I shall have that pleasure when I return. And as I don't understand the musick I shall be better off than the rest of the world.[4]

Jennens responded almost immediately: 'As to the Messiah, 'tis still in his power by retouching the weak parts to make it fit for a publick performance; & I have said a great deal to him on the Subject; but he is so lazy and so obstinate, that I much doubt the Effect'.

When Jennens got hold of a copy of the word-book printed for the first performance of *Messiah* in Dublin his mood blackened further. It was 'printed in Ireland, full of Bulls' – 'bulls' being typographical errors – '& if he does not print a correct one here, I shall do it my Self, & perhaps tell him a piece of my mind by way of Preface. I am a little out of humour, as you may perceive, and want to vent my Spleen for ease'. 'What adds to my chagrin is', he continued, 'that if he makes his Oratorio ever so perfect, there is a clamour about Town, said to arise from the Brs, against performing it'.[5] The 'Brothers' were John and Charles Wesley who had opened two new chapels in London that year. Methodists certainly praised the Lord with 'swift singing' but it was then wholly without instrumental accompaniment; in any case, John Wesley was adamant in his condemnation of the playhouse as a source of sinful corruption.

Handel could afford to shrug off Wesleyan hostility. Much more worrying was powerful opposition from many of those who for years had been loyally attending performances of his compositions.

'I ASK IF THE *PLAYHOUSE* IS A FIT *TEMPLE* TO PERFORM IT IN OR A COMPANY OF *PLAYERS* FIT *MINISTERS* OF *GOD'S WORD*'

Handel arranged to have the London première of *Messiah* on 23 March 1743. The advertisement published in the *Daily Advertiser* four days beforehand was distinctly circumspect:

> A NEW SACRED ORATORIO. With a Concerto on the Organ. And a Solo on the Violin by Mr. Dubourg.

Why did Handel not give his new sacred oratorio its title? The reason was that, shortly after he had announced his intention to stage *Messiah* at Covent Garden, an eloquent denunciation had appeared in the *Universal Spectator*. In a long letter, this correspondent, signing himself 'Philalethes', explained that his purpose was 'to consider, and, if possible, induce others to consider, the Impropriety of Oratorios, as they are now perform'd'. He made it clear that he was nevertheless 'a profess'd Lover of Musick, and in particular of Mr. Handel's Performances, being one of the few who never deserted him. I am also a great Admirer of Church Musick'. Having made that proviso, he launched into a sustained assault:

> An *Oratorio* is either an *Act* of *Religion*, or it is not; if it is, I ask if the *Playhouse* is a fit *Temple* to perform it in or a Company of *Players* fit *Ministers* of *God's Word*, for in that Case such they are made ...
> In the other Case, if it is not perform'd as an Act of *Religion*, but for Diversion and *Amusement* only (and I believe few or none go to an *Oratorio* out of *Devotion*), what a *Profanation* of *God's* Name and Word is this, to make so light Use of them? I wish every one would consider whether, at the same Time they are diverting themselves, they are not accessory to the breaking of the *Third Commandment*. I am sure it is not following the Advice of the *Psalmist, serve the Lord with Fear, and rejoice unto him with Reverence.*

The 'most *sacred Name of God*' was due to be sung 'by a set of People *very unfit to perform* so *solemn* a service. *David* said, *How can we sing the Lord's Song in a strange Land*; but sure he would have thought it much stranger to have it heard it sung in a *Playhouse*'. 'Philalethes' continued:

> But it seems the *Old Testament* is not to be profan'd alone, nor *God* by the *Name* of *Jehovah* only, but the *New* must be join'd with it, and *God* by the most *sacred* and *merciful Name* of *Messiah*; for I'm inform'd that an Oratorio call'd by that Name has already been perform'd in *Ireland*, and is soon to be perform'd here: What the Piece itself is, I know not.

Handel did have his defenders. A poem appeared on 31 March:

> Wrote extempore by a Gentleman on reading the Universal Spectator:
>
> > Cease, Zealots, cease to blame these Heav'nly Lays,
> > For Seraphs fit to sing Messiah's Praise!
> > Nor, for your trivial Argument, assign,
> > 'The Theatre not fit for Praise Divine.'
> >
> > These hallow'd Lays to Musick give new Grace,
> > To Virtue Awe, and sanctify the Place;
> > To Harmony, like his, Celestial Pow'r is giv'n,
> > T'exalt the Soul from Earth, and make, of Hell, a Heav'n.[6]

Messiah had three performances: 23, 25 and 29 March 1743. Lord Shaftesbury, noting that *Samson* was 'received with uncommon Applause', found that *Messiah* was greeted coldly.[7]

'YOU HAVE CONTRIBUTED, BY YR. OWN CONFESSION, TO GIVING POOR HANDEL A FEVER'

Jennens was present at the first performance of *Messiah* in London. While he grudgingly admitted that it was 'a fine Composition', he was still full of bile:

> Messiah was perform'd last night, & will be again to morrow, not withstanding the clamour rais'd against it, which has only occasion'd it's being advertis'd without its Name; a Farce which gives me as much offence as any thing relating to the

performance can give the Brs & other squeamish People. 'Tis after all, in the main, a fine Composition, notwithstanding some weak parts, which he was too idle & too obstinate to retouch, tho' I us'd great importunity to perswade him to it. He & his Toad-eater Smith did all they could to murder the Words in print; but I hope I have restor'd them to Life, not without difficulty.

John Christopher Smith was the composer's long-standing and self-effacing business manager, who arranged the copying of scores and the printing of word-books.

'Handel has had a palsy, and can't compose', Horace Walpole reported. Discovering this himself, Jennens softened his tone: 'I hear Handel has had a return of his Paralytick Disorder, which affects his Head & Speech. He talks of spending a year abroad, so that we are to expect no Musick next year; & since the Town has lost it's only Charm, I'll stay in the Country as long as ever I can'.[8]

Handel recovered quickly and this encouraged Jennens to return to the charge. 'I don't yet despair of making him retouch the Messiah, at least he shall suffer for his negligence'. He admitted that he had contributed to making the composer ill – 'nay I am inform'd that he has suffr'd for he told Ld. Guernsey that a letter I wrote him about it contributed to the bringing of his last illness upon him … I gall'd him: but I have not done with him yet'.[9]

Holdsworth at last tired of these vitriolic attacks. Jennens, he was sure, had been spending too much time on his own in Leicestershire: 'it has had an ill effect upon you, and made you quarrel with your best friends, Virgil and Handel'. He continued: 'You have contributed, by yr. own confession, to give poor Handel a fever; and now He is pretty well recover'd, you seem resolv'd to attack him again … This is really ungenerous, & not like Mr. Jennens. Pray be merciful; and don't you turn Samson, & use him like a Philistine.'[10]

'HANDEL HAS HAD WORSE SUCCESS THAN EVER HE HAD BEFORE'
'I have been long persuaded that perfect friendship is nowhere to be found but in marriage', the widower Rev. Dr Patrick Delany wrote to the widow Mary Pendarves on 23 April 1743, proposing to her. He could offer her 'a good clear income … a good many books, a pleasant garden (better I believe than when you saw it) etc. Would to God

I might have leave to lay them all at your feet'.[11] Mrs Pendarves was eager to accept, but she had to face strong family disapproval. After the passage of 10 days Delany was becoming desperate: 'Permit me, madam to beg to know my fate'.[12] Mary did have the warm support of her sister Anne; on 3 June she offered Dr Delany 'sisterly affection and esteem … as you *make her happy*', and offered 'ardent prayers and wishes for your mutual happiness'.[13] But her brother Bernard remained vigorously opposed to the match. Mary decided to go ahead without his consent; in consequence the couple's marriage ceremony on 9 June 1743 was a very private one. Henceforth, in almost all her correspondence Mrs Delany referred to her husband affectionately as 'D.D.' – initials which became particularly appropriate the following year when he was appointed Dean of Down. Part of the Delanys' honeymoon was spent in London, but Mrs Delany was to be deeply disappointed that she did not have the opportunity to attend a performance of *Messiah*.

'Now boys, now for the honour of England, fire and behave bravely, and the French will soon run!' George II was leading the infantry in person at Dettingen near Frankfurt. It was 16 June 1743. Actually it took 12 hours for them to run, but the French indeed were beaten. This was the last time a British monarch was to be present on a battlefield. Naturally a *Te Deum* had to be composed in celebration and, of course, Handel was the man to compose it. Mary and Patrick Delany were in the Chapel Royal on 27 November to hear it. She found the *Te Deum* 'excessively fine, I was all rapture and so was your friend D.D. … it is heavenly'. Handel had ambitious plans for the following year, 1744. Mary Delany was at the première of his latest oratorio, *Semele*, on 11 February and found it 'a delightful piece of music … But being a profane story D.D. does not think it proper for him to go'. In short, Dr Delany's approach was *exactly* the reverse of that of Philalethes – as a man in holy orders he would only go to the theatre if the subject *was* a religious one. As for Jennens, he judged it 'No Oratorio, but a baudy Opera'.[14]

The 1744 oratorio season could be judged a reasonable success. In addition to *Semele*, it included *Joseph and his Brethren*, *Saul* and *Samson*. But there was one very obvious omission. 'Last night alas! was the last night of oratorio', Mrs Delany wrote; 'it was concluded with Saul: I was in hopes of the Messiah'. But at least Handel did accept her invitation to visit. 'Today I shall have a treat … Handel, my brother and Donnellan *dine here*, and we are to be entertained with *Handel's playing over Joseph to us*'.[15] But when would Handel be able to perform *Messiah* again? First, he needed to restore better relations with Jennens. On 9 June 1744 the composer wrote Jennens a warm letter, asking him if he would like to write the libretto for a new oratorio, *Belshazzar*. Jennens agreed, but only on condition that modifications would be made to *Messiah*. In correspondence Handel felt obliged to add: 'Be pleased to point out these passages in the Messiah which you think require altering'.[16] When he got the libretto for *Belshazzar*, Handel to his dismay found that it was far too wordy. It was with great difficulty that he cajoled Jennens to agree to cuts and alterations. Unsurprisingly, this provoked yet another sour response, evident in a letter to Holdsworth: he disliked having 'to oblige the Man who made me but a Scurvy return for former obligations … if he does not mend his manners I am resolv'd to have no more to do with him'.[17]

Handel's energy was undiminished. He planned a season of no fewer than 24 performances on subscription. But he still faced the vicious opposition of anti-Handelists. And it was by no means certain that, as yet, London audiences had decided that sacred oratorios performed in theatres were to their liking. *Deborah* opened on 3 November but the audiences were too thin. Handel was forced to suspend his performances until 5 January 1745. Susannah Cibber had meanwhile plucked up the courage to return to the London stage, her estranged husband, Theophilus, having dropped his opposition to her reappearance there. After a short spell in Covent Garden, she moved to Drury Lane, there to play alongside David Garrick. Handel was happy to engage her. Unfortunately, she was indisposed for the first performance of *Hercules* and, though she sang a week later, the house was almost empty. Handel felt he had no choice but to abandon his series. He wrote a long letter of apology, published in the *Daily Advertiser*. 'I have the Mortification now to find, that my Labours to please are become ineffectual, when my Expences are considerably greater. To what Cause I must impute the loss of publick Favour I am ignorant, but the Loss itself I shall always lament.'[18]

'Handel has had worse success than ever he had before', Jennens wrote, 'being forc'd to desist after performing but 6 of the 24 Entertainments he had contracted for, & to advertise that the Subscribers might have 3 4ths of their money returned. Most of them refus'd to take back their Money, upon which he resolv'd to begin again in Lent'.[19] Handel put on 10 performances during Lent, including *Messiah* on 9 and 11 April – still advertised as A *Sacred Oratorio* or *The Sacred Oratorio*.

At Jennens's behest, Handel had made some changes to *Messiah*. Jennens wrote to a friend:

> I shall show you a collection I gave Handel call'd Messiah which I value highly, & he has made a fine Entertainment of it, tho' not near so good as he might & ought to have done. I have with great difficulty made him correct some of the grossest faults in the composition, but he retain'd his Overture obstinately, in which there are some passages far unworthy of Handel but much more unworthy of the Messiah.[20]

When he read a copy of this letter many years later, Horatio Townsend, in his account of Handel's visit to Dublin, expressed his gratitude that Jennens had not succeeded in persuading the composer to cut out 'Sinfony', the overture which opens *Messiah*:

> Few will deem the majestic movement which commences the overture, with its grand succession of chords that come rolling on, one after the other, like great billows of the ocean, unimpressive or beneath the dignity of the subject.[21]

Parts of *Messiah* Handel agreed to alter for Jennens with new settings included 'How beautiful are the feet', 'Why do the nations' and 'Their sound is gone out', and, in addition, he reordered the rhythm of 'Rejoice greatly'.[22] Whether or not Susannah Cibber found enough space in her busy schedule to sing in *Messiah* is not known.

Just how the 1745 performances were received is not recorded. An anonymous poem, *Ode to Mr. Handel*, appeared in May 1745 that concludes:

The God who conquers Death,
When, bursting from the Grave,

Mighty he mounts, and wing'd with rapid winds,
Thr' Heav'ns wide portals opening to their Lord
To boundless realms return'd,
The King of Glory reigns.

Powr's, dominations, thrones resound HE REIGNS,
High Hallelujah's of empyreal hosts,
And pealing Praises join
The thunder of the spheres.[23]

It seems, however, that this poet was expressing a minority view. There is no evidence that London audiences were particularly impressed by these two performances of *Messiah*. It is clear that in England this sacred oratorio was regarded for the present as, at best, just another of Handel's minor compositions. Another three years would pass before Handel had the heart to place *Messiah* before the critical eyes and ears of fashionable society in the capital.

Meanwhile, on the other side of the Irish Sea, since Handel's departure, *Messiah* was being given regular performances to enraptured listeners.

'HIS WONDERFUL MESSIAH WILL NEVER BE OUT OF MY HEAD ... MY HEART WAS RAISED ALMOST TO HEAVEN BY IT'

For uninterrupted years after Handel had returned to England, the appetite of Dublin audiences for his music could hardly be sated. Though Thomas Arne found it very profitable to stay in the city, being rewarded with packed audiences, the concert schedules were dominated by Handel's works. During the years 1749-1750, for instance, the only choral or sacred-dramatic works not by Handel given in Dublin were single performances of Giovanni Pergolesi's *Stabat Mater* and a funeral anthem by Giovanni Bononcini. Handel's masque, *Acis and Galatea*, was performed no fewer than seven times that season. In addition, Dublin society was always eager to hear his latest oratorios and anthems, even if some of them were tepidly received in London.[24]

The Charitable Musical Society scheduled *Messiah* for 15 December 1743, but it was trouble with the choir and not lack of audience interest that led to a postponement. Choir members had objected to John Church assuming 'an Authority at all Publick Performances, which he is not entitled unto'. This had caused 'several vexatious Disputes to the prejudice of Musick, and to the great detriment of all publick Charities'. In their insertion in the *Dublin Journal*, the nine 'undernamed Performers do declare that we will not for the Future, engage or perform in any Society or Concert, where the said John Church is any way concerned'. The Charitable Musical Society felt obliged to place a long insertion in *Faulkner's Dublin Journal.* – a notice which confirms that the society had obtained from 'the celebrated Mr. Handell, a copy of the Score of the Grand Musical Entertainment, called the MESSIAH'. It had been 'intended to have it rehearsed on the 12th, and performed on the 16th of December, Inst. for the Benefit and Enlargement of Prisoners confined for Debt pursuant to their advertisements'. 'In order to have it executed in the best Manner', the notice continued, the society had 'prevailed on Mr. Dubourg to give them his Assistance' and got permission to obtain the services of 'members of the Choirs of the two Cathedrals to assist therein'. However,

> after Preparations had been made, at considerable Expence, to the Surprise of the Society, several of the Members of the said Choirs, (some of whom had engaged as before mentioned) thought fit to decline performing, and returned their Parts, for Reason that no way related to or concerned the said Society.

As a result the society was 'obliged to postpone that Entertainment until Friday 3rd day of February next, to the great Detriment and Delay of their Charitable Intentions'. By that date 'the Society will provide such Performers as will do justice to that Sublime Composition'.[25]

Somehow, the dispute was eventually resolved. Then there were other difficulties. It seemed that several ladies coming to the Fishamble Street Musick Hall insisted on wearing hoops in their dresses. Some did at a private rehearsal in the middle of January 'in the Presence of some of the best Judges', necessitating a hopeful insertion in the press that, as at the public rehearsal ' the audience will be very numerous, we hear the Ladies have resolved to come without Hoops, as when the same was performed by Mr. Handel'. Not all the ladies so resolved, prompting another almost desperate appeal in the press:

> From the Charitable Musical Society for the Relief of poor Prisoners.
> The Society beg leave respectfully to address themselves to the Ladies, and to appeal to such of them as were at the publick Rehearsal last Wednesday, for the necessity of this their Request, that had the Ladies laid aside their Hoops, the Musick Hall would contain a hundred Persons more with full ease … they humbly hope the Ladies will not take amiss to be requested to lay aside a *Mode*, (for one evening) however Ornamental on other Occasions.

At least that rehearsal had given 'great satisfaction', the 'most celebrated Band of Vocal and Instrumental Musick' being greeted 'with universal applause'. In any case, 'nothing can come up to the choice of the subject, the Words are those of the sacred Text'.[26]

But once more *Messiah* had to be rescheduled. The performance had been due on 3 February, but that day was set at short notice for the trial of Lord Nicholas Netterville in the Irish House of Lords. Viscount Netterville was charged with murder of a man in Co. Meath. Interest was intense because Lord Santry, a member of the Hellfire Club, had been capitally convicted in 1740 on charge of killing a tavern porter by drunkenly running him through with his sword – only at the last moment had George II given him a royal pardon. The Netterville trial in the Irish House of Lords proved an anti-climax: the two principal witnesses had died and the law of evidence did not permit their depositions to be read. Netterville's peers had no hesitation in giving their verdict: 'Not Guilty'. *Messiah* was eventually performed on 7 February 1744. Another performance, this time to raise funds for the Charitable Infirmary, followed on 27 February.

In spite of *Messiah* being twice postponed, the Charitable Musical Society had been able to announce in January 1744 – that is before the two February performances – that in the previous year 'they released out of the several Marshalseas in and about this City, 142 Prisoners, whose principal Debts and Fees amounted to the sum of £1225 17s. 1d. besides £33 given in Charity to poor creditors and out-going Prisoners'.[27]

Messiah was given its first performance in a church when it was put on in St Fin Barre's Cathedral in Cork on 6 December 1744. Matthew Dubourg conducted *Messiah* in the Fishamble Street Musick Hall for the second time that year on 14 December. This was for the benefit of prisoners 'confined for debt in the several Marshalseas'. In short, in just one year, between 7 February and 14 December 1744, Ireland had hosted four performances of *Messiah*.

A striking feature of musical entertainment in Dublin at this time is that so much of it was arranged for the benefit of charities. This fact goes a long way towards explaining why *Messiah* succeeded immediately in Ireland and was close to being a failure in London. In Dublin from the outset the sacred oratorio was associated with moral improvement and charitable giving. This was emphasised by John Mainwaring, Handel's first biographer:

> The first step that he made, was to perform his *Messiah* for the benefit of the city-prison. Such a design drew together not only all the lovers of music, but all the friends of humanity. There was a particular propriety in this design from the subject of the oratorio itself.[28]

Distinguishing one charitable musical organisation from another is not easy, especially given the propensity for some of them to change their names especially when they moved their organising committees from one tavern to another. In addition to the Charitable Musical Society for the Relief of Debtors (but advertised as the 'Charitable Society for the Relief of poor Prisoners' in 1744) there were: the Philharmonick Society, which had its music room almost facing the Musick Hall in Fishamble Street; the Charitable Musical Society at the Bear, College Green; the Charitable Musical Society in Vicar's Street; the Charitable Musical Society in Crow Street; the Charitable Musical Society for the support of Incurables; and a new one was soon to be formed in the Tailors' Hall in Back Lane. There was an extremely close relationship between Dublin hospitals, the church authorities and these musical societies. The city's hospitals could not have survived without funds raised in benefit concerts. In addition, the participation of the two cathedral choirs for concerts of any consequence was greatly helped, as we have seen, by the fact that the Sub-Dean of St Patrick's and the Dean of Christ Church both helped to run Mercer's Hospital, one as a governor and the other as a trustee. Virtually every Irish performance of Handel's masques and oratorios, starting with *Acis and Galatea* on 17 December 1742, was for the benefit of a public or private charity. For example, the oratorio *Deborah* (incidentally, not staged, not even once, in London in those years) had seven performances in Dublin between 1745 and 1753, and four of these were to raise funds specifically for the Charitable Infirmary on Inns Quay. All five Dublin performances of *Judas Maccabeus* between 1748 and 1752 were in aid of charities. *Joshua* was performed in 1751 and 1752, both of them for the benefit of the Hospital for Incurables.[29]

Dublin audiences, unlike those in London, had no experience of *opera seria* (literally 'serious opera'), that is, Italian operas on heroic or tragic subjects, for long the main musical diet of the upper classes in London.[30] The success or otherwise of operas in the English capital depended almost entirely on the aristocracy and the gentry. In Dublin there were no opera houses and no titled promoters, and Handel's public performances, including *Messiah*, were all given in purpose-built concert halls. On his return from Ireland, Handel had directed his oratorios at the King's Theatre in the Haymarket, and then in Covent Garden, where his operas had been staged for so long. Performances of *Messiah* were given in London in 1743, 1745, 1749 and 1750, 'but on each occasion', the musicologist Harry White observes, 'the work alienated rather than sublimated its audience'. Because in Ireland the composer's sacred oratorios were not staged in opera houses, White continues, the 'Dublin performances were thus contextually isolated from the puritanical suspicions and associations which dogged Handel's biblical dramatizations in in England'.[31]

In any case, the composition of audiences not only in the Fishamble Street Musick Hall but also in the Aungier Street and Smock Alley theatres, was rather different from that in London. Those who filled the seats and boxes in the Haymarket and Covent Garden theatres were overwhelmingly members of the gentry and aristocracy. In Dublin the 'quality' sat alongside merchants, shopkeepers, university fellows, clergy and lawyers of all ranks, and included at least one school teacher, Laurence Whyte, who celebrated in verse Handel's presence in the city. Admittedly, the admission ticket price of half a guinea to *Messiah* did ensure the absence of artisans and labourers.

The first time Mary Delany got to hear *Messiah* was at a rehearsal at noon on 16 December 1745 in the Fishamble Street Musick Hall. She wrote:

> Last Monday the Dean and I went to the rehearsal of the Messiah for the relief of poor debtors; it was very well performed, and I much delighted. You know how much I delight in music, and that piece is very charming; but I had not courage to go to the performance at night, the weather was so excessively bad, and I thought it would hazardous to come out of so great crowd so far, that is my kind guardian thought so for me.

Indeed the weather was so bad that the public performance – as always in the Fishamble Street Musick Hall – had to be postponed to 19 December, and Mrs Delany was able to be there after all. 'Though *voices* and *hands* were wanting to do it justice', she had no hesitation letting her brother know that it 'gave me great pleasure 'tis heavenly'. Thereafter she had many more opportunities to attend performances of the sacred oratorio and, as a letter to her brother Bernard Granville made clear, she became a passionate admirer of the work:

> I hope you find Mr. Handel well. I beg my compliments to him: he has not a more real admirer of his great work than myself; his wonderful Messiah will never be out of my head; and I may say my heart was raised almost to heaven by it… If anything can give us an idea of the last day it must be that part 'The trumpet shall sound, the dead shall be raised'. It is few people I can say so much to as this, for they would call me an enthusiast; but when I wish to raise my thoughts above this world and all its trifling concerns, I look over what oratorios I have, and even my

poor way of fumbling gives me pleasing recollections, but I have nothing of the Messiah, but 'He was despised'.[32]

That letter was written in December 1750. Only by then – eight years after its first performance in Dublin – was *Messiah*, at last, being fully appreciated on the other side of the Irish Sea.

Chapter 12
Messiah Secured for Posterity

'THE MESSIAH ... WAS BUT INDIFFERENTLY RELISH'D'
'Handel, once so crowded, plays to empty walls in that opera house, where there used to be a constant *audience* as long as there were any dancers to be *seen*'. This was the melancholy observation of Elizabeth Carter, one of the composer's most loyal admirers, in a letter to a friend on 2 April 1745. She had just returned from the première of *Belshazzar* in the Haymarket theatre. 'Unfashionable that I am', she continued, 'I was I own highly delighted', but there were few others who agreed with her.[1] It did seem that London's élite had not been won over to sacred oratorio.

This failure seems to have affected Handel's health and the composer retreated to the country to recover. Then, that summer, news reached Handel that Charles Edward Stuart, the 'Young Pretender', long after remembered as 'Bonnie Prince Charlie', was on the march to seize back the Crown for the Stuart line. Having come ashore at Eriskay in July, this grandson of James II had taken Edinburgh, then Manchester and by early December 1745 had reached Derby. That was as far south as the Jacobites got; thereafter they were forced to retreat. Handel was galvanised into writing a string of patriotic oratorios – *The Occasional Oratorio*, *Joshua*, *Alexander Balus* and *Judas Maccabaeus* – the last one, in effect, to mark the Duke of Cumberland's triumph at Culloden in April 1746, the very bloody end of the Jacobite rebellion in the Highlands.

Three years later the conclusion of the War of the Austrian Succession was celebrated by an outdoor performance in Vauxhall of *Musick for the Royal Fireworks*, specially composed by Handel for the occasion. Only a very few of the enormous crowd heard a single note played by the hundred-strong orchestra, due to a violent thunderstorm and to attention being dramatically diverted to flames and explosions as an entire pavilion stuffed with fireworks accidentally burned down.

And what of *Messiah*? It did get staged as the very last of 12 oratorios in Handel's 1749 Lenten season: even though the sacred oratorio was given its proper title for the first time in England, it was received with no special warmth. The Earl of Shaftesbury later attempted an explanation:

> [Handel] afterwards performed The Messiah but partly from the scruples, some Persons had entertained, against carrying on such a Performance in a Play House, and partly for not entering into the genius of the Composition, this Capital Composition, was but indifferently relish'd.[2]

Then the whole future of *Messiah* was altered, secured forever, however unintentionally, by the benevolence of an old sea dog.

Messiah at the Foundling Hospital: a pivotal moment

Thomas Coram, after spending his early life sailing the north Atlantic and then building ships in Massachusetts, returned to become a successful merchant in London. There he was appalled by the sight of abandoned, homeless children in the streets of the capital, many of these discarded, hapless creatures found dying in alleys and on the pavements. After 17 years of dogged campaigning, Coram got George II in 1739 to grant a royal charter to establish a 'hospital for the reception, maintenance and education of exposed and deserted young children'.[3] Building began in 1742 on a site in Lamb's Conduit Fields in Bloomsbury and by 1745 the Foundling Hospital was finished.

John Walsh, one of Handel's publishers, contributed £50 to the charity in 1748. Almost certainly it was he who persuaded the composer to become involved. Handel attended a special meeting at the hospital on 4 May 1749 and there 'generously and charitably offered a performance of vocal and instrumental musick to be held at this Hospital'.[4] The Prince and Princess and their children, and a 'prodigious concourse of the Nobility and Gentry' attended the concert on 27 May which, in addition to an anthem specially composed for the occasion, included the Royal Fireworks Music, the Dettingen Anthem and, just one piece from *Messiah*, the 'Hallelujah' chorus.

Handel, soon to be one of the charity's governors, at his own expense contracted Jonathan Morse of Barnet to build an organ for the Foundling Hospital. The composer agreed to give a special recital on the instrument on 1 May 1750, but the organ was not quite ready. Instead, Handel decided to present his *Messiah*. As at Fishamble Street Musick Hall eight years before, members of the audience, who had paid half a guinea for each ticket, were requested not to wear hoops or swords. Dublin had been far better organised, however: a shortage of stewards led to traffic chaos and far more patrons had been sold tickets than could possibly be accommodated in the chapel. A second performance was hastily arranged for 15 May.

This was a pivotal moment, the turning-point in *Messiah*'s fortunes. These two Foundling Hospital performances transformed the standing of this sacred oratorio in the eyes of the English public. As it had been in Ireland from the outset, *Messiah* was now associated inextricably with good works, moral improvement and religious devotion. The oratorio was now being staged more frequently at Covent Garden, indicating a melting away of opposition to staging scriptural works in a playhouse. Performances of *Messiah* at the Foundling Hospital and for its benefit became an annual event without interruption from 1750 to 1777. Handel's donation of the oratorio's score to the hospital in 1754 did result in an awkward stand-off: the Treasurer reported to the governors that he understood that it was the composer's wish 'that it should be perform'd nowhere else' but in the Foundling Hospital. The governing body actually resolved to apply for an Act of Parliament to secure the benefaction 'to the sole use & benefit of this Hospital'.[5] Of course this had not been Handel's intention. According to Burney, he burst out:

> Te teufel! for what sall de Foundlings put mein oratorio in de Parliament? Te teufel! mein moosic sall not go to de Parliament!

With some difficulty the composer persuaded the governors to back down. In any case, Handel had given the score, gratis, to the Charitable Musical Society and Mercer's Hospital in Dublin years before. As well as the fact that with Handel's approval Niccolò

Pasquali, having moved from Ireland to Scotland, had taken most of the oratorio's choral pieces to the rooms of the Edinburgh Musical Society.[6]

14 APRIL 1759: 'AT 8 O'CLOCK IN THE MORN DIED THE GREAT AND GOOD MR. HANDEL'

'How dark, O lord, are thy decrees, all hid from mortal sight!': Handel was midway through writing music for this chorus in his oratorio *Jephtha* when he broke off to write in German, 'reached here on 13 Febr. 1751 unable to continue owing to a relaxation of the sight of my left eye'.[7] 'Noble Handel hath lost an eye', Sir Edward Turner wrote a month later; 'but I have the Rapture to say that St. Cecilia makes no complaint of any Defect in his Fingers'.[8] Nevertheless, it took him until August to finish the work, at the end of which he added his age: *aetatis* 66.[9] 'Poor Handel!', Mary Delany wrote on 25 November 1752 (in a reference to Milton's words 'Total eclipse! no sun, no moon!' in his oratorio *Samson*) 'how feelingly must he recollect the "total eclipse": I hear he has now been couched'.[10] The composer had, ill-advisedly, subjected himself to an operation on his right eye, which involved the surgeon piercing the cornea with a thorn. As a result, Handel became completely blind and his composing days were over.

The annual performance of *Messiah* in the Foundling Hospital became a highlight in London's social calendar. Not only had Handel periodically made some adjustments to the score but he had increased the number and the range of instruments in the orchestra to well beyond what had been available to him in Dublin. Mustered for the annual Foundling Hospital performance on 15 May 1754, for example, were: fifteen violins; five violas; three cellos; two double basses; four bassoons; four oboes; two trumpets; two horns; and drums. On that occasion, as was usual then, there were two sopranos, Giuilia Frasi and Christina Passerini, making up a total of five soloists. By this stage John Christopher Smith junior, son of Handel's manager, had taken over responsibility for making all the necessary arrangements. Handel's servant, Peter Le Blond, was also much involved, being given a guinea for his help which included paying the organ blowers four shillings. Mrs Delany was in London for the Foundling Hospital *Messiah* the following year; she thought the music '*too fine*, I never heard it so well performed'.[11] In December 1756 she was in London again and called on her friend Anne Donnellan. 'I promised Don. to call on her and meet Mr. Handel, which I did; he was not in spirits any more than myself, but his playing is *always* delightful'.[12] In fact, the composer had become seriously ill.

On 6 April 1759 the *Whitehall Evening Post* reported that 'this Day Mr. Handel proposed setting out for Bath, to try the Benefit of the Waters, having been for some Time past in a bad State of Health'. He was unable to go. That evening, after attending the last of three performances of *Messiah* at Covent Garden, the 74-year-old composer took to his bed. There he added a final codicil to his will which included a bequest to Matthew Dubourg, £1,000 to the Society for the Support of Decay'd Musicians and £600 for a monument, should his request that he be buried in Westminster Abbey be accepted. According to Charles Burney:

> He had most seriously and devoutly wished, for several days before his death, that he might breathe his last on Good-Friday, 'in hopes', he said, 'of meeting his Good God, his sweet Lord and Saviour, on the day of his resurrection'.

Handel survived until Easter Saturday morning, 14 April 1759. James Smyth wrote to Mary Delany's brother, Bernard Granville, on 17 April:

> According to your request to me when you left London, that I would let you know when our good friend departed this life, *on Saturday last at 8 o'clock in the morn died the great and good Mr. Handel.* He was sensible to the last moment … I had the pleasure to reconcile him to his old friends; he saw them and forgave them, and let all their legacies stand! In the codicil he left many legacies to his friends, and among the rest he left me £5000, and has left you the two pictures *you formerly gave him* … He died as he lived – a good *Christian*, with a true sense of his duty to God and man, and in perfect charity with all the world.

Charles Burney, though he noticed that Handel had become 'studious and sedentary' in his later years, was at pains to remind his readers that the composer, 'with his other excellencies, was possessed of a great stock of humour; no man ever told a story with more'.[13] Handel did not get the private funeral he had requested: at least 3,000 were present when he was buried in Westminster Abbey on 24 April.

Three days earlier '*An Attempt towards an* EPITAPH' had appeared in the *Universal Chronicle*. This anonymous correspondent's words were not those that were to appear on Louis François Roubiliac's fine memorial. Nevertheless, they state elegantly and succinctly how Handel was remembered by his contemporaries and ever since then by lovers of his music:

> Beneath this Place
> Are reposited the Remains of
> GEORGE FREDERICK HANDEL
> The most excellent Musician
> Any Age ever produced:
> Whose Compositions were a
> Sentimental Language
> Rather than mere Sounds;
> And surpassed the Power of Words
> In expressing the various Passions
> Of the Human Heart.

Roubiliac's monument, unveiled in 1762, depicts Handel with the open score of 'I know that my Redeemer liveth'.

By 1759 *Messiah* had already become the most cherished of all of Handel's compositions. 'And from this time to the present,' Burney wrote in 1785, 'this great work has been heard in all parts of the kingdom with increasing reverence and delight; it has fed the hungry, clothed the naked, fostered the orphan, and enriched succeeding managers of the Oratorios, more than any single production in this or any country'.[14]

Without Charles Jennens there would have been no *Messiah*. This lonely and rather odd English gentleman of leisure had the imagination and determination to devise a new way to reach out to those who believed neither in divine intervention nor in biblical revelation. His strikingly original idea was to put together a 'Scripture Collection' for a musical entertainment to be performed, not in a church, but in a theatre. Jennens was convinced that only Handel possessed the incomparable genius to compose music to his word-book so powerful, so moving, so sublime that sceptics would be so moved by the emotional dynamism and beauty of the oratorio that they could be enticed back from their irreligious, unbelieving ways. In turn Jennens had already convinced the composer that he had the literary prowess and sympathetic understanding of his music to be sure that the *Messiah* libretto – unasked for though it was – would be given serious consideration.

The role of the city of Dublin in bringing this sacred oratorio to life is pivotal. After a couple of decades of dazzling success, Handel had the humiliation to find that London audiences were tiring of his Italian operas. And, at the same time, they were not yet certain that static performances of the composer's oratorios on stage were to their taste. An invitation from a respectable, though modest, charitable musical society in Dublin arrived at just the right moment: Handel was spurred into action. Jennens's word-book for *Messiah* may have been sitting in his Brook Street House unread for as long as 18 months. Though the musical society had not specified what should be performed in a concert to raise money to help imprisoned debtors, the composer now seized the opportunity to take up Jennens's libretto, set this drama on revealed religion to music and present it to a fresh, new audience, in a venue where he could be certain he would not be to be dogged and pestered by arrogant, hostile Anti-Handelian nobles as he was so frequently in London.

When Handel came to Dublin as the year 1741 was drawing to a close, he must have been aware that the cultural tastes of the city's élite were not too different from those of London and, indeed, from those in the cities on the European mainland favoured by sons of the gentry undertaking the Grand Tour. It cannot be doubted that Matthew Dubourg, Mary Pendarves and Anne Donnellan had convinced Handel that, not only would Dublin society make sure that he would be warmly received, but also that this second largest city of George II's Hanoverian dominions could muster sufficient musical resources to stage his works in a way that would meet his approval.

Jennens must have been fully aware that Handel, the grandson of a Lutheran pastor, had an intimate and thorough knowledge of the context and meaning of the biblical text he had carefully selected for the word-book. He also took the decision that even the most outspoken sceptics knew Bible stories sufficiently well to make it unnecessary to link the extracts he had chosen from the scriptures with linking narrative. The oratorio was therefore composed without the need for any tiresome explanatory recitative. Edward Synge, the Bishop of Elphin, was to give as one of the reasons 'for the Superior Excellence' of *Messiah*, ''Tis this there is no Dialogue'. The entire libretto was made up solely of biblical extracts, these chosen with meticulous care to give Handel the scope to write a score to portray joy, tragedy, pathos, anger, celebration, eager expectation, exultation and, indeed, every possible emotion.

For very different reasons in each case, a number of clergymen in Dublin removed any hint that attending a sacred oratorio in a music hall was inappropriate. And, at the same time, they helped to remove obstacles in the way of the first performance of *Messiah* in the city. They included Patrick Delany, Charles Cobbe, Robert Clayton and Matthew Pilkington. The one thing these very different men all shared was a love of contemporary music, Handel's music in particular. Jonathan Swift was open about his indifference to the attractions of music, and he came very close to making that première impossible. But it must be remembered that, during his many years of service as Dean of St Patrick's, he had conscientiously and successfully striven to improve the quality of choral music in his cathedral, raising it to a standard high enough for Handel to request the participation of its choristers.

It is possible that, but for the rapturous reception it was given in Dublin, *Messiah* would have lain in storage, unheard for very many years until, inevitably, it would have been discovered as a work of genius by later generations. Handel waited nearly five months in the city before he had the confidence to present his new sacred oratorio. Until 13 April 1742 he staged no new compositions: all the performances in Dublin up to then were of works that had won approval years before on the other side of the Irish Sea.

Had Handel never come to Ireland and, as Jennens intended, given *Messiah* its first performance in London, it seems very likely that it would have attracted hostile criticism from the outset. It certainly became evident that there was a vocal group in the English capital – unlike the Irish capital – that thought the very secular venue of a theatre was no place for a musical entertainment incorporating biblical text. Dublin had given Handel the confidence to persist in his efforts to have *Messiah* performed in England after he had returned from Ireland. When his sacred oratorio was castigated in London as a profanation of God's name and word, Handel could remind himself that the audience in the Fishamble Street Musick Hall had no such squeamish objections. And he carried back to England the reassuring letter from the Bishop of Elphin that *Messiah* was 'a Species of Musick different from any other', certain 'to please all who have Ears & will hear, learned and unlearn'd'.[15] Dublin, therefore, gave Handel the confidence to persist in his efforts to win the English audiences over to his sacred oratorio. Dublin had also demonstrated how he could achieve that. In Ireland the first performance had been for charity. Only when *Messiah* was detached from the theatre, associated in the minds of many with foreign depravity, and performed for a good cause in London's Foundling Hospital was this matchless sacred oratorio secured for posterity.

Epilogue:
'An Idea of Heaven, Where Everybody is to Sing'

MESSIAH'S OUTSPREADING: 'TEARS ... TRICKLING DOWN THE FACES OF MANY'

Less than a year after Handel's death, the rector of Church Stretton in Shropshire, John Mainwaring, published anonymously his *Memoirs of the life of G.F. Handel*. It was actually the first full-length biography of any composer in any language. Riddled with inaccuracies though it was, Mainwaring's book unhesitatingly placed *Messiah* centre-stage as the greatest of Handel's compositions, a composition which it asserted had rescued the Foundling Hospital in London from financial ruin. 'The very successful application of this wonderful production of his genius to so beneficent a purpose', Mainwaring believed, 'reflected equal honour on the Artist and the Art'. So began the near-beatification of Handel in the decades following his death.

The mood of mid-eighteenth-century England was shifting: application of Longinus's rules of rhetoric was doing its work. So, too, were the 'Brothers', John and Charles Wesley. Above all, *Messiah* was no longer the preserve of members of a narrow élite capable of paying half a guinea each for a ticket. Horace Walpole was perhaps the first to predict that ordinary people as well as trained choristers and soloists would long to take part in singing Handel's oratorio music. Momentarily dropping his usual pose as someone rather fastidiously uninterested in music, Walpole, with great prescience, had written in 1743 that the composer's oratorios 'give me an idea of heaven, where everybody is to sing whether they have voices or not'.[1]

The music publisher, John Walsh, helped to make the score of *Messiah* available across the country, starting out in 1743 with a printing of 'Sinfony', the oratorio's overture. He published Volume

I of *Handel's Songs Selected from his Oratorios* in 1749, and by the time Volume V had appeared in 1759 it included all the *Messiah* arias.[2] *Messiah* was no longer confined to a metropolis. If enough competent instrumentalists and singers could be brought together, a provincial performance could be staged, provided four or five trained soloists could be enticed down from the city. In England the first performance of *Messiah* outside London was given on 14 April 1749 in Oxford to mark the opening there of Dr Radcliffe's Library (now the Radcliffe Camera).

Methodists, having dropped their opposition to instrumental accompaniment, had now become amongst the most avid admirers of *Messiah*. The oratorio, either in part or as a whole, was being heard regularly in their chapels. John Wesley went to a performance in Bristol Cathedral in August 1758. He recorded in his Journal: 'I doubt if that congregation was ever so serious at a sermon as they were during this performance'.[3]

Enthusiasts could accelerate *Messiah*'s outspreading into the very heart of the countryside. The Reverend William Hanbury, the eccentric Rector of Church Langton, a tiny village in Leicestershire, was planning a music festival to raise money for an ambitiously huge new parish church when he heard of Handel's death. *Messiah* was quickly added to the programme and got a performance in the village on 27 September 1759. It was a dazzling success. 'The foot-roads from every quarter were lined with common people, and the quality and gentry in their different carriages rattled in from every part' – more than 200 wheeled conveyances, in fact. 'The music, on so solemn a subject, by so good a band' had a powerful emotional impact. 'Tears then with unconcern were seen trickling down the faces of many; and then indeed, it was extremely moving to see the pity, compassion, and devotion, that had possessed the greater part present'. After the performance, part of it was put on again in the open 'for the entertainment of the common people'.[4]

'THE CHORUS AND KETTLE DRUMS FOR FOUR HOURS WERE SO THUNDERFULL, THAT THEY GAVE ME A HEAD-ACHE'

Ever since *Messiah* had been given its first performance in Dublin, Handel had tweaked, adjusted, revised, and re-composed parts of the score. Some changes he regarded as improving refinements; a few but significant alterations had been made at Jennens's behest; and other tinkering is largely accounted for by the strengths or shortcomings Handel had perceived in individual soloists he had engaged for particular performances. The composer certainly bequeathed ample work to musical scholars who much later took up the challenge of judging what surviving scores of the oratorio were the finest or the most authentic – or, indeed, both.[5]

After Handel's death, *Messiah* was constantly retouched and reshaped to adapt the oratorio to tastes and developments as they altered over time. J. C. Bach, Haydn and Mozart were amongst those who felt entitled to tamper with or 'improve' the score. The range of orchestral instruments available was ever widening and many conductors could not resist the temptation to include some of the newest ones (such as clarinets, trombones and bass drums) into performances they were directing. Above all, with every passing year the size of the chorus and the orchestra seemed to just keep on growing and growing.

In 1784 members of the 'Noblemen's Concert of Antient Music' organised a Handel centenary commemoration in aid of the Society for Decay'd Musicians and the Westminster Infirmary. Actually, the composer had been born in 1685, not 1684; the noblemen had not questioned the incorrect date provided both by Mainwaring and the Westminster Abbey monument. A performance of *Messiah* was to be the high point of this commemoration in the Abbey, Handel's final resting place. Much of the venerable building had to be fitted out with elaborate temporary galleries, platforms and an extremely large stepped tribune not only to accommodate a huge audience but also a chorus of 257 and an orchestra of 250. The choir was made up of 53 trebles, 45 altos, 80 tenors and 79 basses. All but six of the trebles were boys and all the altos were men. The orchestra consisted of: 48 first violins, 47 second violins, 26 violas, 21 cellos, 15 double basses, 26 oboes, 26 bassoons, 12 trumpets, 4 timpanist, 6 flutes, 12 horns, 6 trombones and a double bassoon. Mary Delany, a widow again since 1768, was present in the abbey on that occasion; she was observed listening to 'I know my Redeemer liveth' with 'tears … trickling down her venerable cheeks'.[6]

The urge to field even larger musical forces could not be skewered. The tally of performers in the 1785 anniversary concert was 616. After the 1786 anniversary performance of *Messiah*, when the number had risen to 640, Horace Walpole observed:

> The sight was really very fine, and the performance magnificent; but the chorus and kettle-drums for four hours were so thunderfull, that they gave me a head-ache, to which I am not at all subject.

There were no fewer than 1,068 musicians deployed in the monumental 1791 Westminster Abbey anniversary performance – almost twice as many as in 1784.[7]

These commemoration performances, Richard Luckett concludes, 'were to give a licence for almost any kind of maltreatment of *Messiah* in the future'. 'In England', he adds, 'the Victorian cult of Handel can only be characterised, physically as well as morally, as a case of sustained enormity'. For Luckett the 'moral enormity' was the 'elevation of Handel to divine status, while at the same time accepting all kinds of drastic modifications of what he wrote'.[8] The meaning of the words of Scripture chosen by Jennens was increasingly overlooked. Victorian gravity and solemnity led to a steady slowing down to an almost somnolent pace and, therefore, a great lengthening of performances. This was largely due to the fact that public response to *Messiah* had become mainly religious – in the words of Christopher Hogwood, 'reactions to the music were being filtered through a thick gauze of devotional sentiment'.[9]

It has long been assumed that the custom of standing for the 'Hallelujah' chorus was instituted by George II. This is based on an unsubstantiated anecdote told decades later and, actually, there is no evidence that the King was ever present at a performance of *Messiah*. The first reference to standing for the 'grand choruses' (the second being 'Worthy is the Lamb') was made in a letter written by Catharine Talbot in 1756 after she had been to a performance in Covent Garden, in spite of feeling even at this late date that this theatre was 'an unfit place for such a solemn performance'.[10]

Meanwhile *Messiah* was becoming ever more accessible, having a particular appeal for the rapidly-growing number of musical societies. In Handel's day both instrumentalists and singers had to perform from single-line part books. Then, during the early nineteenth century, inexpensive vocal scores brought the oratorio within the reach of amateur singers. Tonic sol-fa (a technique for teaching sight-singing invented by Sarah Ann Glover) had been devised for those unable to read musical notation. Later, Vincent and J. Alfred Novello sold cheap, clearly-printed and easily-held editions of most of Handel's oratorios.

At the conclusion of the 1851 Great Exhibition in London the huge Crystal Palace was re-erected at Sydenham. The Sacred Harmonic Society, an amateur choral society formed in 1833, responded to a request to perform *Messiah* there in 1857, and 48,114 people came to hear it. Then in June 1859 81,319 came to listen and to watch Sir Michael Costa conduct a chorus of 2,765 and 460 instrumental musicians. Thereafter, the Crystal Palace hosted triennial Handel festivals right into the 1920s. Gargantuan performances of *Messiah* in the metropolis must not be allowed to obscure the fact that the oratorio could be heard and deeply appreciated on a much more modest scale sung by dedicated amateurs, accompanied by ad hoc orchestras of amateur players or simply by an organ.

'GLAD TO HEAR THE WORK SERIOUSLY PERFORMED ONCE BEFORE WE DIE'
It was an Irishman, a Dubliner indeed, who was the first to issue a heart-felt appeal for a return to *Messiah* as Handel had written it. Writing in 1891, George Bernard Shaw, a music critic as well as a playwright, began by expressing his feeling of frustration at 'the impossibility of obtaining justice' for *Messiah* in a Christian country. 'Import a choir of heathens', he continued, 'restrained by no considerations of propriety from attacking the choruses with unembarrassed sincerity of dramatic expression, and I would hasten to the performance if only to witness the delight of the public and the discomfiture of the critics'. The problem was that we 'have all had our Handelian training in church, and the perfect church-going mood is one of pure abstract relevance. A mood of active intelligence would be scandalous':

> Thus we get broken in to the custom of singing Handel as if he meant nothing; and as it happens that he meant a good deal, and was tremendously earnest about it, we know rather less about him than they do in the Andaman Islands, since

the Andamans are only unconscious of him, whereas we are misconscious … Why, instead of wasting huge sums on the multitudinous dullness of a Handel Festival does not somebody set up a thoroughly rehearsed and exhaustively studied performance of the Messiah in St. James's Hall with a chorus of twenty capable artists? Most of us would be glad to hear the work seriously performed once before we die.[11]

More than half a century was to pass before determined attempts were being made, after Shaw had delivered his broadside, to rediscover an authentic *Messiah*. The ground had to be prepared by careful investigative work, and this was not carried out in a sustained way by scholars until the 1950s, notably by Jens Peter Larsen, Winton Dean, O. E. Deutsch and William C. Smith. In short, these men were publishing *after* the issue of very popular recordings by Malcolm Sargent in 1946 and by Thomas Beecham in 1947 – versions weighed down with nineteenth-century accretions, disappointingly far distant from the kind of performance Shaw wanted to hear before he expired.

John Tobin, conductor of the London Choral Society, proved to be a pioneer. Tobin performed *Messiah* in St Paul's Cathedral on 18 March 1950, as he explained, 'presented swept free of textual errors, garnished by the conventions of eighteenth-century performance, and in the chamber music style which was an essential part of Handel's conception of the work'.[12] 'It glows in fresh colours and moves us anew', one critic acknowledged, if somewhat hesitantly.[13] The search for authentic, lighter and sprightlier performances had begun and was much assisted by the early music campaigners and further scholarly work, by H. Watkins Shaw and Donald Burrows, in particular. At the Stour Music Festival on 25 June 1966 Alfred Deller conducted Concentus Musicus from Vienna in what was the first performance of *Messiah* in Britain using original instruments. In 1984 Christopher Hogwood published what is still one of the very best biographies of Handel. By then Hogwood had won international renown as a conductor and as a leading champion of authentic interpretation. He prepared the 'London version' of *Messiah*, based on research into the performances given between 1743 and 1749. For a recording made in 1976 by Neville Marriner and The Academy of St. Martin-in-the-Fields, Hogwood recreated one particular performance of *Messiah*, that at the Foundling Hospital in 1754. This was with the Choir of Christ Church Cathedral, Oxford and The Academy of Ancient Music, issued as a recording in 1980.[14]

THE WORLD'S MOST POPULAR PIECE OF CLASSICAL MUSIC

'We are looking for all parts but especially Tenors and Basses'. This was an appeal put out during the summer of 2013 by Cór Mhaigh Eo, a choral society based in the town of Castlebar in the west of Ireland. 'The Handel Challenge' had been launched to provide an opportunity for amateur choral singers to raise much-needed funds for a local charity. The challenge was for the choir members, directed by Kathy Fahy, to master all 21 choruses of *Messiah* in 12 weeks in preparation for a public performance of the oratorio in its entirety. Each participant was obliged to raise a minimum of 200 in sponsorship for the Mayo Roscommon Hospice Foundation, a voluntary organisation set up to provide palliative care for the people of the two counties. The immediate aim was to fund a 14-bed specialist unit in Castlebar and an 8-bed specialist unit in Roscommon Town.

The first of 10 rehearsals began on 2 September in the Galway-Mayo Institute of Technology, next to the General Hospital in Castlebar. For good measure each chorister was issued with a score training CD. The venue was to be the Church of the Holy Rosary, Castlebar (which as an indication of the changing composition of Irish society now had a Polish Mass, with Father Krzysztof as celebrant, on the first Sunday of every month). On the night of 8 December the church was packed to capacity, each person there having paid 25 for a ticket. RTÉ's Mary Kennedy introduced the Celtic Concert Orchestra, the 100 members of the chorus, and the soloists: Regina Nathan, soprano; Anne Marie Gibbons, alto; Eamon Mulhall, tenor; and Owen Gilhooly, bass. The performance was rapturously received and, as a sign of the times, part of it (in a somewhat shaky mobile-phone recording) was immediately posted on www.youtube.com, where it can still be found.

This single performance of *Messiah*, in a sparsely-inhabited part of Ireland still reeling from the impact of the global financial crisis of 2008, raised the extraordinarily large sum of 30,000 for charity.[15] It was also an indication of how all sections of Irish society had taken this oratorio to their hearts. After all, the Fishamble Street Musick Hall performances in 1742 – and, indeed, those put on in Ireland throughout the remainder of the eighteenth century – had been organised by Protestants for audiences that had been overwhelmingly Protestant.

In the eighteenth century only Dublin and Cork had been offered the opportunity to hear *Messiah*. Belfast got its first performance in 1813 in Dr Drummond's Meeting House, the Second Presbyterian Church. It was conducted by Edward Bunting, the celebrated collector of Irish airs. Performances at the 1831 Dublin Musical Festival, the Cork Exhibitions of 1852 and 1883, the 1873 Dublin Musical Festival and by societies such as the Antient Concerts Society, the Royal Choral Institute and the Armagh Musical Society did much to give *Messiah* a central place in Irish public esteem. In 1914 the composer Charles Villiers Stanford approvingly remarked that he had identified 'Dublin traditions' of *Messiah* performance that excised 'all the feelings of stodginess which a strict adherence to the printed note-values emphasises'.

Five combined choral societies at the Gaiety Theatre in Dublin marked the *Messiah* bicentenary in 1942, and the first period-instrument performance in Ireland was given in the Royal Hospital Kilmainham by The Sixteen in 1992, one of several major concerts to celebrate the 250th anniversary. Any hint that *Messiah* was in any way a Protestant preserve had vanished long since. Indeed, the organisation now most associated with the oratorio in the public mind was Our Lady's Choral Society. Following a performance of *Messiah* by an amalgamated group of choirs in the diocese of Dublin in December 1945, this society was formed a few months later with Archbishop John Charles McQuaid as president. In addition to a performance of *Messiah* at the National Concert Hall in Dublin each December, Our Lady's Choral Society in 1989 inaugurated the tradition of marking the historic first performance of 1742 by singing excerpts from the oratorio in the open air in Fishamble Street on 13 April and on the same date every year thereafter.[16]

'A Sacred Oratorio, on the Prophecies concerning Christ … Never performed in America'. This advertisement confirms that it was not until 16 January 1770, at a concert given in George Burns's Music Room in the New York City Tavern on Broadway, that *Messiah* crossed the Atlantic. This was made up of extracts only and, largely due to the War of Independence and other conflicts, a full performance (given by the Massachusetts Musical Society and spread over three evenings) had to wait until 1817. The first complete performance in one evening was given on Christmas Day, 1818, at Boylston Hall, Boston. The Sacred Music Society gave New York its first full *Messiah* on 18 November 1831 in St Paul's Chapel.

Meanwhile on the European mainland Thomas Arne's son, Michael, had selections from *Messiah* put on in Hamburg in 1772, and then it was given in full by C. P. E. Bach three years later. The poet J. G. Herder translated Jennens's text for performances in the Court Theatre at Weimar in 1780 and 1781. The writer Johann Goethe was so moved by hearing it that later his friends arranged to have it put on in a special performance in his own house. While listening to the oratorio in the company of the Crown Prince of Prussia in Potsdam in 1783, Carl Friedrich Zelter decided on the spot to give up being a stone mason and to become a composer. He was so moved that he gave voice to his emotions in 'loud, indeed in painful exclamations' and then rushed out into the night there to 'shed tears of emotion on the lonely road'. However, for most of the nineteenth century Germans – unlike the Danes and the Swedes – seemed to prefer Handel's *Joshua* and *Israel in Egypt* to *Messiah*. Lord Mount-Edgecumbe was at a concert in Paris in 1784, which included pieces from *Messiah*. His verdict was clear: 'The French had not the taste to like it'. France did not get a complete *Messiah* until 1873. It was well into the twentieth century before Italians began to take any serious interest in the oratorio. Meanwhile, British imperial expansion had seen to it that *Messiah* was heard in places as far apart as Jamaica and India even before the eighteenth century had closed.[17]

By the twenty-first century the oratorio was being appreciated in the most unlikely places. In 2006 *The Really Big Chorus*, a choir made up of amateur singers from all over the United Kingdom, travelled to China with their conductor, Brian Kay. On 16 October in Beijing they joined forces with the Choir of the China Conservatory of

Music, with Wu Lingfen as Chorus Mistress. There in the Forbidden City Concert Hall, accompanied by the Xinkongqi Orchestra, they performed *Messiah*. One of the visiting choristers, John Hunter from Belfast, afterwards recalled with some astonishment that officials in the concert hall insisted that everyone present stand for the 'Hallelujah' chorus.[18]

Both Handel and his librettist, Charles Jennens, had intended *Messiah* as a musical entertainment to be staged during Lent. Ireland, along with the rest of the world, decided instead that *Messiah* should be an integral part of Christmas festivities. The performance of *Messiah* in the Church of the Holy Rosary, Castlebar, in 2013 was only one of at least 20 performances of the oratorio across Ireland during the Christmas season that year. Anyone turning to the internet in an attempt to tot up the number of performances of *Messiah* across the globe between November and January in any recent year would be reduced to a state of exhausted incoherence before coming anywhere near an accurate figure.

If Handel could be brought back down to earth what would he think of the extraordinary range of performances on offer in the second millennium? It is certain that he would warmly approve of those who were striving to achieve authentic renderings of his score unencumbered with later accretions. He might even feel that soloists, choristers and instrumentalists – benefitting from more thorough training and longer rehearsal time than was ever available in his day – were able to perform the sacred oratorio both to his great liking and to a standard higher than he had previously thought possible. At the same time he would surely be a little impatient with those modern purists who in a jaundiced way look down on the very many who have their own different ways of staging and enjoying *Messiah*.

Open-minded and irrepressibly gregarious, Handel could not but be touched by the enormous enthusiasm and commitment of amateur choristers across the globe who delight in singing his masterpiece. It is more than likely, it has to be admitted, that performances of *Messiah* with huge choruses and orchestras in, for example, Westminster Abbey in 1791 and the Crystal Palace in 1859, would not have been to the composer's taste. The deployment of such enormous musical forces in those venues could only have resulted in muffled, distorted and generally unbalanced renderings – quite apart from the certainty that he would have loathed the growing taste for solemn snail-like tempi and the general inattention paid to Jennens's words drawn from Scripture. However, modern auditoria and theatres, with interiors specifically designed to ensure clarity and equipped with sophisticated sound systems, have created the opportunity to present *Messiah* with choirs and orchestras far larger than Handel had ever envisaged without distorting his original design.

Handel delighted in new instruments: if brought back to earth the man who introduced hunting horns and the carillon into his compositions might be tempted to write a concerto for a sousaphone (preferably the latest hybrid brass/fibreglass version), possibly accompanied by lambeg drums from Ulster in place of kettledrums, which he regularly borrowed from the Tower of London. If taken to a music shop he would most likely head straight for the very latest in digital synths and then would listen, fascinated, as the sales assistant explained how he could record, edit and mix his music on a DAW (digital audio workstation). Handel was also a promoter. Could *Messiah*, on a scale never before attempted, be performed on a scale in Dublin's Croke Park or Aviva Stadium?

'Enough!' as Lord Chief Justice Sir William Lee was prompted to exclaim during the Cibber-Sloper trial in December 1738.

Ben Finane concludes that after '250 years of continuous performance, having bent to and having survived every conceivable and inconceivable manner of orchestration, having accommodated choirs of a dozen to choirs of thousands … Handel's *Messiah* thrives as ever'.[19]

A survey made in 2014 revealed that *Messiah* had become the world's most popular piece of classical music. This is all the more extraordinary since the libretto is made up solely of biblical text. Those words set to music to become 'a fine Entertainment' were specifically intended to convey the mystery, the revelation, the prophesies contained in Holy Writ bringing the assurance of redemption, salvation and everlasting life. To millions *Messiah* does indeed convey such assurance, but in an increasingly secular age millions of others are simply enchanted by the emotional power of the oratorio, by the sublime beauty of the music Handel composed.

Appendix 1:
The *Messiah* Word-Book

PART ONE

1. Orchestra
   Sinfony (Overture)

2. Recitative (tenor)
   Comfort ye, my people, saith your God. Speak ye comfortably to Jerusalem, and cry unto her, that her warfare is accomplish'd, that her iniquity is pardon'd. The voice of him that crieth in the wilderness, 'Prepare ye the way of the Lord, make straight in the desert a highway for our God'. (Isaiah 40:1-3)

3. Air (tenor)
   Ev'ry valley shall be exalted, and ev'ry mountain and hill made low, the crooked straight and the rough places plain. (Isaiah 40:4)

4. Chorus
   And the glory of the Lord shall be revealed, and all flesh shall see it together: for the mouth of the Lord hath spoken it. (Isaiah 40:5)

5. Recitative (bass)
   Thus saith the Lord, the Lord of Hosts: Yet once, a little while, and I will shake the heav'ns and the earth, the sea and the dry land. And I will shake all nations, and the desire of all nations shall come. (Haggai 2:6, 7)
   The Lord, whom ye shall seek, shall suddenly come to his temple, ev'n the messenger of the covenant, who ye delight in: behold, he shall come, saith the Lord of Hosts. (Malachi 3:1)

6. Air (alto)
   But who may abide the day of his coming? And who shall stand when he appeareth? For he is like a refiner's fire. (Malachi 3:2)

7. Chorus
And he shall purify the sons of Levi, that they may offer unto the Lord an offering in righteousness. (Malachi 3:3)

8. Recitative (alto)
Behold, a virgin shall conceive, and bear a son, and shall call his name Emmanuel, 'God with us'. (Isaiah 7:14, Matthew 1:23)

9. Air (alto and chorus)
O thou that tellest good tidings to Zion, get thee up into the high mountain; O thou that tellest good tidings to Jerusalem, lift up thy voice with strength; lift it up; be not afraid; say unto the cities of Judah, Behold your God! O thou that tellest good tidings to Zion, arise, shine, for thy light is come, and the glory of the Lord is risen upon thee. (Isaiah 40:9 & 60:1)

10. Recitative (bass)
For behold, darkness shall cover the earth, and gross darkness the people; but the Lord shall arise upon thee, and his glory shall be seen upon thee. And the Gentiles shall come to thy light, and kings to the brightness of thy rising. (Isaiah 60:2, 3)

11. Air (bass)
The people that walked in darkness have seen a great light: and they that dwell in the land of the shadow of death, upon them hath the light shined. (Isaiah 9:2)

12. Chorus
For unto us a child is born, unto us a son is given, and the government shall be upon his shoulder: and his name shall be called Wonderful, Counsellor, the mighty God, the everlasting Father, the Prince of Peace. (Isaiah 9:6)

13. Orchestra
Pifa (Pastoral Symphony)

14. 15. 16. Recitative (Soprano)
There were shepherds abiding in the field, keeping watch over their flock by night. (Luke 2:8)
And lo, the angel said unto them, Fear not: for behold, I bring you good tidings of great joy, which shall be to all people. For unto you is born this day in the city of David a Saviour, which is Christ the Lord (Luke 2:10, 11)
And suddenly there was with the angel a multitude of the heavenly host praising God, and saying (Luke 2:13)

17. Chorus
Glory to God in the highest, and peace on earth. Good will toward men. (Luke 2:14)

18. Air (soprano)
Rejoice greatly, O daughter of Zion, shout, O daughter of Jerusalem: behold, thy King cometh unto thee: he is the righteous Saviour, and he shall speak peace unto the heathen. (Zechariah 9:9, 10)

19. Recitative (alto)
Then shall the eyes of the blind be open'd, and the ears of the deaf unstopped. Then shall the lame man leap as an hart, and the tongue of the dumb shall sing. (Isaiah 35: 5, 6)

20. Duet (alto and soprano)
He shall feed his flock like a shepherd: and he shall gather the lambs with his arm, and carry them in his bosom, and gently lead those that are with young. (Isaiah 40:11)
Come unto him, all ye that labour; come unto him that are heavy laden, and he will give you rest. Take his yoke upon you, and learn of him: for he is meek and lowly of heart; and ye shall find rest unto your souls. (Matthew 11:28, 29)

21. Chorus
His yoke is easy, his burthen is light. (Matthew 11:30)

Part Two

22. Chorus
    Behold the Lamb of God, that taketh away the sin of the world.
    (John 1:29)

23. Air (alto)
    He was despised and rejected of men; a man of sorrows, and
    acquainted with grief. (Isaiah 53:3)
    He gave his back to the smiters, and his cheeks to them that
    plucked off the hair: he hid not his face from shame and
    spitting. (Isaiah 50:6)

24. Chorus
    Surely, He hath borne our griefs, and carried our sorrows. He
    was wounded for our transgressions, he was bruised for our
    iniquities; the chastisement of our peace was upon him; (Isaiah
    53:4, 5)

25. Chorus
    And with his stripes we are healed
    (Isaiah 53:5)

26. Chorus
    All we like sheep have gone astray; we have turned ev'ry one to
    his own way, and the Lord hath laid on him the iniquity of us
    all. (Isaiah 53:6)

27. Recitative (tenor)
    All they that see him laugh him to scorn: they shoot out their
    lips and shake their heads, saying: (Psalm 22:7)

28. Chorus
    He trusted in God that he would deliver him; if he delight in
    him, let him deliver him. (Psalm 22:8)

29. Recitative (tenor)
    Thy rebuke hath broken his heart; he is full of heaviness. He

looked for some to have pity on him, but there was no man, neither found he any to comfort him. (Psalm 69:20)

30. Air (tenor)
Behold and see if there be any sorrow like unto his sorrow (Lamentations 1:2)

31. Recitative (tenor)
He was cut out of the land of the living: for the transgressions of thy people was he stricken. (Isaiah 53:8)

32. Air (tenor)
But thou didst not leave his soul in hell, nor didst thou suffer they Holy One to see corruption. (Psalm 16:10)

33. Chorus
Lift up your heads, O ye gates; and be ye lift up, ye everlasting doors; and the King of glory shall come in. who is this King of glory? The Lord strong and mighty in battle. Lift up your heads, O ye gates; and be ye lift up, ye everlasting doors; and the King of glory shall come in. Who is this King of glory? The Lord of hosts, he is the King of glory. (Psalm 24:7-10)

34. Recitative (tenor)
Unto which of the angels said he at any time: Thou art my Son, this day have I begotten Thee? (Hebrews 1:5)

35. Chorus
Let all the angels of God worship him. (Hebrews 1:6)

36. Air (alto)
Thou art gone up on high; thou hast led captivity captive, and received gifts for men; yea, even for thine enemies, that the Lord God might dwell among them. (Psalm 68:18)

37. Chorus
The Lord gave the word: great was the company of preachers. (Psalm 68:11)

38. Air (soprano)
   How beautiful are the feet of them that preach the gospel of peace, and bring glad tidings of good things! (Romans 10:15)

39. Chorus
   Their sound is gone out into all lands, and their words unto the ends of the world. (Romans 10:18)

40. Air (bass)
   Why do the nations so furiously rage together: why do the people imagine a vain thing? The kings of the earth rise up, and the rulers take counsel together against the Lord, and against his Anointed. (Psalm 2:1,2)

41. Chorus
   Let us break their bonds asunder, and cast away their yokes from us. (Psalm 2:3)

42. Recitative (tenor)
   He that dwelleth in heaven shall laugh them to scorn: the Lord shall have them in derision. (Psalm 2:4)

43. Air (tenor)
   Thou shalt break them with a rod of iron; thou shalt dash them in pieces like a potter's vessel. (Psalm 2:9)

44. **Hallelujah!** for the Lord God omnipotent reigneth. The kingdom of this world is become the kingdom of out Lord, and of his Christ; and he shall reign for ever and ever, King of Kings, Lord of Lords, Hallelujah! (Revelation 19:6, 11:15, 19:16)

PART THREE

45. Air (soprano)
   I know that my redeemer liveth, and that he shall stand at the latter day upon the earth. And though worms destroy this body, yet in my flesh shall I see God. (Job 19:25,26) For now is Christ risen from the dead, the first fruits of them that sleep. (1st Corinthians 15:20)

46. Chorus

Since by man came death, by man came also the resurrection of the dead. For as in Adam all die, even so in Christ shall all be made alive. (1st Corinthians 15:21, 22)

47. Recitative (bass)

Behold, I tell you a mystery: we shall not all sleep, but we shall all be chang'd, in a moment, in the twinkling of an eye, at the last trumpet. (1st Corinthians 15:51, 52)

48. Air (bass)

The trumpet shall sound and the dead shall be raised incorruptible, and we shall be changed. For this corruptible must put on incorruption, and this mortal must put on immortality. (1st Corinthians 15:54)

49. Recitative (alto)

Then shall be brought to pass the saying that is written: Death is swallow'd up in victory. (1st Corinthians 15:54)

50. Duet (alto and tenor)

O death, where is thy sting? O grave, where is thy victory? The sting of death is sin, and the strength of sin is the law. (1st Corinthians 15:55, 56)

51. Chorus

But thanks be to God, who giveth us the victory through our Lord Jesus Christ. (1st Corinthians 15:57)

52. Air (soprano)

If God be for us, who can be against us? Who shall lay anything to the charge of God's elect? It is God that justifieth. Who is he that condemneth? It is Christ that died, yea rather, that is risen again, who is at the right hand of God, who makes intercession for us. (Romans, 8:31, 33, 34)

53. Chorus

Worthy is the Lamb that was slain, and hath redeemed us to God by his blood, to receive power, and riches, and wisdom, and strength, and honour, and glory, and pow'r, be unto him that sitteth upon the throne, and unto the Lamb for ever and ever, Amen. (Revelation 5:9, 12, 13)

Appendix 2:
How Did Fishamble Street Get its Name?

A ridge of well-drained ground, 50 feet above the tide at its highest point, formed the ancient nucleus of Dublin. By the black pool – in Irish, *Dubhlinn* – formed where the Poddle stream flowed in from the south to meet the River Liffey, Viking raiders back in the ninth century had pulled their longships onto a dry bank, covered them, lashed them down, and erected a stockade around their vessels for protection. Here, they decided to stay. Two centuries later their descendants had made their settlement, Dublin, the largest city in the Viking world. Another two hundred years after that a fresh wave of newcomers, the Normans, seized the city. They turned Dublin into the capital of their latest acquisition, which they named the Lordship of Ireland. The Normans brought a mix of peoples with them, including Welsh, Flemings and English (the city being 'granted and confirmed to his men of Bristol' by Henry II in 1171). John, King of England and Lord of Ireland, commissioned Dublin Castle, a great fortress built on the remains of the Viking stockade.

At the western edge of the ridge, a Viking King of Dublin, Sitric Silkenbeard, had founded the city's first cathedral, Christ Church. Sitric Silkenbeard had become a Christian when his father king Olaf had agreed to be baptised in 979. When he was in Dublin with a great army in 1210, King John had ordered that this should be pulled down and replaced with a more magnificent structure. The steep and crooked lane running down the east side of the cathedral was to become Fishamble Street. Here, during the thirteenth century, at the foot of the lane where it met the Liffey, tidal mud was reclaimed to raise it above the high spring tide mark. First a post and wattle fence was erected and debris piled behind it; then great uprights of oak were driven into the estuarine mud, supported by struts; and finally heaps of stones, soil and rubbish of all kinds were laid behind retaining walls until dry firm land was pushed out into the deep river channel to create a good anchorage. It was this extensive timber revetment that gave the anchorage its name: Wood Quay.

Alongside vessels tied up at the quay, local fishermen pulled up their boats onto a slip at the eastern end of Wood Quay. The lane became the city's fish shambles where the catch was gutted and filleted and sold. Nearby the tanners were busy at the top of Fishamble Street in Skinners' Row and in Winetavern Street, and the butchers had their flesh shambles in High Street. Entrails, hides and fish guts cast down to fester on the cobbles heaved with bluebottle maggots, constantly endangering the health of citizens. In 1459 the Dublin Assembly, fearing epidemics, enacted this order for the street's fish market:

> every fisher that has a board in the fishambles and casts guts under their boards, and wash not their boards after they have done their markets, that they pay a groat as oftentimes as they be found guilty thereof.

Strict regulations for the fish market were made half a century later. Only wholesalers could buy from the boats until three o'clock; charges were imposed of a halfpenny per horseload of fish and a farthing for every load of eels carried on a man's back. Every stall-holder in Fishamble Street, and every woman selling from a basket, had to pay for cleaning up after the market.

In 1595 latrines were ordered for this crowded area: 'the masters of the cittie works to have a common jackes made upon such place of the Wod Key Mr. Maior and his bretherne, such as he shall call for that purpose shall think convenyent'.[1] The final subjugation of Ireland to the English Crown was now under way. On 11 March 1597 400 barrels of gunpowder hoisted onto the quay accidentally detonated. 'The ruyne of the town is exceeding great', Sir John Norris informed Queen Elizabeth, and the Mayor and sheriffs reported that those 'who fortuned to be in the last misfortune happened within the cittie of Dublin, lost to the number of six skoare, besides sondrie headles bodies, and heads without bodies that were found and not known'.[2] In 1684 Ormond Bridge was completed to span the Liffey at Wood Quay. This was the work of Sir Humphrey Jervis, a wealthy shipowner, who had built Capel Street and erected Essex Bridge further downstream, and developed Ormond Market on the north side of the river. Jervis convinced the city corporation to compel the fishmongers, butchers and tanners to transfer their activities to the new market.

At a stroke Fishamble Street was transformed. The 'excessive and noxious stenches' arising from the shambles had been removed. Only row boats and vessels which could unstep their masts could negotiate the bridges to reach Wood Quay upstream. Fishamble Street became one of Dublin's most fashionable streets. Sir Daniel Bellingham, the first man elected with the new elevated title of Lord Mayor, put up an 'elegant building' with ten hearths at the top end of Fishamble Street. In a cul-de-sac near the foot of the street, Smock Alley flourished as the city's leading theatre. And it was in this street that members of the Charitable Musical Society, meeting here in the comfortable rooms of the Bull's Head tavern, decided to erect their Musick Hall.

Appendix 3:
Fishamble Street Developers Help to Shape Georgian Dublin

North of the River Liffey, Henrietta Street had become the showcase for the latest town house style: tall terraces constructed predominantly of warm red brick with plain, elegant facades, well-proportioned elevations, recessed windows and roofs hidden by parapets. Here, Luke Gardiner, a man who had risen from an obscure background in Fishamble Street to bring order to the state's finances and to be appointed to the lucrative post of Receiver and Paymaster, was turning land once possessed by St Mary's Abbey into the city's choicest residential area. Laid out in 1721, Henrietta Street was still being developed 20 years later. Gardiner had his own magnificent house at the top of the street and at an early stage he persuaded Archbishop Hugh Boulter to have his town house built on a plot directly opposite. Boulter insisted that the street should be at least 50 feet wide. This became known as 'Primate's Hill – indeed four successive archbishops of Armagh lived here. The two terraces of residences, one on each side of the street, were palatial, with four storeys over a basement and five bays.

On the south side, St Stephen's Green, created on the initiative of Dublin Corporation from city commons, had become Dublin's most fashionable square. The Corporation retained control of the Green, surrounding wall and paved walks that led, eventually, to an equestrian statue of George II in the centre. Here the 'quality' promenaded – in the evenings during the week and after two o'clock on Sundays. Adjacent to the Green, Viscount Robert Molesworth, son of a merchant who had made his fortune supplying tents and baggage to Oliver Cromwell, also from Fishamble Street, developed land in close collaboration with Joseph Dawson, secretary to the Lords Justices. Between them they laid out: Grafton, Dawson, Molesworth, Anne, Duke and Nassau streets. Dawson sold his own grand town house to the Corporation, below what it had cost him to put up, as a residence for the lord mayors of the city – now known as the Mansion House. West of St Stephen's Green, Francis Aungier, 1st Earl of Longford, had overseen the construction of a grid of streets on land confiscated in the sixteenth century from the Whitefriars. Here, Aungier Street was the main thoroughfare, connected to the Green by lanes, including Goat Alley, Love Lane and Beaux Lane.

Overseas visitors were struck by the comparatively austere frontages of the rows of terraced residential housing rising up in the city suburbs. Gardiner, who had set this fashion in Dublin, was motivated largely by economy since the cost of stone was far higher than it was, for example, in Edinburgh and Bath. Stone decoration greatly increased the expense of construction. Those entitled to sit in the House of Lords, MPs and rich landowners made sure that they picked the choicest town houses but they were far outnumbered by lesser mortals, including merchants, lawyers and other professionals. Most of Gardiner's houses were either sold or rented off the peg and often divided into flats or even single rooms.

Those with large disposable incomes rarely attempted to alter exteriors; instead they made sure that rooms were lavishly furnished and decorated and that they were provided with commodious stables to the rear and elegant horse-drawn carriages to be driven out of arched stable lanes to drive in style through the city streets.

Appendix 4:
Dublin, Sweet City

The pulsing heart of Ireland's day-to-day administration was not to be found in the Irish Parliament nor in Dublin Castle but in a comparatively modest building on the quays, the Custom House. The government could hardly have functioned for a day but for the business conducted in this building. Here, the seven Commissioners of the Revenue met three times a week to assess and collect the country's taxes. All but a trifling amount of the funds needed to run the country were gathered from duties levied on incoming seaborne trade. And more than half of all the vessels sailing in to Ireland's ports in these years tied up in the waters just downstream of Essex Bridge.

The Revenue Commissioners employed a veritable army of men, over a thousand. At Dublin port the Customer, the Controller and the Searcher were the senior officials responsible for the checking of cargoes, the issuing of warrants and the counter-signing of documents. Surveyors boarded vessels with a book of rates; tide-waiters recorded cargoes item by item; and then land-waiters opened casks and other containers to record what was in them. Gaugers were on hand to measure the alcoholic content of rum, brandy, claret, port and other wines. Out at sea revenue cutters kept a constant watch on the Irish coast to suppress smuggling, not always with success.

The élite in Ireland had made sure it was not over-burdened with taxation. Land-owners paid a quit rent to the Crown for their estates, a modest charge not increased at all since the time of Charles II. The hearth tax notoriously fell most heavily on the shoulders of the poor. The levying of an income tax lay far in the future and – unlike Westminster – the Irish Parliament had successfully resisted the introduction of a land tax. As a result, the government depended to an extraordinary extent for its income on duties levied on sugar, tobacco and rum, that is, on the produce of the slave plantations on the other side of the North Atlantic.

Of course Westminster had ruled that colonial goods must be carried in British ships and landed at British ports. But these mercantilist restrictions, if anything, were to Dublin's benefit. Duty paid – principally at Bristol, Chester, Liverpool, London and Glasgow – was fully returned if this produce from the British West Indies and North American colonies was re-exported to Ireland. The most convenient destination on the other side of the Irish Sea, where duty now had to be paid, was Dublin.

By the 1740s sugar had become the single most valuable import and the most lucrative source of Ireland's revenue. Dubliners, it seemed, could not get enough of this exotic tropical product. Sugar arrived as muscovado, the wet, dark brown substance formed by boiling down the juice from cane crushed by slaves on the Caribbean plantations. Dozens of sugar houses across the city heated vats of muscovado to reduce it carefully to a crystalline form. Only specialist English refiners had the expertise to make loaf and lump white sugar, which had to be imported into Ireland; but local processors had a ready market for their less expensive powdered brown or 'bastard' sugar.

Appendix 5:
The Phoenix Park

Back in 1662, James Butler, the newly created Duke of Ormond, had entered Dublin in triumph as Lord Lieutenant, Charles II's viceroy. The people trusted that he would bring with him a new era of peace, toleration and prosperity. Ormond did not disappoint. King Charles had every intention of visiting Ireland and, to ensure he could provide suitable entertainment for his nobility and courtiers, he asked his viceroy to create a royal deer-park adjacent to the city.

The 2,000 acres Ormond purchased for his monarch were intended for the chase, but from the outset citizens without restriction or payment were encouraged to walk or ride in the grounds. One nobleman went to England to bring back fallow deer; another travelled to Wales to fetch partridges; and the duke's son provided pheasants from his Tipperary estates. It was not long before poachers from the city hunted down every last game bird, but descendants of the fallow deer still graze there today. By 1669 the park had cost over £31,000, and before it was finished it had cost half as much again. Phoenix Park got its name from a spring – providing *fionn uisce*, 'clear water' in Irish – though one suspects that Charles II never knew that. Of course, Charles never came to Ireland, but he toyed with the idea of giving the park to his mistress, Barbara Villiers, the Countess of Castlemaine. Ormond talked the king out of it. The mistress was furious: as the Jacobite historian, Thomas Carte, recalled, she fell upon the Duke 'with a torrent of abusive language, loaded him with all the reproaches that the rancour of her heart could suggest … and told him in fine, that she hoped to live to see him hanged'.[1] From the outset Phoenix Park was a public park where citizens could take their ease. They could also gather to watch parades and reviews of troops marched out from the nearby Royal Barracks. Ormond liked it too, and – finding Dublin Castle dingy and dank – built himself a viceregal residence close by. Nathaniel Clements, Luke Gardiner's deputy in the Custom House and later his successor as

Deputy Vice-Treasurer and Deputy Paymaster General, lived in 'Parisian luxury' at his home in 7 Henrietta Street. Soon after he had been appointed Chief Ranger of the Phoenix Park, Clements built himself a three-bay palladian mansion in the park. This was bought over by the government and extended in 1782 to become the Viceregal Lodge. Extended further in the nineteenth century, today it is Áras an Uachtarain, the official residence of the President of Ireland. The government set aside land for the Royal Zoological Society of Ireland, and in 1831 the zoological gardens opened – the second-oldest (after Regent's Park, London) privately-owned zoo in the world. In 1742 Phoenix Park was the largest city public park in Europe and, well into the second millennium, it still is.

Appendix 6:
Badger Flambé, Anyone?

Robert Jocelyn, Lord Chancellor and one of the three lords justices at the time of Handel's visit to Dublin, had a house in St Stephen's Green and another property well beyond the city's southern suburbs at Mount Merrion. He had a crucial role to play in forging political alliances and in promoting government policy, especially as he had a decidedly tricky relationship with a fellow lord justice, the Speaker, Henry Boyle. Entertaining distinguished guests – including, on at least one occasion, the Lord Lieutenant, the Duke of Devonshire – was a serious business.

From the year 1740, Jocelyn kept a dinner book. Most of his dinners were for men but they did include women such as Lady Betty Ponsonby and Lady Ross. Often the meals he had served ran only to four dishes (for *each* course), but dozens of dishes were presented on grander occasions. Guests were not expected to try every dish but simply to help themselves to a selection. Jocelyn was anxious to emulate French fine dining in spite of the political risks of aping the manners of the enemy. He had elaborate table plans sketched out with notes of what was to be served, including 'removes' – a remove was a dish replaced and replenished after it had been removed.

Jocelyn's table plan for a *first* course on one occasion had no fewer than 22 dishes. They included:

Crawfish soop remove; Haunch of Vennison Roast; Chickins Boild wth Rice and Stewd Turneps; Lambs ears Ragoued; Blanket collops; Badger Flambe wth Colleflowr; Pottery of Lobsters; Boild Rabbitts onions; Beef alla Doabe; Turkey Pye; Remove Boild mackerall; fillis of Fowls; fricease of frogs; Ducks alla Dolfini; Pigons Baseleed with Sorrel & Eggs; frickndoes of Lambe; Soop Loraine; Remove to the Chine of Beef'.

On other occasions he served 'Cods tongues', 'Boyld Fowls wth Oyster', 'Mushrooms friceasai', 'asparaguss', 'Leverett', 'Puffins in pickle', 'potted Grouse', 'Doabe Goose', 'french partridge pye', 'battery of Trouts' and 'Pyramid of Sweet meats.'[1]

Such sumptuous repasts were put in the shade by the fare presented in Dublin Castle by the Duke of Devonshire. His state dinners included a first course – and this was only the first course – made up of thirty-four dishes and six removes with fourteen dishes of sweetmeats separately placed on a long middle table. Some of these official dinners were 'largesse' days, when the poor were invited in to take away what remained. The Pursuivant shouted out 'largesse, largesse, largesse' and the doors were thrown open to admit women of the town, the guests, already satiated themselves, sitting back to enjoy the antics of the shrieking, jostling rabble.

Appendix 7:
'Did He Ever Blaze?' Duelling in Dublin

The Irish MP Sir Jonah Barrington observed in his memoirs that a
duel was considered so much a necessary piece of a young gentleman's
education that the first two questions always asked as to a young
man's respectability and qualifications, especially when he proposed
for a wife, were, 'What family is he of? and 'Did he ever blaze?'

No gentleman was well dressed unless he appeared with a
sword (hence the need for appeals to leave these weapons at home
for the two performances of *Messiah*). Only Protestant gentlemen
were entitled to bear arms. Since there was no police force in
Dublin other than a handful of elderly watchmen, the authorities
were unlikely to intervene when a gentleman felt that his honour
had been besmirched. Eventually duels became so frequent that
duelling clubs were established. In the early eighteenth century
most duels were fought with swords but the use of a brace of pistols
was becoming increasingly popular. Dubliners enjoyed taking the
air in Phoenix Park but local press reports make it clear that this
could be a hazardous business. Here, combatants did not always
confine themselves to secluded spots, but often 'stood up' on the
roads, endangering passers-by with stray bullets. Duels fought in
St Stephen's Green must have been an even bigger threat to public
safety. Lucas's Coffee-House on Cork Hill (at the top of Dame Street
facing the entrance to Dublin Castle) was much favoured by duellists,
where bullies went deliberately to pick fights. Duels were often fought
in the back yard, and so many dead bodies ended up on its tables that
the coffee house became known as 'Surgeon's Hall'.

Quarrels resulting in mortal combat were usually fuelled by strong
drink and generally had trivial causes. Typical was a dispute over a
card game at the Golden Bottle Inn in St Nicholas Street in 1730
that resulted in a duel in which the attorney William Todd killed his
relative, Pierce Rice. Customary rules of etiquette were frequently
broken, for example, following a quarrel over dinner in December
1716, Adam Cusack, a justice of the peace in Dublin, challenged his
relative, Lieutenant Brice. Instead of waiting for the following day,

the two men straight away picked up their weapons and fought to a standstill. Brice died of his wounds the next day, and Cusack died a few days later. Ten years later the son of a prosperous brewer, Pat Kelly, fell into dispute with Lieutenant James Smith in a tavern and – again without waiting or seeking out seconds – they fought to the death with their swords on Ormond Quay. Smith was run through the heart and it was reckoned that Kelly could not recover from his wounds.

Provided surviving combatants were well-connected and had powerful friends to speak for them, it was unlikely that they would be punished. After a coroner's inquest, a trial either before the Court of King's Bench or the local assizes would follow a few months later. If the duel was judged to have been fought within the accepted rules, the survivor was convicted of manslaughter in his own defence, in which case he could walk free. In 1725 Nicholas Jones, an army captain fought a duel with Hon. Colonel Nugent at Lucas's Coffee-House and killed him. William Pulteney, later Earl of Bath, personally intervened on Jones's behalf. He wrote to the Lord Chancellor, Richard West, arguing that Jones was so provoked that he was 'forced to fight' and asked that the captain be dealt with leniently as he was 'a particular friend of mine'.[1] Convicted of manslaughter though he was, Captain Jones walked out of the court a free man.

The frequency of duels increased as the century progressed, especially amongst the leaders of society. For example, in November 1726 the MP for Blessington, John Slattery, was killed in a duel fought with swords and pistols by the MP for Clonmel, Stephen Moore. A good many duels seem to have been little more than ritualised murder, opportunities to exact bloody vengeance without the threat of the noose. In the 1730s and 1740s the code of honour was most frequently breached by failing to allow some hours, at least, to elapse between a challenge and a duel. In January 1737 Harry St Lawrence, brother of Lord Howth, was so outraged when the man he was visiting in Meath, Hamilton Gorges, described his sister-in-law, Lady Howth, as 'silly', that he threw down a challenge. Refusing to wait for seconds, the two men fought behind closed doors. Gorges was mortally wounded, but fortunately for St Lawrence, as he was expiring, Gorges before witnesses absolved him from having done any wrong. As a result, St Lawrence was only convicted of manslaughter and walked free.

Dean Jonathan Swift did not feel that the authorities should concern themselves over much, shrugging his shoulders to observe that duellists should be allowed to continue exterminating each other. Samuel Madden disagreed: in 1738 he published *Reflections and resolutions proper for the gentlemen of Ireland.* In this widely-read tract, warmly supported by *Faulkner's Dublin Journal,* Madden deplored the fact that it was 'safer to kill a man' in a duel 'than steal a sheep or a cow'.

If anything, duelling became more popular in Ireland as the eighteenth century wore on. The five Grattan brothers, brought up in Fishamble Street, were amongst Swift's closest friends. Henry Grattan was to become one of Ireland's most famous patriots. Born in Fishamble Street in July 1746, the son of James Grattan MP, he was baptised in the nearby parish church of St John's. The Irish Parliament's most distinguished orator, he led the successful campaign for legislative independence in 1782. A man of high moral principle, he was nevertheless not averse to an occasional 'blaze'. His most notorious duel took place in 1800, after an 'abominable personal' exchange with Isaac Corry, Chancellor of the Exchequer, in the Irish House of Commons. Corry had supported the Bill for Union, which had just been passed, and accused Grattan, opposed to the measure, of 'being the associate of traitors'. Grattan, denouncing the charge, declared 'it was false, it was utterly, totally, and meanly false' and challenged Corry to a duel. Corry missed completely but Grattan left a bullet in the Chancellor's arm. After the duel, Grattan said that Corry 'gave me his bloody hand; we had formerly been friends'.[2] Many duels in Dublin did not end in such a gentlemanly way once honour had been satisfied.

Appendix 8:
The Blasters: The Dublin Hellfire Club

The wealthy and often titled members of the original Hellfire Club, founded in London around 1720, were deists and freethinkers who went much further than other 'enlighteners' who argued that it was through education, science and reason that mankind could be liberated from ignorance, superstition and religious repression. Since they did not expect an afterlife in which they would be punished by God, these Hellfire Club members saw no reason why they should not devote themselves to a delightful and sinful existence characterised by unrestrained self-indulgence.

The Prime Minister's son Edward Walpole, quite unlike his younger brother Horace, mixed with the hard-drinking hedonistic set in London. In 1737 he was appointed secretary to the Lord Lieutenant of Ireland, the Duke of Devonshire. Edward Walpole encouraged a member of the Hellfire Club in London, the portrait painter James Worsdale, to join him in Dublin. Matthew Pilkington, curate of St Anne's parish church on Dawson Street, who openly conducted affairs with other women, had befriended Worsdale during the year when he had been chaplain to the Lord Mayor of London and they now renewed their acquaintance in the Irish capital.

Edward Walpole introduced Worsdale to Dublin's most celebrated libertine, Richard Parsons, the extraordinarily dissolute Earl of Rosse. The Earl was so contemptuous of institutional religion that on one occasion he stripped himself completely naked to receive the moralist, Rev. Dr Samuel Madden, in his town house. Some time during the year 1737 Rosse and Worsdale founded the Dublin Hellfire Club in the Eagle tavern, opposite Lucas's Coffee-House, on Cork Hill. This was an exclusive circle: Worsley was to paint a group portrait of some members which included: Henry, 4th Baron Barry of Santry; Captain (later Colonel) Henry Clements; Simon Luttrell (later the 1st Earl of Carhampton); Colonel Richard St George and Colonel Henry Ponsonby. The wild behaviour of members soon made it plain that the Dublin Hellfire Club was even more scandalous and outrageous than its London counterpart.

The members' own footmen and the Eagle tavern's waiters or 'drawers' made sure that there they had ample supplies of punch and claret on tap. Each man had a commemorative wine glass engraved with his name and club title. Worsdale's survives: it is inscribed 'The Hell Fire Club' and 'James Worsdale Master of the Revels'. Drink alone was not enough to make them depraved. According to a contemporary pamphlet, members being initiated had to swear an oath to Pluto promising to 'let nothing share the least part of my favour, but what is solely urg'd by my most vicious and libidinous desires'. Once enrolled the new member was assured that the club met only 'to satiate our constant craving appetites … nor do we meet but when our lusts run high'. Worsdale's role was to find women to feed these appetites. Obtaining prostitutes from the brothels of Smock Alley was not difficult but Rosse and other members were eager to seduce 'women of quality'. Once her adultery had become public knowledge towards the end of 1737, Laetitia Pilkington, abandoned by her husband Matthew, became a chosen victim. She described how Rosse and other 'worthy peers' broke into her lodgings. She locked herself in a room and could not be found; 'being disappointed, they were forced to decamp, cursing, and vowing revenge against the woman of the house'. No doubt other vulnerable women were not as fortunate as Mrs Pilkington and fell hapless victims of these rakehells.

The Dublin Hellfire Club specialised in ridiculing institutional Christianity in a bizarre variety of rituals and by blaspheming – which is why they often referred to themselves as 'Blasters'. This became so blatant that the Irish House of Lords' Committee for Religion met in February 1738 to discuss the 'present notorious immorality and profaneness' and, a month later, to describe the Blasters as an 'impious society'. On 24 March the Lord Lieutenant and Privy Council of Ireland issued a proclamation offering a reward for the arrest of Peter Lens, the most notorious Blaster who had prayed to the Devil and 'uttered the most daring and execrable blasphemies against the sacred name and majesty of God'.

Lens managed to escape to London. In the end the Dublin Hellfire Club was undone by the drunken and violent excesses of its members. In the most grisly fashion Santry murdered a sedan chairman who was lying sick in bed. He forced the chairman to

drink a quart of brandy 'and then, with kindled spirits, he set fire
to the sheets, &c. the wretch lay in, who soon expired in the most
excruciating torture'.[1] Astonishingly, he escaped prosecution. Then
on 9 August 1738 in a drunken rage Santry plunged his sword into
a porter, Laughlin Murphy, who had accidentally got in his way.
The unfortunate man died on 23 September. Santry was imprisoned
in Newgate.

Santry was tried in the Irish House of Lords in April 1740, 23
of his fellow peers sitting as judges. Robert Jocelyn, then still the
Attorney-General, led the prosecution. The evidence against Santry
was overwhelming and he was duly convicted and sentenced to
death. His friends launched a campaign for clemency, arguing that
Murphy was of lowly status. Only at the last moment, on 17 June
1740, did George II issue a full royal pardon.

In June 1741 the Earl of Rosse lay dying in his Molesworth
Street town house. This prompted the vicar of St Anne's to
write him a letter to remind him of his past life, which included
'profligacy, gaming, drinking, rioting, turning day into night,
blaspheming his Maker, and, in short, all manner of wickedness' and
'to employ the last moments left that remained to him in penitently
confessing his manifold transgressions and soliciting his pardon
from an offended Deity'.[2] It was entirely in Rosse's character that he
asked for a fresh envelope and readdressed the letter to the Earl of
Kildare. By the time the outraged Kildare had discovered the truth,
Rosse was dead. He was only 39 years old.

The ruined building on Montpelier Hill in the Dublin
Mountains is universally known as 'The Hellfire Club'. Built in
the 1720s by William Conolly, then Speaker of the Irish House
of Commons, it may have been used later by the club. In 1739 an
army officer told of an incident on Montpelier Hill: 'a whole Hellfire Club was actually put to flight, and chaced out of the house,
by a goose dropped down a chimney that was on fire'. 'Whatever
the Club's relationship with Montpelier', the historian David
Ryan concludes, 'apocryphal tales of sinister orgies, black masses
and encounters with the devil became widespread in the locality'.[3]
Montpelier Hill is now owned by the state forestry company,
Coillte, and is open to the public. Parents, after taking their children

up the nature trail or orienteering course, and approaching the ruins of the Hellfire Club, like to tell them of the ghost of a very large black cat lurking there.

Appendix 9:
A British Sixpence ... Half a Guinea
... How Much?

In 1701 the Irish Pound was fixed by proclamation at £108 6s 7d to £100 British sterling, and 13 Irish pennies were to be equivalent to a British shilling, that is, 12 pennies.

It is reckoned that the value of one British pound in 1742 was about £139. 50 in 2014. The value of a guinea (approximately a quarter ounce of gold) was supposed to be equal to a British pound sterling. In practice, rises in the price of gold relative to silver caused the value of the guinea to rise to about 30 shillings (£1 10s 0d) by 1742.

The cost of a *Messiah* word-book was 'a British Sixpence', equal to sixpence halfpenny Irish. The modern equivalent, using exchange rates at the close of trading on 11 June 2015, would be:

British sterling	euro	US dollars
£3. 49	€4. 81	$5. 41

The admission ticket for the first performance of *Messiah* on 13 April 1742 was 'Half a Guinea'. The modern equivalent would be:

British sterling	euro	US dollars
£104. 63	€144. 34	$162.16

The money collected from the first performance was £400, of which £381 remained after expenses, providing £127 for each of the three charities. The modern equivalent would be:

British sterling	euro	US dollars
£400 = £55,800. 00	€76,981. 68	$86,484. 42
£381 = £53,149. 50	€73,325. 05	$82,376. 41
£127 = £17,716. 50	€24,441. 68	$27,458. 80

Be cautious before drawing definite conclusions from these figures. A respectable number of us today would be prepared to pay €144.34 to attend a première by a great composer and conducted by him or her. But we have to remind ourselves that an adult male labourer in 1742 could expect only 6d Irish (€4.44, 2015 equivalent) for a day's work and he could not be certain of employment every week day throughout the year. Those employed on the Newry Navigation 1731–1742 were paid 7d Irish (€4.85, 2015 equivalent) a day provided they had with them 'one good working tool, such as spade, pick, stubbing axe or shovel'.

Bibliography

Anderson, Keith, *Naxos: The A to Z of Opera*, London, 2000

Anon, *The Tryal of a Cause for Criminal Conversation, between Theophilus Cibber, Gent., Plaintiff, and Willam Sloper, Esq., Defendant*, London, 1739

Bardon, Jonathan, *A History of Ireland in 250 Episodes*, Dublin, 2008

— and Stephen Conlin, *Dublin: One Thousand Years of Wood Quay*, Belfast, 1984

Barnard, T. C., 'Grand metropolis or "The anus of the world"? The cultural life of eighteenth-century Dublin', in *Proc. BA*, London, 2001

— *A new anatomy of Ireland: the Irish protestants, 1649-1770*, Yale, 2003

— *Making the grand figure: lives and possessions in Ireland, 1641-1770*, Yale, 2004

— 'The Gentrification of Eighteenth-Century Ireland', *Eighteenth-Century Ireland*, 12, 1997

Boyd, Gary, *Dublin 1745-1922: Hospitals, Spectacle & Vice*, Dublin, 2006

Boydell, Barra, *A History of Music at Christ Church Cathedral*, Dublin, 2004

Boydell, Brian, *A Dublin Musical Calendar, 1700-1760*, Dublin, 1988

— 'Organs Associated with Handel's Visit to Dublin', *BIOS Journal*, 19, 1995

Brady, Joseph and Anngret Simms (eds), *Dublin Through Space and Time*, Dublin, 2001

Brimley, Johnson R., *Mrs Delany at Court and Among the Wits*, London, 1925

Burrows, Donald, *Handel: Messiah*, Cambridge, 1991

— 'Handel's Dublin Performances', in Patrick F. Devine and Harry White (eds), *Irish Musical Studies 4, The Maynooth International Musicological Conference 1995, Selected Proceedings: Part One*, Blackrock, 1996

Casey, Christine (ed.), *The Eighteenth-Century Dublin Town House, Form, Function and Finance*, Dublin, 2010

Castlebar News, September-December 2013

Clark, Peter and Raymond Gillespie (eds), *Two Capitals: London and Dublin 1500-1840*, Oxford, 2001

Clarke, Norma, *Queen of the Wits: A Life of Laetitia Pilkington*, London, 2008

Connolly, S. J., *Religion, law and power: the making of protestant Ireland, 1660-1760*, Oxford, 1992

— *The Oxford Companion to Irish History*, Oxford, 1998

Craig, Maurice, *Dublin 1660-1860*, Dublin, 1969

Cullen, L. M., *Anglo-Irish trade, 1660-1800*, Manchester, 1968

Culwick, James, *Handel's Messiah: Discovery of the original Word-Book*, Dublin, 1891

Damrosch, Leo, *Jonathan Swift: His Life and His World*, New Haven and London, 2013

Day, Angélique, *Letters from Georgian Ireland: The correspondence of Mary Delany 1731-68*, Belfast, 1991

Dean, Winton, *Handel's Dramatic Oratorios and Masques*, London, 1959

Deane, Séamus, Andrew Carpenter and Jonathan Williams (eds), *The Field Day Anthology of Irish Writing*, Vol. I, Derry, 1991

Delany, Patrick, *Revelation examined with candour, or A fair enquiry into the sense and use of several revelations expresly declared, or sufficiently implied, to be given to mankind from the creation as they are found in the Bible*, London, 1745

Deutsch, Otto Erich, *Handel: A Documentary Biography*, New York, 1955

Dickson, David, *DUBLIN: The Making of a Capital City*, Dublin, 2014

— *Arctic Ireland: The extraordinary story of the Great Frost and Forgotten Famine of 1740-41*, Dundonald, 1997

— 'The Place of Dublin in the Eighteenth-Century Irish Economy' in T. M. Devine and David Dickson (eds), *Ireland and Scotland 1600-1850*, Edinburgh, 1983

— (ed.), *The Gorgeous Mask: Dublin 1700-1850*, Dublin, 1987

Donnelly, James S. jr, and Kerby A. Miller (eds), *Irish Popular Culture, 1650-1850*, Dublin, 1998

Fagan, Patrick, *The Second City: Portrait of Dublin 1700-1760*, Dublin, 1986

Finane, Ben, *Handel's Messiah and his English Oratorios*, New York and London, 2009

FitzGerald, Alison, '*Taste in high life*: dining in the Dublin town house', in Christine Casey (ed.), *The Eighteenth-Century Dublin Town House, Form, Function and Finance*, Dublin, 2010

Gilbert, J. T., *A History of Dublin*, 3 vols., Dublin, 1854-1859

— (ed.), *Calendar of the Ancient Records of Dublin in possession of the municipal corporation*, 19 vols., Dublin, 1899

Gilbert, J. T., 1854-59, vol. I, p. 69 – 'A Poetical Description of Mr. Neal's New Musick-Hall in Fishamble-street, Dublin' by Laurence Whyte. Original Poems on Various Subjects, Serious, Moral and Diverting, by Laurence Whyte, Dublin, 1742

Gilligan, H. A., *A History of the Port of Dublin*, Dublin, 1988

Grattan Flood, W. H., 'Dublin "City Music" from 1456 to 1786, *SIMG* 11: 1 (1909)

'Dublin Harpsichord and Pianoforte Makers of the Eighteenth Century', *JRSAI* 39 (1909)

'Fishamble Street Music Hall, Dublin, from 1741 to 1777', *SIMG* 14: 1 (1912)

Grindle, W. H., *Irish Cathedral Music: A History of Music at the Cathedrals of the Church of Ireland*, Belfast, 1989

Guinness, D., *Georgian Dublin*, London, 1979

Hayton, D. W., *Ruling Ireland, 1685-1742: Politics, Politicians and Parties*, Woodbridge, Suffolk and Rochester, New York, 2004

Hogwood, Christopher, *Handel*, London, 1984

Hunter, David, 'The Irish State Music from 1716 to 1742 and Handel's Band in Dublin', *Göttinger Händel-Beiträge* 9, ed. Marx Göttingen, 2006

— 'Inviting Handel to Ireland: Laurence Whyte and the Challenge of Poetic Evidence', *Eighteenth-Century Ireland* 20 (2005)

Hussey, John, 'Granite as a building material in Dublin in the early eighteenth century, *History Ireland*, November/December 2014, vol. 22, No. 6

Jacobi, Peter, *The Messiah Book: The Life and Times of G.F. Handel's Greatest Hit*, New York, 1982

James, Francis G., *Lords of the ascendancy: the Irish House of Lords and its members, 1600-1800* Dublin, 1995

Johnston-Liik, Edith M., *Ireland in the eighteenth century*, Dublin, 1974

— *MPs in Dublin: Companion to the History of Parliament 1692-1800*, Belfast, 2006

Jones, G. and E. Malcolm, (eds), *Medicine, disease and the state in Ireland, 1640-1940*, Cork, 1991

Journals of the House of Commons of the Kingdom of Ireland, Vols VI and VII, Dublin MDCCLXXXII

Keates, Jonathan, *Handel: The Man & His Music*, London, 2009

Kelly, James, *'That Damn'd Thing Called Honour': Duelling in Ireland 1570-1860*, Cork, 1995

— and Martyn J. Powell (eds), *Clubs and Societies in Eighteenth-Century Ireland*, Dublin, 2010

Kirkpatrick, T. P., *The foundation of a great hospital: Steevens' in the XVIII century*, Dublin, 1933

Klein, Suzy (presenter), *A Night at the Opera: Rule Britannia – Music Mischief and Morals in the Eighteenth Century*, BBC4, 9 p.m., 7 April 2014

Larsen, Jens Peter, *Handel's 'Messiah': Origins, Composition, Sources*, London, 1957. Second edition with additions and revisions, New York, 1972

Lennon, Colm, *DUBLIN 1610 to 1756: The Making of the Early Modern City*, Dublin, 2009

— and John Montague, *John Rocque's DUBLIN: A Guide to the Georgian City*, Dublin, 2010

Llanover, Lady (ed.), *The autobiography and correspondence of Mary Granville, Mrs Delany* ... 6 vols., London, 1861-2

Luckett, Richard, *Handel's Messiah: A Celebration*, New York, San Diego and London, 1992

Lyons, J. B., *The quality of Mercer's: the story of Mercer's Hospital*, Dublin, 1991

McBride, Ian, *Eighteenth Century Ireland: The Isle of Slaves*, Dublin, 2009

McCracken, Eileen, *Irish Woods since Tudor Times: Their Distribution and Exploitation*, Newton Abbot, 1971

MacLoughlin, Adrian, *Guide to Historic Dublin*, Dublin, 1979

McNally, Patrick, *Parties, Patriots and Undertakers: parliamentary politics in early Hanoverian Ireland*, Dublin, 1997

Malcomson, A. P. W., *Nathaniel Clements: Government and the Governing Elite in Ireland, 1725-75* Dublin, 2005

Maxwell, Constantia, *Dublin under the Georges*, London, 1936

Magennis, Eoin, *The Irish Political System 1740-1765*, Dublin, 2000

Morash, Christopher, *A History of Irish Theatre 1601-2000*, Cambridge, 2002

Nash, Mary, *The Provoked Wife: The Life and Times of Susannah Cibber*, London, 1977

O'Brien, E. (ed.), *The charitable infirmary, Jervis Street, 1718-1987: a farewell tribute*, Dublin, 1987

O'Connor, Frank, *A Book of Ireland*, London & Glasgow, 1959

O'Mahony, Charles, *The viceroys of Ireland*, London, 1912

O'Toole, Fintan, *A Traitor's Kiss: The Life of Richard Brinsley Sheridan*, New York, 1998

Pakenham, Thomas and Valerie (eds), *Dublin: a travellers' companion*, London, 1988

Pilkington, Laetitia, *Memoirs*, London, 1748

Post, John D., *Food Shortage, Climatic Variability, and Epidemic Disease in Preindustrial Europe*, Ithica and London, 1985

Robins, Joseph, *Champagne and silver buckles: the viceregal court at Dublin Castle, 1700-1922* Dublin, 2001

Rodgers, Nini, *Ireland, Slavery and Anti-Slavery 1612-1865*, particularly Chapter 8, 'Dublin, Sweet City', Basingstoke, 2007

Ryan, David, 'The Dublin Hellfire Club', in James Kelly and Martyn J. Powell (eds), *Clubs and Societies in Eighteenth-Century Ireland*, Dublin, 2010

Scott, David, *The Rise of Britain as a World Power*, London, 2014

Shaw, Watkins, *A textual and Historical Companion to Handel's 'Messiah'*, London, 1965

Somerville-Large, Peter, *Dublin*, St Albans, 1979

Smith, Ruth, *Charles Jennens: The Man Behind Handel's* Messiah, London, 2012

— *Handel's Oratorios and Eighteenth-Century Thought*, 1995, Cambridge

Tarling, Judy, *Handel's Messiah: a Rhetorical Guide*, St Albans, 2014

Townsend, Horatio, *An Account of the Visit of Handel to Dublin: with incidental notices of his life and character*, Dublin and London, 1852

Walsh, T. J., *Opera in Dublin, 1705-1797: The Social Scene*, Dublin, 1973

Warburton, J., Whitelaw, Rev. J., and Walsh, Rebert, Rev., *History of the city of Dublin from the earliest accounts to the present time*, 2 vols., London, 1818

Watson Stewart, John, *The Gentleman's and Citizen's Almanack*, Dublin, 1730-86

Williams, Harold (ed.), *The correspondence of Jonathan Swift, V: 1737-1745*, Oxford, 1965

White, Harry, 'Handel in Dublin: A Note', in *Eighteenth-Century Ireland*, Vol. II, 1987

— and Barra Boydell (eds), *The Encyclopaedia of Music in Ireland*, Dublin, 2013

Woolley, David (ed.), *The Correspondence of Jonathan Swift*, 4 vols., Frankfurt, 1999-2007

Notes

Where the title of the book, article or pamphlet is not given, the complete reference will be found in the bibliography.

CHAPTER 1

1 Fiona Aryan, one of the midsummer climbers, informed the author of this annual event on Killiney Hill; Dickson, 1997, pp 42, 70; MacLoughlin, 1979, p. 212.
2 Dickson, 1997, p. 14.
3 Dickson, 1997, pp 12-16.
4 Post, 1985, pp 23, 52-53, 59, 62, 64-67.
5 Dickson, 1997, pp 19-20.
6 ibid.
7 Dickson, 1997, p. 19.
8 Dickson, 1997, p. 23.
9 Dickson, 1997, pp 23-24.
10 Dickson, 1997, pp 17, 22-24; Post 1985, p. 68.
11 Dickson, 1997, pp 27-29.
12 Dickson, 1997, p. 33.
13 Dickson, 1997, pp 32-33; Post, 1985, pp 71-72, 125.
14 Dickson, 1997, p. 35.
15 Dickson, 1997, p. 36.
16 Dickson, 1997, pp 35-38.
17 Dickson, 1997, p. 48.
18 Dickson, 1997, p. 50.
19 Dickson, 1997, pp 48, 50, 51.
20 Johnston-Liik, 2006, p. 70; Dickson, 1997, pp 51-53; Post, 1985, pp 23, 26-27, 230-231.
21 Dickson, 1997, pp 69, 72.
22 Post, 1985, pp 122, 145, 160-161, 183, 193.
23 Dickson, 1997, p. 53.
24 ibid.
25 Dickson, 1997, pp 53-55.
26 *House of Commons Journals (Ireland)*, Vol. V, 1723-1731, pp 1027, 1034, 1059, 1062.
27 David Kelly, 'The Conditions of Debtors and Insolvents in Eighteenth-Century Dublin', in Dickson (ed.), 1987, pp 98-100.
28 Bernadette Doorly, 'Newgate Prison', in Dickson (ed.), 1987, p. 121.
29 ibid.
30 David Kelly in Dickson (ed.), 1987, p. 108.
31 ibid.
32 David Kelly in Dickson (ed.), 1987, p. 108.
33 Dickson, 1997, p. 54.
34 *Irish House of Commons (Journal)*, Vol. VII, 1737, pp 766, 770.
35 Lisa Parker, 'Neal [Neale] family', in Harry White and Barra Boydell (eds), 2013, p. 731; Gilbert, 1854-1859, vol. I, pp 67-68; Brian Boydell, 1988, pp 38, 39, 46.
36 Dickson, 2014, p. 148; Gilbert, 1854-1859, vol. I, pp 59-60, 65-68.
37 Gilbert, 1854-59, vol. I, p. 69.
38 ibid; 'A Poetical Description of Mr. Neal's New Musick-Hall in Fishamble-street, Dublin' by Laurence Whyte. *Original Poems on Various Subjects, Serious, Moral and*

Diverting, by Laurence Whyte, Dublin, 1742.

39 Maria McHale, 'Whyte, Laurence', in Harry White and Barra Boydell (eds), p. 1058; Gilbert, 1854-1859, vol. I, p. 69.

40 Gilbert, 1854-1859, vol. I, pp 72-73; Craig, 1969, pp 36-37, 131.

41 Rachel Talbot, 'Fishamble Street' in Harry White and Barra Boydell (eds), 2013, vol. I, p. 386; Townsend, 1852, footnote, p. 61.

42 Townsend, 1852, p. 35.

43 O'Brien, 1987. pp 4-5. The six surgeons were: Francis and George Duany, Patrick Kelly, Nathaniel Handson, John Dowdall and Peter Brenan.

44 Bennett, 1991, p. 134.

45 Barnard, 2003, p. 33; Bennett, 1991, p. 134; Fagan, 1986, p. 27; Townsend, 1852, pp 37-38.

46 David Hunter, 'Inviting Handel to Ireland: Laurence Whyte and the Challenge of Poetic Evidence', *Eighteenth-Century Ireland* 20 (2005), p. 158.

47 David Hunter, 'Inviting Handel', *Eighteenth-Century Ireland* 20 (2005), pp 156-168; Barra Boydell, 'Handel, George Frideric', in Harry White and Barra Boydell (eds), 2013, vol. I, p. 459.

CHAPTER 2

1 Keith Anderson, *The A to Z of Opera*, Naxos, 2000, pp 479-480.

2 Keates, 2009, p. 62.

3 Suzy Klein, *A Night at the Opera: Rule Britannia – Music Mischief and Morals in the Eighteenth Century*, BBC4, 9 p.m., 7 April 2014; Keates, 2009, pp 60-63; Hogwood, 1984, pp 62-66.

4 Hogwood, 1984, pp 11-48; Keates, 2009, pp 1-48; Finane, 2009, pp 3-9; Burrows, 1991, pp 2-3.

5 Keates, 2009, p. 50.

6 Keates, 2009, p. 57.

7 Keates, 2009, p. 78.

8 Keates, 2009, p. 59.

9 Keates, 2009, pp 59, 83-84.

10 Ragnild Hatton, *George I: Elector and King*, London, 1978, pp 129-132.

11 Hogwood, 1984, p. 81.

12 Hogwood, 1984, p. 83; Keates, 2009, p. 121.

13 Keates, 2009, p. 122.

14 Keates, 2009, p. 57.

15 ibid.

16 Smith, 1995, p. 74.

17 Smith, 1995, p. 75.

18 Smith, 1995, pp 74-75.

19 Keates, 2009, p. 161.

20 Hogwood, 1984, p. 129.

21 Keates, 2009, p. 190.

22 Keates, 2009, p. 238.

23 Finane, 2009, pp 26-30.

24 Smith, 1995, p. 83.

25 Smith, 1995, pp 44, 83.

26 Smith, 1995, p. 84.

27 Smith, 1995, p. 157.

28 Smith, 1995, pp 157, 159.
29 Hogwood, 1984, p. 193.
30 Smith, 1995, p. 168.
31 Smith, 1995, p. 86.
32 Keates, 2009, p. 74.
33 Keates, 2009, p. 188.
34 Hogwood, 1984, p. 98; Finane, 2009, pp 30-32.
35 Hogwood, 1984, p. 187.
36 Keates, 2009, p. 198.
37 Keates, 2009, p. 199.
38 Keates, 2009, pp 187, 198-199.
39 Hogwood, 1984, p. 121.
40 Keates, 2009, p. 209.
41 Keates, 2009, p. 217.
42 Keates, 2009, p. 34.
43 Hogwood, 1984, p. 153; Smith, 2012, pp 28-29, 58-59.
44 Hogwood, 1984, pp 156-158.

CHAPTER 3
1 McCracken, 1971, pp 29 and 83-84; Smith, 2012, p. 3.
2 Smith, 2012, pp 1-8, 13.
3 McBride, 2009, p. 71.
4 ibid.
5 McBride, 2009, p. 71.
6 McBride, 2009, pp 70-76.
7 Smith, 1995, pp 142, 144.
8 Scott, 2014, p. 271.
9 Smith, 1995, p. 142.
10 Smith, 1995, pp 142-143.
11 Smith, 1995, p. 149; Luckett, 1992, p. 77.
12 Smith, 2012, p. 17.
13 Smith, 2012, pp 21-22.
14 Smith, 2012, pp 41-43.
15 Luckett, 1992, p. 70.
16 Smith, 2012, p. 22, p. 50; Keates, 2009, p. 203.
17 Smith, 2012, p. 17.
18 Hogwood, 1984, p. 156.
19 Keates, 2009, p. 259.
20 Hogwood, 1984, p. 161; Keates, 2009, pp 263-265.
21 Smith, 2012, p. 51; Keates, 2009, pp 269-270.
22 Hogwood, 1984, p. 163.
23 Hogwood, 1984, pp 162-163.
24 Keates, 2009, p. 272.
25 Keates, 2009, p. 273.
26 Keates, 2009, p. 275.
27 Hogwood, 1984, pp 165-166.
28 Hogwood, 1984, p. 167.
29 Luckett, 1992, pp 70-71.

30 Finane, 2009, pp 63-64.
31 Smith, 2012, pp 52-53; Smith, 1995, p. 149.
32 Smith, 2012, p. 59.
33 Smith, 2012, p. 57; Luckett, 1992, pp 73-78; Hogwood, 1984, p. 167.
34 Tarling, 2014, p. vii.
35 Luckett, 1992, pp 73-74; Finane, 2009, pp 64-65.
36 Smith, 1995, pp 95-96, 108.

CHAPTER 4
1 Dickson, 2014, p. 152.
2 Barnard, 2003, pp 2-3.
3 Jonathan Bardon, *The Plantation of Ulster*, Dublin, 2011, pp 305-307.
4 Connolly (ed.), 1998, pp 127, 218, 251.
5 Dickson, 2014, pp 112-113.
6 Bennett, 1991, p. 118; Dickson, 2014, pp 112-114,140.
7 Brian Boydell, 1988, pp 38-41.
8 Brian Boydell, 1988, pp 44, 47, 63, 266.
9 Brian Boydell, 1988, pp 11-12.
10 Brian Boydell, 1988, p. 36.
11 David J. Rhodes, 'Cousser [Kusser], John Sigismond [Johann Sigismund]', in Harry White & Barra Boydell (eds), 2013, pp 258-259; Brian Boydell, 1988, pp 14-15.
12 Barra Boydell, 2004, pp 39, 41, 47, 104-105; Estelle Murphy, 'Catch and glee clubs', p. 171, and Frank Lawrence & Paul Arbuthnot, 'Vicar choral', p. 1028, in Harry White & Barra Boydell (eds), 2013.
13 Estelle Murphy, 'Crow Street', in Harry White & Barra Boydell (eds), 2013, pp 267-268.
14 David J. Rhodes, 'Geminiani, Francesco', in Harry White & Barra Boydell (eds), 2013, p. 427.
15 David J. Rhodes, 'Geminiani, Francesco', in Harry White & Barra Boydell (eds), 2013, pp 426-427; Brian Boydell, 1988, pp 23-24.
16 Frank O'Connor, *A Book of Ireland*, London & Glasgow, 1959, pp 180-182.
17 David J. Rhodes, 'Beggar's Opera, The', in Harry White & Barra Boydell (eds), 2013, p. 75; Brian Boydell, 1988, p. 44.
18 Brian Boydell, 1988, p. 46.
19 ibid.
20 Brian Boydell, 1988, p. 46.
21 Brian Boydell, 1988, pp 46, 292.
22 David J. Rhodes, 'Dubourg, Matthew', in Harry White & Barra Boydell (eds), 2013, p. 32.
23 Hogwood, 1984, p. 131.
24 Hogwood, 1984, p. 133.
25 David J. Rhodes, 'Dubourg, Matthew', in Harry White & Barra Boydell (eds), 2013, pp 332-333; Hogwood, 1984, pp 131,133.
26 Brian Boydell, 1988, pp 38, 39, 46.
27 Paul McKeever, 'Cuvillie, John Baptiste', p. 274, and Andrew Johnstone, 'Harris, Renatus', p. 469, in Harry White & Barra Boydell (eds), 2013; Barra Boydell, 2004, p. 115.
28 Brian Boydell, 1988, p. 39.
29 Brian Boydell, 1988, p. 54.

30 Brian Boydell, 1988, pp 44, 54, 62-64.
31 Brian Boydell, 1988, p. 64.
32 Brian Boydell, 1988, pp 54, 70; Estelle Murphy, 'Scarlatti, Francesco', in Harry White & Barra Boydell (eds), 2013, p. 919.

Chapter 5

1 Keates, 2009, p. 309.
2 Hogwood, 1984, pp 122-123.
3 Day (ed.), 1991, p. 87.
4 Day (ed.), 1991, p. 25.
5 Day (ed.), 1991, pp 32-33.
6 Day (ed.), 1991, pp 25, 32-33, 87.
7 Day (ed.), 1991, p. 125.
8 Barnard, 2003, p. 284; Lennon and Montague, 2010, pp 63-65.
9 Deane (ed.), 1991, pp 341-350; Bardon, 2008, pp 244-245.
10 Damrosch, 2013, pp 357-378, especially p. 372.
11 O'Toole, 1998, p. 12.
12 O'Toole, 1998, pp 5-9,13-17.
13 Day (ed.), 1991, p. 65.
14 Damrosch, 2013, pp 426-427.
15 ibid.
16 Damrosch, 2013, pp 427-428.
17 Day (ed.), 1991, p. 27.
18 Clarke, 2008, p. 53.
19 Clarke, 2008, p. 46.
20 Day (ed.), 1991, p. 27.
21 Clarke, 2008, p. 48.
22 Clarke, 2008, p. 50.
23 Clarke, 2008, p. 73.
24 Clarke, 2008, pp 64-73.
25 Clarke, 2008, p. 99.
26 Clarke, 2008, p. 127.
27 Clarke, 2008, pp 126-132.
28 Clarke, 2008, p. 131.
29 Clarke, 2008, pp 129-131.
30 Clarke, 2008, pp 159-160, 197-200.
31 Day (ed.), 1991, p. 87.
32 Aidan Clarke et al (eds), *Dictionary of Irish Biography*, 2009, Vol II, p. 564.
33 Smith, 1995, p. 273.
34 Delany, 1745, pp i- xlvi.
35 Smith, 1995, p. 145; Hogwood, 1984, p. 194.
36 Day (ed.), 1991, p. 8.
37 Day (ed.), 2008, p. 67
38 ibid.

Chapter 6

1 *Faulkner's Dublin Journal*, 22-26 September 1741.
2 Craig, 1952, p. 76.

3 Craig, 1952, pp 86-87; Dickson, 2014, p. 86.

4 *Faulkner's Dublin Journal*, 22-26 September 1741.

5 Bardon, 1984, p. 14.

6 Craig, 1980, p. 127.

7 *Faulkner's Dublin Journal*, 22-26 September 1741.

8 Hayton, 2004, p. 266.

9 Barnard, 2004, p. 1.

10 Hayton, 2004, p. 266.

11 Barnard, 2004, pp 9, 12.

12 Robins, 2002, pp 11, 24.

13 *Journals of the House of Commons of the Kingdom of Ireland*, Dublin, MDCCLXXXII, Vol. VII, pp 703-704.

14 ibid.

15 McBride, 2009, pp 106, 236; Barnard, p. 203.

16 Johnston-Liik, 2006, chap. 3, pp 63-132; Rodgers, 2007, p. 166.

17 McBride, 2009, p. 221.

18 McBride, 2009, pp 216, 220-221.

19 Barnard, 2003, p. 32.

20 John Hussey, 'Granite as a building material in Dublin in the early eighteenth century' in *History Ireland*, November/December 2014, Vol. 22, No. 6; Susan Roundtree, 'Brick in the eighteenth-century Dublin town house', pp 73-79, and Tony Hand, 'Supplying stone for the Dublin house', pp 82-84, in Christine Casey (ed.), *The Eighteenth-Century Dublin Town House*, 2010.

21 Hayton, 2004, p. 257.

22 Morash, 2002, p. 13.

23 Morash, 2002, p. 35.

24 Discussed in David Hunter, 'Inviting Handel to Ireland: Laurence Whyte and the Challenge of Poetic Evidence', *Eighteenth-Century Ireland*, 20 (2005).

CHAPTER 7

1 Luckett, 1992, pp 17, 86-87; Hogwood, 1984, pp 167-170, 287; Keates, 2009, pp 282-283; Burrows, 1991, p. 12.

2 Smith, 2012, p. 53.

3 Luckett, 1992, pp 62, 67.

4 Hogwood, 1984, p. 168; Luckett, 1992, p. 67.

5 Keates, 2009, pp 283-284; Finane, 2009, pp 40, 74; Hogwood, 1984, pp 168-170; Luckett, 1992, p. 88.

6 Tarling, 2014, p. 89.

7 Finane, 2009, pp 76-79.

8 Finane, 2009, p. 82; Tarling, 2014, p. 89.

9 Finane, 2009, pp 82-87; Luckett, 1992, pp 89-95.

10 Tarling, 2014, pp vii, 200.

11 Finane, 2009, p. 88; Luckett, 1992, p. 95.

12 Finane, 2009. pp 88-93; Luckett, 1992, pp 95-97; Tarling, 2014, pp 53-54, 59, 65, 72-73.

13 Finane, 2009, pp 95-100; Luckett, 1992, pp 100-101.

14 Luckett, 1992, p. 102; Finane, 2009, pp 100-102; Tarling, 2014, p. 190.

15 Finane, 2009, pp 102-105.

16 Tarling, 2014, p. 200.

17 Luckett, 1992, p. 106.

18 Finane, 2009, p. 1.

19 Hogwood, 1984, pp 171-172 (Hogwood points out that Charles Cudworth has cast doubt on the latter part of this story in 'Mythistorica Handeliana' in *Festkrift Jens Peter Larsen*, Copenhagen, 1972); Luckett, 1992, pp 106-107.

20 Luckett, 1992, p. 108.

21 Townsend, 1852, pp 44-45.

22 Brian Boydell, 1988, p. 70.

23 Burrows, 1996, p. 53.

24 Townsend, 1852, pp 46-47.

25 Burrows, 1996, pp 54-55.

26 Hogwood, 1984, pp 172-173; Brian Boydell, 1989, pp 75-76; Townsend, 1852, p. 49.

27 Deutsch, 1955, p. 530.

28 ibid.

29 Luckett, 1992, p. 115.

30 Deutsch, 1955, p. 531.

31 Luckett, 1992, pp 114-115; Hogwood, 1984, pp 172-173; Townsend, 1852, pp 45-46, 48-52.

32 David Hunter, 'Inviting Handel to Ireland: Laurence Whyte and the Challenge of Poetic Evidence', *Eighteenth-Century Ireland*, Vol. 20 (2005), p. 158; Hogwood, 1984, pp 140, 177-178.

33 Burrows, 1996, p. 47.

34 Townsend, 1852, pp 52-53.

35 Burrows, 1996, p. 54.

36 Townsend, 1852, p. 60, taken from *Faulkner's Dublin Journal*, 9–16, February 1742.

37 Townsend, 1852, pp 58-62; Luckett, 1992, p. 119; Brian Boydell, 1988, p. 77.

38 Hogwood, 1984, p. 176.

39 Townsend, 1852, p. 61.

40 Tighearnan Mooney and Fiona White, 'The Gentry's Winter Season', in Dickson (ed.), 1987, pp 1-2.

CHAPTER 8

1 Nash, 1977, p. 31.

2 Nash, 1977, p. 35.

3 Nash, 1977, pp 14-15, 62-108.

4 Anon, *A Tryal of Two Causes…*, 1739, p. 25.

5 Anon, *A Tryal of Two Causes…*, 1739, pp 26-27.

6 Anon, *A Tryal…*, 1739, pp 33-34.

7 Nash, 1977, p. 140.

8 Nash, 1977, pp 139-140; Anon, *A Tryal of Two Causes … ,* 1739, p. 34.

9 Anon, *A Tryal of Two Causes …*, 1739, p. 44.

10 *A Tryal of Two Causes…,* 1739, pp 34, 44.

11 Nash, 1977, pp 130-134.

12 Nash, 1977, pp 78-79, 81-84, 168-169.

13 Nash, 1977, pp 167-168.

14 Brian Boydell, 1988, p. 72.

15 Brian Boydell, 1988, pp 72-73.

16 Nash, 1977, p. 170.

17 Luckett, 1992, p. 112.

18 Brian Boydell, 1988, p. 76, 78, 79; Luckett, 1992, p. 119.

19 Anon, 1740, p. 29; Luckett, 1992, p. 199.

20 Burrows, 1996, p. 46.

21 Keates, 2008, p. 281.

22 Keates, 2008, p. 281; Luckett, 1992, p. 130.

23 Nash, 1977, pp 39-40.

CHAPTER 9

1 McBride, 2009, p. 277.

2 McBride, 2009, p. 277; Damrosch, 2013, p. 271.

3 Damrosch, 2013, pp 271, 415.

4 Mason, 1820, footnote p. 407.

5 Damrosch, 2013, p. 269.

6 Mason, 1820, pp 91-92.

7 Mason, 1820, p. 92.

8 Mason, 1820, pp 91-93; Estelle Murphy, 'Catch and glee clubs', p. 171, and Frank
   Lawrence and Paul Arbuthnot, 'Vicar choral', p. 1028, in Harry White & Barra Boydell
   (eds), 2013.

9 Brian Boydell, 1988, pp 38, 57.

10 Grindle, 1989, pp 39-40; Brian Boydell, 1988, pp 38, 57.

11 Woolley, 1999-2007, Vol.I, p. 638, 16 April 1726; Grindle, 1989, p. 41.

12 Barra Boydell, 2004, pp 104-111, 114, 131-132; Grindle, 1989, p. 42; Woolley, 1999-
   2007, Vol. I, p. 639, 16 April 1726.

13 Damrosch, 2013, p. 460.

14 ibid, p. 274.

15 Damrosch, 2013, p. 406.

16 Deane, Carpenter and Williams (eds), 1991, pp 386-391.

17 Damrosch, 2013, pp 464-465.

18 Townsend, 1852, p. 54.

19 Damrosch, 2013, p. 271.

20 Townsend, 1852, pp 54-55.

21 Hogwood, 1984, p. 174.

22 Deutsch, 1954, pp 536-537; Townsend, 1852, p. 56; Luckett, 1992, p. 117.

CHAPTER 10

1 Luckett, 1992, p. 121.

2 Luckett, 1992, pp 123-124.

3 For a thoroughly-researched discussion of who sang in *Messiah* on 13 April and 3 June
   1742, see Burrows, 1996, pp 56, 62, 70. Musicologists are not in agreement: Barra
   Boydell, 2004, p. 121, concludes that 'it would seem that the choirboys did not take
   part, the top line being sung by female sopranos'; and Richard Luckett, 1992, p. 125,
   writes that 'there were also sixteen boy choristers'; see also Townsend, 1852, p. 85.

4 Burrows, 1996, p. 62; Luckett, 1992, pp 114-115.

5 Luckett, 1992, p. 124.

6 Burrows, 1996, pp 57-58; Townsend, 1852, pp 84-85; Luckett, 1992, pp 124-125.

7 Townsend, 1852, pp 86-88.

8 Townsend, 1852, pp 88-90.

9 Luckett, 1992, pp 129-130, 132-133; Hogwood, 1984, pp 178-179.

10 *Faulkner's Dublin Journal*, 13–17 April 1742.

11 Burrows, 1991, p. 21; Luckett, 1992, p. 130; Nash, 1977, pp 175-176, 342-343; Deutsch, 1955, pp 554-555.

12 Townsend, 1852, pp 95-96.

13 Brian Boydell, 1988, pp 82-85; Luckett, 1992, p. 132.

14 Burrows, 1996, pp 46-47.

15 Townsend, 1852, pp 97-98. The Vernons built the present Clontarf Castle, now a hotel, a century after Handel's visit.

16 Burrows, 1996, pp 47, 52.

17 Luckett, 1992, p. 132.

18 Townsend, 1852, p. 101.

19 Luckett, 1992, pp 132-133.

20 *Faulkner's Dublin Journal*, 10–14 January 1743-44.

CHAPTER 11

1 Hogwood, 1984, pp 180-181.

2 Townsend, 1852, p. 109.

3 Hogwood, 1984, pp 179-182.

4 Hogwood, 1984, p. 182.

5 Hogwood, 1984, p. 183.

6 Hogwood, 1984, pp 180-183.

7 Luckett, 1992, pp 142-143.

8 Hogwood, 1984, p. 183.

9 Hogwood, 184, p. 184.

10 Hogwood, 1984, pp 183-184.

11 Day (ed.), 1991, p. 10.

12 Day (ed.), 1991, p. 11.

13 Day (ed.), 1991, pp 10-12.

14 Keates, 1985, pp 292, 295; Hogwood, 1984, p. 194.

15 Hogwood, 1984, p. 195.

16 Hogwood, 1984, p. 197.

17 Hogwood, 1984, p. 198.

18 Hogwood, 1984, pp 199-200.

19 Hogwood, 1984, p. 200.

20 Luckett, 1992, p. 153.

21 Townsend, 1852, p. 121.

22 Luckett, 1992, pp 240-241.

23 Luckett, 1992, p. 156.

24 Harry White, 'Handel in Dublin: A Note', in *Eighteenth-Century Ireland*, Vol. II, 1987, p. 185.

25 Brian Boydell, 1988, pp 95-96; Townsend, 1852, p. 114.

26 Townsend, 1852, p. 115.

27 Townsend, 1852, pp 114-116; Brian Boydell, 1988, pp 95, 97.

28 Harry White, 'Handel in Dublin: A Note', in *Eighteenth-Century Ireland*, Vol. II, 1987, p. 183.

29 Harry White, 'Handel in Dublin: A Note', in *Eighteenth-Century Ireland*, Vol. II, 1987, pp 183-185; Brian Boydell, 1988, pp 94-95.

30 Finane, 2009, p. 123.

31 Harry White, 'Handel in Dublin: A Note', in *Eighteenth-Century Ireland*, Vol. II, 1987, p. 184.

32 Day (ed.), 1991, pp 261-263.

CHAPTER 12

1 Hogwood, 1984, p. 201.

2 Luckett, 1992, p. 143.

3 Hogwood, 1984, p. 217.

4 Luckett, 1992, p. 163.

5 Luckett, 1992, p. 172.

6 Townsend, 1852, p. 123; Luckett, 1992, pp 172-174.

7 Hogwood, 1984, p. 222.

8 ibid.

9 Hogwood, 1984, p. 222-224.

10 Townsend, 1852, p. 124; Day, 1991, p. 266.

11 Luckett, 1992, pp 171-172, 174.

12 Day (ed.), 1991, p. 266.

13 Hogwood, 1984, pp 7-8, 230-231.

14 Luckett, 1992, pp 178-9; Finane, 2009, p. 25; Burrows, 1991, p. vii.

15 Luckett, 1992, p. 129.

EPILOGUE

1 Hogwood, 1984, p. 180.

2 Luckett, 1992, p. 162.

3 Luckett, 1992, p. 183.

4 Luckett, 1992, pp 185-186.

5 Burrows, 1991, p. 40.

6 Hogwood, 1984, caption to Plate 58.

7 Luckett, 1992, p. 197; Hogwood, 1984, pp 242-243.

8 Luckett, 1992, pp 198, 219-220.

9 Hogwood, 1984, p. 250.

10 Luckett, 1992, pp 174-175.

11 Luckett, 1992, pp 223-224.

12 Luckett, 1992, p. 232.

13 Luckett, 1992, p. 233.

14 Luckett, 1992, pp 232-239; Burrows, 1991, p. 54 and p. 116, endnote 30; Finane, 2009, p. 111.

15 *Castlebar News*, 18 September 2014; www.mayochoral.com/wp-content/uploads/2013/08/handel.challenge.blue_.background.pdf; www.castlebar.ie/'Hallelujah-Handel's Messiah returns to Castlebar' by Vivienne Lee; www.youtube.com/watch?v=ET3xFpc6NS4; www.facebook.com/pages/The-Handel-Challenge/493235794102899 ; www.castlebar.ie/parish

16 Lisa Parker, 'Messiah', p. 665, and David Connolly, 'Our Lady's Choral Society', pp 815-816, in Harry White White and Barra Boydell (eds), 2013.

17 Luckett, 1992, pp 205-217.

18 Information provided by John and Rosemary Hunter, 3 June 2015.

19 Finane, 2009, pp 114-115.

APPENDICES

How Did Fishamble Street Get its Name?

1 Bardon, 1984, pp 12–14.

2 Bardon, 1984, p. 14; Somerville-Large, 1979, p. 137.

Fishamble Street Developers Help to Shape Georgian Dublin

1 Toby Bernard, Brendan Twomey, Christine Casey and Edward McPartland in Casey (ed.) 2010, pp 2–11, 37, 46–58, 128–129.

2 Dickson, 2014, pp 139–144.

3 Craig, 1969, pp100–105.

Dublin, Sweet City

1 Rodgers, 2007, pp 159–168.

2 Dickson, 2014, pp 125–126.

The Phoenix Park

1 T. and V. Pakenham (eds), 1988, p. 127.

2 McLoughlin, 1979, p. 131; Craig, 1969, pp 13–16; Somerville-Large, 1979, p. 133; Bardon, 2008, pp 206–207.

Badger Flambé, Anyone?

1 Alison FitzGerald, 'Taste in high life: dining in the Dublin town house' in Casey (ed.), 2010, Plates 14-17 and pp 120–121; Robins, 2001, pp 38–39.

'Did He Ever Blaze?' Duelling in Dublin

1 Kelly, 1995, p. 51.

2 Patrick M. Geoghegan, *The Irish Act of Union*, Dublin, 1999, p. 107.

The Blasters: The Dublin Hellfire Club

1 David Ryan, 'The Dublin Hellfire Club', in Kelly & Powell (eds), 2010, p. 339–341.

2 David Ryan, 'The Dublin Hellfire Club', in Kelly & Powell (eds), 2010, p. 349.

3 David Ryan, 'The Dublin Hellfire Club', in Kelly & Powell (eds), 2010, p. 352.

Index